A TRAVEL A[...]
BI[...]
OF COSTA RICA

WITH SIDE TRIPS TO PANAMA AND NICARAGUA

MW00790667

A TRAVEL AND SITE GUIDE TO
BIRDS
OF COSTA RICA
WITH SIDE TRIPS TO PANAMA AND NICARAGUA

Written by
Aaron D. Sekerak

Illustrated by
Elissa Conger

LONE
PINE

EDICIONES
NATURALEZA

THE PUBLISHER: LONE PINE PUBLISHING

206, 10426-81 Avenue	202A, 1110 Seymour Street	16149 Redmond Way, #180
Edmonton, Alberta	Vancouver, British Columbia	Redmond, Washington
Canada T6E 1X5	Canada V6B 3N3	U.S.A. 98052

Canadian Cataloguing in Publicaton Data

Sekerak, Aaron D.
    A travel and site guide to birds of Costa Rica

ISBN 1-55105-084-6

    1. Birding sites—Costa Rica—Guidebooks. 2. Birdwatching—Costa Rica—Guidebooks. 3. Costa Rica—Guidebooks. I. Title.

QL687.C8S44 1996   598'.072347286   C96-910667-X

DEDICATION

To my mother, the best there ever was,
and Nell, for her love and support these many years.

Senior Editor: Nancy Foulds

Editorial: Linda Caldwell, Lee Craig

Production Manager: David Dodge

Design, Layout and Production: Gregory Brown, Carol S. Dragich

Maps: Volker Bodegom, Carol S. Dragich

Scanning: Elite Lithographers Co. Ltd., Edmonton, Alberta, Canada

Printing: Quebecor Jasper Printing Inc., Edmonton, Alberta, Canada

The publisher gratefully acknowledges the support of Alberta Community Development and the Department of Canadian Heritage.

CONTENTS

ACKNOWLEDGEMENTS

Many thanks are due to the people of Costa Rica who extended innumerable small and large kindnesses to me and my companions during our travels in their country. Special thanks are extended to Romelio Compos, manager of Oro Verde Lodge; the Delgado family, especially Don Fernando and his wife Merceditas, for their hospitality during home stays in San Antonio de Belen; Lidier and Elieth Elizando for their kindness while staying at Los Angeles; Herman Geest of Cabinas La Rivera in Fortuna; Martin Geza for a memorable walk in the jungle near Punta Uva; Luis Diego Gomez, director of Las Cruces Biological Station; Peter Kaltenegger of Cooperacion Austriaca in Managua, Nicaragua; Sergio Leon, director of Tapantí National Park; the Murillo family—Joaquin, Hugo, Carlos and especially Anna—for their helpfulness and hospitality while staying at their farm; Edgar Quiros, manager of Las Tablas Research Station; Adelina Schutt at Curú Hacienda and Wildlife Refuge; Jan Segleau of Jardin Botanico Las Cusingas; Alberto Taylor for a pleasurable paddle in Tortuguero National Park; Rob Taws, Peace Corps volunteer, for helpful information on the Colorado region; and Alexander Villegas for special efforts in birding in the Monteverde region.

Extra special thanks are due to George Armistead, who kindly supplied his observations on birds in several areas for use in this book; Hector Montenegro and Juan Martinez for arranging a birding trip up the Changuinola River in northwestern Panama; Oscar Rojas of Los Chiles for his help with birding in Nicaragua; Bill Ross and Gabriel Sanchez of Las Ventanas de Osa for their help and hospitality while birding in southwestern Costa Rica, and Alexander Skutch for his thoughtful comments and the sharing of a pleasurable conversation while birding on his porch at Finca Los Cunsingos.

Thanks are also due to Nancy Foulds for guidance through the publishing process, to Linda Caldwell and Lee Craig for their careful edit of the text, to Greg Brown for his design and layout skill, to Shane Kennedy for his enthusiastic support, to Volker Bodegom and Carol Dragich for their final mapping, and to all the Lone Pine Publishing crew.

The efforts of Nell Stallard, who word-processed the manuscript, prepared bird list upon bird list, commented on various drafts, prepared draft maps from which final versions were produced, and assisted in every way, are most greatly appreciated.

INTRODUCTION

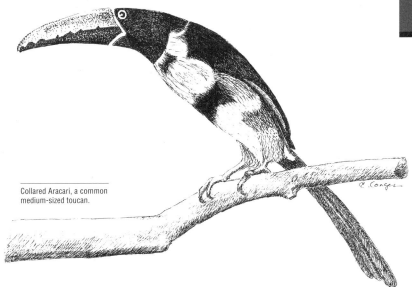

Collared Aracari, a common medium-sized toucan.

Costa Rica is a unique destination for birders because of the large number of birds that inhabit the country year-round, are winter residents, or are here only a brief time as passage migrants. Many of the birds of Costa Rica are large, extremely colorful tropical varieties, such as parrots, toucans and trogons—so foreign and thrilling to watch. Others, such as the antbirds and woodcreepers, are more drab, shy and secretive, but attract birders from around the world because of their unusual nature and restricted distributions.

Costa Rica also serves as a major migration corridor for many species of birds that winter in South America. Although most of these birds are small and are apparent only to keener observers, spectacular migrations of **Turkey Vultures** and hawks—sometimes numbering in the tens of thousands—stream across the Costa Rican sky every spring and fall. These features, together with the ease of air travel to San José, the capital of Costa Rica, and the overall friendliness of the Ticos, make Costa Rica one of the foremost birding destinations in the world. If you go, you'll want to return—as I have many times.

Costa Rica contains one of the most complex and varied avian communities in the world, all packed into an extremely small area the size of a modest U.S. state or European country. Although tiny, only 51,000 square kilometers (20,000 square miles), Costa Rica is in the enviable position of having more than 850

Costa Rica

─⟨10⟩─ highway; major highway
• ✱ town or city; provincial capital

species of birds recorded within its boundaries. In comparison, an equal number of birds, about 850, has been recorded in all of North America north of Mexico, an area more than 400 times the size of Costa Rica!

How has nature loaded this incredible diversity into such a small area? Several factors work together: tropical location, varied climatic conditions, isolated high mountains and valleys and proximity to both North and South America. Tropical systems normally contain more species (but sometimes fewer individuals of each species) than more temperate ones, but Costa Rica is quite different from other adjacent tropical countries in a number of ways. First, no other central American country is as mountainous as Costa Rica. Several peaks attain altitudes of more than 3,200 meters (10,500 feet) and Cerro Chirripó, at 3,820 meters

(12,530 feet), in southern Costa Rica, is the highest mountain in Central America. These mountains stand between great lowland areas in Nicaragua and Panama and have been centers of speciation for a substantial number of birds. Many of these species are unique to Costa Rica and northern Panama because they have been unable to disperse across the great lowlands to the north and south. Such great changes in altitude also give rise to equally great differences in climate, plant and animal communities and, of course, habitats for birds.

Climate in Costa Rica ranges from frosty (yes, frosty) mornings in the high mountains to year-round, hot tropical conditions along coastlines, with a gamut of conditions in between. Thus, the stunted tundra-like vegetation (called *páramo*) of the highest mountains yields to predominantly oak forests in moderate elevations and then to more characteristic tropical forest communities at lower elevations. Even the two coasts of Costa Rica have quite different climates because of the intervening mountains, with the Pacific coast having a more pronounced dry season, especially in the northwestern province of Guanacaste. Mangrove swamps, savannas, freshwater swamps, rivers, pasture and crop land, black water swamps and saline ponds are a few of the many other micro-habitats available for birds.

Costa Rica is also in a unique geographical position because plant and animal species of North American origin merge and overlap with those of South America in the southwestern portion of the country, especially on the Osa Peninsula. This overlap gives rise to one of the highest diversities of plants and animals in the world. Finally, Costa Rica serves as a migration route or a wintering area for many bird species that raise young in North America—including warblers, vireos, raptors, kingfishers, thrushes, and a large number of shorebirds. Some species, such as the **Piratic Flycatcher**, even come from South America to breed in Costa Rica.

All in all, Costa Rica is a marvelous country of smiling people, volcanoes, sunny beaches, humid jungles and cool, misty mountain tops. And the ecological wonders don't stop with birds. The country has recently been declared the world's leader in the combined biodiversity of birds and mammals, with 615 species per 10,000 square kilometers (4,000 square miles), even surpassing African countries such as Rwanda and Gambia, with 596 and 574 species of birds and mammals, respectively. Within Latin America, only Colombia has more plants—7,074 in Costa Rica as opposed to 10,735 plant species per 10,000 square kilometers (4,000 square miles). Costa Rica has more species of butterflies than the entire continent of Africa, not to mention numerous species of amphibians, reptiles, fish and untold multitudes of weird and wonderful insects. So concentrate on birds by all means, but don't forget to enjoy the culture of the country and its other ecological treasures.

DISTRIBUTION OF COSTA RICAN BIRDS

To make birding in Costa Rica more manageable, considering the very large number of species involved, I have categorized the 856 species into 21 groups according to their distributions (see Appendix I). Most groups are based on major habitat types, which in turn are related to the seven geographic regions featured on the map opposite. Thus, the **Northwestern Lowlands** are defined as the dry region below 1,000 meters (3,300 feet) in elevation, which extends north from about Carara to the Nicaraguan border. Owing to prevailing winds, the dry Northwest also includes lowlands adjacent to Lake Nicaragua, even though they are east slope drainages. As shown in the table below, 47 species of birds are mainly restricted to the Northwestern Lowlands within Costa Rica. The **Southwestern Lowlands** is the area south of Carara. It receives much higher rainfall and is more humid than the northwest, although it also has a pronounced dry season. The **Valle Central** is a relatively high, cool, dry plateau, most of which lies to the west of the Continental Divide. This region has relatively few species not found in other parts of Costa Rica. Its avifauna mainly consist of a mixture of wide-ranging birds and modest

DISTRIBUTION OF BIRDS IN COSTA RICA
(All lowland areas are <1,000 m (3,000 ft) in elevation)

Group	Main Area of Distribution	Number of Species
1	Country-wide—except perhaps in the high mountains	275
2	Country-wide—except NW	101
3	Country-wide—except SW	8
4	Country-wide—except NE	0
5	Country-wide—except SE	1
6	Eastern lowlands —except dry areas south of Lago de Nicaragua	84
7	Northeastern Lowlands	9
8	Southeastern Lowlands	3
9	Western Lowlands	10
10	Northwestern Lowlands —includes dry areas south of Lago de Nicaragua	47
11	Southwestern Lowlands	39
12	Northern Lowlands	4
13	Southern Lowlands	5
14	Valle Central	4
15	Mountains—usually above 1,000 m (2–3,000 ft)	83
16	Highlands—greater than 1,700 m (5,000 ft)	40
17	Pacific Coast—oceanic	11
18	Both coasts—oceanic	4
19	Cocos Island	8
20	Northwest and Valle Central	15
21	Very rare, accidental, extinct in Costa Rica	75

rooms tend to be small and you often have a choice of a private bathroom or sharing one down the hall. Ask to see the room before you decide. For the price, you will often be pleasantly surprised. Beware of hotels with attached bars or discos unless you want to join the party.

Very cheap hotels and *cabinas*, costing from $5–$15 per night, usually have small rooms, poor lighting, a fan if you are lucky, and shared bathrooms. Some are spotlessly clean and well run, some are not. It's well worth checking them out if you are on a limited budget. To make it easier for you to choose accommodations, the table on pages 20–22 compares characteristics of the birding locations discussed in this book.

In this book, when referring to cost of hotels or *cabinas,* I use the following categories: low=less than $15–$25 per person; moderate=$25–$40 per person; expensive=more than $40 per person. All prices are in U.S. dollars.

Restaurants

In general, food is cheap in Costa Rica. Many restaurants (*sodas*), especially those serving Tico food, are very inexpensive. Most Tico restaurants serve good food, the staple being black beans, rice, some salad and a modest portion of meat (beef, pork or chicken)—and the whole affair is called *casados*. For a change of pace, try a pizzeria—some are quite good—or try some seafood. Sea bass with garlic (*corvina con ajo*) is absolutely delicious at many restaurants. Fruit plates are often available, cheap and delicious. Stop at stands and buy fruit for an early morning breakfast before or during your birding excursion.

Restaurant meals generally cost about one half or less than meals in North American restaurants. Some lodges where guests are more or less captive, there being no other choices nearby, offer breakfasts for $7 or $8 and lunch and supper for $10 or $15—very expensive for Costa Rica.

The following are some of the better restaurants I've come upon:

Turrialba:	Try the Pollo a la Eleña la Giralda in the centre of town for a very tasty and large serving of fajitas—hard to come by in Costa Rica.
San José:	Tin Jo (C11, A6 & 8) has excellent Thai food at reasonable prices.
Escazú:	Restaurante Parillada Argentina in Escazú has the very best steak I've had in Costa Rica—also very reasonable in price. However, if you prefer no or little salt, be sure to tell the waiter.
Sabana:	Giardino Restaurante Italiano is a three-year-old restaurant under new management. It has great Italian food, not pizza, at reasonable prices. 25 meters east of Sabana Sur del Colegio de Medicos.
Ciudad Quesada: **(San Carlos)**	Try the Coca Loca for good to excellent steak, fish and stir fries. It's next to Hotel Central on the street bordering the central park.

CHARACTERISTICS OF
MAJOR BIRDING DESTINATIONS

[1] Mod=Moderate; MD=Moderately difficult; D=difficult; N/A=not applicable
[2] Camping or staying with park personnel
[3] Numerous guided day tours available to region
[4] Charge for boat transport
[5] Air-conditioning available

NORTHWESTERN LOWLANDS

| Destination | Access | ACCOMMODATIONS | | Comfort Level | Expert Guide Availability | Difficulty of Birding | Comments |
		On-Site	Cost				
Curú Hacienda Wildlife Refuge	Easy	Yes	Low	Low	Possibly	Easy-MD	Alternative accommodation available in Paquera; birding along roads & well-developed trail system
Palo Verde National Park	M-D	Yes[2]	Low	Low	No[3]	Easy-MD	Birding along trails & roads
Santa Rosa National Park	Easy	Yes[2]	Low	Low	No	Easy-MD	Bird densities low during dry season
Colorado	Easy	Yes	Low	Low	No	Easy	Birding near salinas & mangroves
Los Chiles	Easy	Yes	Low-Mod	Low-Mod	Yes	Easy	Birding on farms, roads & trails
Río Frío –Caño Negro	Boat access	No	Mod[4]	N/A	Yes[3]	Easy	Birding rivers & wetlands normally with Los Chiles as base

SOUTHWESTERN LOWLANDS

| Destination | Access | ACCOMMODATIONS | | Comfort Level | Expert Guide Availability | Difficulty of Birding | Comments |
		On-Site	Cost				
Tárcoles	Easy	Yes	Low	Low-Mod	No	Easy	Birding along roads & paths
Tarcol Lodge	Easy	Yes	High	Mod	Yes	Easy-MD	Expert guides & tours included in daily rates; bird estuary from lodge
Carara Biological Reserve	Mod	No	Low day fee	N/A	No[3]	Easy-D	Few public trails; park can quickly become crowded
Villa Lapas	Easy	Yes	High	High[5]	No	Easy-D	Easy walking trails; birding from grounds or trails
Finca Los Cusingos	MD	No	Low day fee	N/A	No	Easy-MD	One main trail through well-developed second growth; gardens; clearings
Palmar Norte	Easy	Yes	Low-Mod	Low-Mod[5]	No	Easy-MD	Birding along roads & trails
Las Ventanas de Osa	MD[1]	Yes	High	Mod-High	Yes	Easy-MD	Expert guides & tours included in daily rate; birding from lodge & along trails
Golfito	Easy	Yes	Low-High	Low-High[5]	No	Easy-MD	Birding mostly along roads in area
Esquinas Rainforest Lodge	MD	Yes	High	Mod	Possibly	Easy-D	Easy birding in gardens & farmlands; difficult in forests

NORTHEASTERN LOWLANDS

Destination	Access	ACCOMMODATIONS On-Site	Cost	Comfort Level	Expert Guide Availability	Difficulty of Birding	Comments
Fortuna	Easy	Yes	Low-Mod	Low-Mod	Possibly	Easy	Birding along roads & trails; many guides in area but few expert birders
Arenal Observatory	Mod	Yes	High	Mod	Yes	Easy-MD	Birding from observation area & along trails
Murillo Farm	Mod	Yes	Low	Mod	No	Easy	Birding in orchards, farmland, gardens & along river
Puerto Viejo de Sarapiquí	Easy	Yes	Low-Mod	Low-Mod	No	Easy	Birding along roads & trails
La Selva	Mod	Yes	High	Mod	Yes[3]	Easy-D	Well-developed trails through primary lowland forest
Los Angeles	D	Yes	Low	Low	No	Easy	Birding along trails; wet walking
Oro Verde	D	Yes	Mod	Mod	Yes	Easy-D	Birding along trails; wet walking
Tortuguero	D	Yes	Low-High	Low-High[5]	Possibly	Easy	Expertise of guides with luxury lodges varies; birding is normally from boats
Virgen Del Socorro	Easy	No	N/A	N/A	No[3]	Easy-MD	Most birding from main road
Quebrada Gonzales	Easy	No	Low day fee	N/A	No	MD-D	Birding along one short trail & from around park buildings
Jardin Botanico Las Cusingas	Mod	Yes	Mod	Low-Mod	No	Easy-MD	Birding in garden & along trails through forest

SOUTHEASTERN LOWLANDS

Destination	Access	ACCOMMODATIONS On-Site	Cost	Comfort Level	Expert Guide Availability	Difficulty of Birding	Comments
Turrialba	Easy	Yes	Low-Mod	Low-Mod	No	Easy	Birding in farming countryside
CATIE	Easy	No	No	N/A	No	Easy	Birding in large grounds of research station
Puerto Viejo de Talamanca	Easy	Yes	Low-High	Low-High[5]	Yes	Easy-MD	Many side roads, trails, nicely forested in many areas
Hitoy-Cerere	D	Yes	Low	Low	No	Easy-MD	Trails through secondary & primary foothills forest, farmlands nearby

VALLE CENTRAL

Destination	Access	ACCOMMODATIONS On-Site	Cost	Comfort Level	Expert Guide Availability	Difficulty of Birding	Comments
Paraiso –Lankester Gardens	Easy	No	Day fee	N/A	No	Easy	Birding in gardens & adjacent wetlands

MOUNTAINS

Destination	Access	ACCOMMODATIONS On-Site	Cost	Comfort Level	Expert Guide Availability	Difficulty of Birding	Comments
Monteverde	MD	Yes	Low-High	Low-High[5]	Yes	Easy-D	Wide variety of birding walks & hikes in area
Vara Blanca	Easy	Yes	Low	Mod	No	Easy	Birding along roads & paths in mixed farmland
Santa Cruz	Easy	No	N/A	N/A	No	Easy-MD	Birding in steep mountains; mixed farmland
Tapantí National Park	MD	Possibly	Low	Low	No	Easy-D	Good road up valley with side trails; crowded on holidays & weekends
San Vito	Easy	Yes	Low-Mod	Low-Mod	No[3]	Easy-MD	Birding in mixed farmland & Wilson Botanical Gardens (includes forest)
Alturas	MD	Yes	Mod	Low	No	Easy-D	Birding along edge of forest & in adjacent farmland; trails in primary forest

HIGHLANDS

Destination	Access	ACCOMMODATIONS On-Site	Cost	Comfort Level	Expert Guide Availability	Difficulty of Birding	Comments
Póas Volcano	Easy	No	Low day fee	N/A	No	Easy-MD	Park gets very crowded; good birding away from main trails & on land adjacent to park
Cerro de La Muerte	Easy	Yes	Low	Mod	No	Easy-MD	Birding along roads & trails, páramo near tops of peaks
Albergue de Montaña Tapantí	Easy	Yes	Mod	Mod	No	Easy	Birding mainly from country roads
El Empalme	Easy	Yes	Low	Mod	No	Easy	Birding on acreage & surrounding roads & trails
Monte Sky	MD	Yes	Low	Low	Possibly	Easy-MD	Newly developed, possibly good birding in steep primary forest

PANAMA

Destination	Access	ACCOMMODATIONS On-Site	Cost	Comfort Level	Expert Guide Availability	Difficulty of Birding	Comments
Bocas del Toro	Mod	Yes	Low	Mod	No	Easy-MD	Birding on islands & in nearby main park
Changuinola River	MD	No	N/A	N/A	Yes	Easy-MD	Birding through mixed farmland along river

NICARAGUA

Destination	Access	ACCOMMODATIONS On-Site	Cost	Comfort Level	Expert Guide Availability	Difficulty of Birding	Comments
Esperanza	MD	No	Mod[6]	N/A	No	Easy-MD	Birding on old Somosa ranch, future tourist development; currently no infrastructure
Solentiname Islands	MD	No	Mod	N/A	No	Easy	Island is refuge for bird colonies

Water

Water in most Costa Rican towns is safe to drink. A notable exception is Puntarenas, which has had a chronic problem with bad water. As you get farther into the "back country," use discretion, especially in lowland areas. The water in Sierpe near Corcovado was bad when I was there. Be especially careful when flooding overloads drainage systems and mixes with town water supplies. It's time to stock up on bottled water when locals line up along streams to watch the floodwater rush by. Ticos also buy bottled water at these times, so watch for line-ups at stores that stock water.

Pests and Other Nasties

Mosquitoes can be bothersome in Costa Rica, although I've never seen the hordes that are so common in temperate and northern regions. Many species of mosquitoes are quite small and you may be supplying them with a feast without even knowing, until a few hours later when the itching starts! A good insect repellent containing DEET will deter them. At low-cost accommodations or when camping, mosquito netting will save you a lot of discomfort.

Midges are small insects, called *parrujas* in Costa Rica and "no-see-ums" in parts of North America. They are especially bothersome towards dawn and dusk at low elevations, especially along the southwest coast of Costa Rica. Avon "Skin-so-Soft" bath oil does a fairly good job of repelling these pests. Some livestock supply stores stock this product because farmers have found it to be effective in reducing bothersome insects on livestock! If you're going to be camping, especially in the southwest, be sure your mosquito netting is fine mesh. *Parrujas* can squeeze through the mesh of standard netting.

Chiggers are one of my worst enemies in Costa Rica because I have a fairly strong reaction to their bite. These insects are small biting mites that cling to you as you brush them off their perches on grass or twigs. They love to crowd into areas where clothing is fairly snug against the skin, such as along belt lines and especially under the tops of socks. There they feast on a bit of your skin for a few days before dropping off to begin another part of their life cycle. Their bite causes itching and scratching causes more itching! Insect repellents do not repel chiggers. Non-wettable elemental sulfur powder (available at large pharmacies) liberally dusted on socks, pant legs and belt lines deters these pests, although if you're in infested country it's difficult not to end up with a bite or two. Rubber boots are also an effective deterrent. Chiggers are seldom a problem in heavy forest, since they tend to infest pastures, grasslands, roadsides and other disturbed areas.

Ants are nearly everywhere in Costa Rica and most of them bite. Aside from flying insects, this is the pest most likely to bite you. Watch where you put your feet. If you step across an ant trail you can get hordes of them on you in a very short time. Don't sit on anything without careful inspection!

There are poisonous snakes in Costa Rica. Fortunately, most are nocturnal and seldom seen. Scorpions abound, especially in drier areas. Watch where you put your hands and feet. Stay on trails. Never put your feet (or hands) in underbrush or grass where you cannot see them. Africanized bees are becoming a problem, especially in dry areas such as Guanacaste. If you see bees or a nest, avoid loud noises and sudden movements and quietly leave the area. A mesh head net in a handy pocket is a useful precaution.

Safety and Crime

Although Costa Rica is still much safer than much of North America and Europe, crime and crime involving personal injury are increasing. San José, like any big city, has its problems. The northwest part of the city is fairly unsavory, but unfortunately it is where many bus terminals are. It's usually safer to take a taxi through this neighborhood, and don't walk it at night.

In general, safety increases as city size decreases, although there is a very unfortunate trend towards robbery of tourists in more remote areas. Trail-side robberies have occurred in Braulio Carrillo National Park (perhaps because of its proximity to San José). Read up on this subject in guide books and buy copies of the English-language newspaper *Tico Times* while in Costa Rica for current information.

Theft has always been a very large problem in Costa Rica. Be aware that if you are a *gringo* tourist, you are immediately singled out as a possible mark. Remember that you are likely very rich compared to most Ticos. The camera around your neck may have cost more money than many Ticos see in a year. Try not to present obvious targets. Use a money belt; never carry a wallet in a baggy pocket or a rear pocket. Beware of pick-pockets, especially at the Coca-Cola bus terminal (named after a bottling plant that once occupied the site). Be especially cautious in line-ups where people press up against one another— the pressure being released from your body may also be relieving you of your wallet. Don't leave things lying around and don't leave possessions in cars—if you absolutely have to, put them in the trunk. An unattended rental car can be a target for thieves.

Money

Currency in Costa Rica is based on the *colone*. Because of the government's policy of currency devaluation over the past serveral years, the value of the *colone* has been changing constantly. In early 1996, $1 U.S. equaled about 200 *colones.*

The only foreign currency that is readily accepted in business establishments is the U.S. dollar, but you are not likely to get a favorable exchange rate in anything other than a bank. The best thing to do is to get U.S. travelers' cheques and change small amounts as you need cash.

Money changers ply the streets of San José, but it is not a good idea to use them to change money or to cash travelers' cheques. Although some of them are honest and they do offer a slightly higher exchange rate than banks, many are con artists who pass out counterfeit money—U.S. $20 bills are a favorite. The scam is to take your U.S. dollars in hand and then, on some pretext like not having enough *colones* to make the transaction, return them to you. The returned money will often contain counterfeit bills that they have exchanged for your real ones.

GETTING AROUND IN COSTA RICA
Taxis

Taxi line-ups are usually near major bus stops or town plazas. Fares are supposed to be metered in San José, but there are some exceptions (e.g., special high rates seem to apply to and from the airport). Tourists are commonly gouged. When getting a taxi, settle the fare before starting out, or ask if he has a meter: *¿Tiene Maria?* or *¿Maria funcional?* (yes, a meter is called a Maria). Metered rates are generally lower than quoted flat rates. If a driver is returning to his home base after dropping off a passenger at an outlying community, you can often negotiate a very cheap "back-haul" fare. He's returning with or without you and the accepted practice is to return with you and add a few hundred *colones* to his day. If you get a taxi from one of the swanky hotels, fares will magically double. However, even when paying seemingly exorbitant rates, taxi fares in Costa Rica are generally substantially cheaper than in North America or Europe.

Road Conditions and Driving

Costa Ricans have some of the world's worst driving records for accidents and injuries to pedestrians. In addition, there are many dangerous conditions, even on major highways, ranging from roadways crumbling off into steep valleys, landslides (especially in Braulio Carrillo Park), narrow bridges without railings and missing planks, poorly marked construction zones and deep potholes. If you drive very defensively and are used to negotiating country backroads, you probably won't have any difficulties. If you are the type that breezes along a superhighway and you take it for granted that it will remain a superhighway around the next bend, you are in for trouble. Potholes are very dangerous at night, especially when lights from oncoming traffic reduce visibility. You don't have to be in constant terror driving in Costa Rica, but remember to be extra cautious and drive defensively.

In this book, I mention conditions of dirt roads and whether or not they are passable with normal small cars. Road conditions can change overnight, so what may have been passable when I drove the road may not be now. Minor improvements can also open up poor roads to normal traffic. Unless you're a pretty good driver when it comes to backroads, don't attempt some of the rough dirt roads I mention. In addition, be aware that rain can change conditions dramatically.

LITTER

Litter is a big problem in Costa Rica, not only with a few plastic cups thrown out of the car window, but with loads of household garbage stuffed in garbage bags. Many small communities simply don't have any garbage disposal system and pick-up in some areas of larger cities is not sufficient to keep up with garbage generation. Before being too critical, think about what you would do with your garbage if you had to dispose of it personally and there was no sanitary landfill nearby (or far away for that matter). Disposal often follows the NIMBY philosophy ("not in my backyard"), so that wide shoulders along public roads are used as dumps, while household yards are generally clean—often immaculately so. There is also a prevailing attitude that roadside garbage will eventually be picked up by public government workers, so it is sort of all right to create that need for employment. Sadly, rivers and streams are also used to carry away garbage.

Education programs are underway and the government is trying to upgrade disposal systems, but funds are sorely limited and the problem will remain for some time. Meanwhile, modern technology generates more and more seemingly indestructible plastics and other noxious or downright toxic compounds with little or no responsibility for their final disposal or break-down. Things were much more simple when nearly all household garbage was quickly biodegraded, especially in the tropics!

CHANGES TO EXPECT

The annual inflation rate in Costa Rica has been running at about 25 percent and wages have not risen equally. At the same time, tourism in the country has blossomed in the last 15 years, so that it is now the leading economic industry in the country, ahead of bananas, coffee and beef! With ever-rising costs and lots of tourists, there has been a tendency to increase prices disproportionately for services related to tourism.

However, the rate of increase of tourism in Costa Rica slowed appreciably in 1995, and there are signs that the bloom is off the banana. The number of tourists in the first three months of 1996, the peak season, actually decreased slightly compared with 1995. At the same time, the number of hotels, *cabinas*, resorts, etc., has steadily grown, so that many are now actually lowering their prices. Ticos were quick to raise prices when they could, but they are fiercely competitive and hard-working, and will do what they can to get business. I expect a considerable number of bankruptcies in the next few years, if this trend continues. At any rate, many bargains are now available in Costa Rica, compared to three or four years ago.

The recent strong growth in industries, agriculture and tourism has necessitated rapid changes in everything from bus schedules and ferry services to a multitude of government services. Every telephone number in the country changed in 1994, because an antiquated system had to be revamped to accommodate astronomical growth in the number of telephones. The number of automobiles in Costa Rica has also increased dramatically. I have provided names and rates of accommodations and other details to assist you in your travels, but please try not to be surprised or exasperated when a number or name turns out to be wrong. Arm yourself with the most recent good travel guide book you can find, and large doses of patience and flexibility, and you will be fine.

A FINAL NOTE

Maps in this book use the following legend:

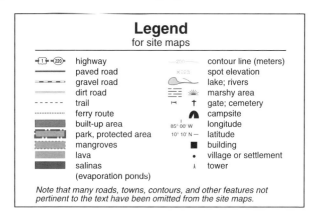

Remember that C=*Calle*=Street and A=*Avenida*=Avenue.

When telephoning to Costa Rica, dial 011 then the area code, 506, then the number.

As mentioned earlier, area lists in this book are based on my own observations when I was at a particular site. Therefore, if I was there in only April to June, only that column will be filled in and the columns for January to March and July to September will be blank.

THE NORTHWESTERN LOWLANDS

Turquoise-browed Motmots nest in burrows in road cuts, stream embankments and steep hillsides.

For our purposes, the Northwestern Lowlands, usually called Guanacaste by the locals, includes land generally less than 1,000 meters (3,300 feet) above sea level, in the northwestern portion of Costa Rica. All of this region is on the Pacific slope, except for a narrow strip between the Nicaraguan border and Cordillera de Guanacaste, which drains to the Caribbean via the Río San Juan. The area includes the Peninsula de Nicoya and Golfo de Nicoya and extends southward approximately to the small coastal town of Tárcoles and Carara National Park. The Interamerican Highway bisects the region as it passes from Nicaragua southwards to San José. Liberia is the major inland community, while Puntarenas is the major seaport. The town of Nicoya serves as a business center for the peninsula. Areas above 1,000 meters (3,300 feet) in the Cordillera de Guanacaste and Cordillera Tilarán are excluded from the region because of the different climatic conditions and avifauna at higher elevations.

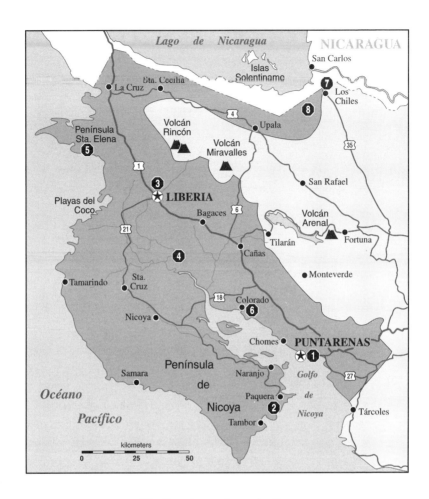

Birding Locations in the
Northwestern Lowlands of Costa Rica

① Puntarenas
② Curú Hacienda and Wildlife Refuge
③ Liberia
④ Palo Verde National Park
⑤ Santa Rosa National Park
⑥ Colorado
⑦ Los Chiles
⑧ Río Frío—Caño Negro Wildlife Refuge

Guanacaste has a pronounced dry season, usually from January to mid-March, and a more variable wet season for the remainder of the year. Because of the intensity and regularity of the dry season, actually the southernmost extension of the climate that produces the great deserts to the north, true dry tropical forest is found in the Guanacaste region. This climate has dramatic effects on bird distribution within the area and therefore we treat the region as a unit. Dry tropical forest once covered much of Guanacaste, but logging, farming and ranching have greatly altered the landscape. Fortunately, national parks have been created to protect or re-establish large tracts of forest, the most significant being Santa Rosa National Park at 49,515 hectares (122,300 acres), Guanacaste at 700 square kilometers (280 square miles) and Rincon de la Vieja at 14,083 hectares (34,785 acres). All are located north of Liberia, the area where natural dry forest once predominated.

The area around Liberia and to the north is the land of the cowboy and large cattle ranches. The Peninsula de Nicoya and land south of Cañas on the mainland are wetter and more fertile and farming becomes more important in these regions. Guanacaste is a land with an openness unusual in the tropics, created by the annual shedding of leaves of many trees during the dry season and by burning to maintain grasslands. However, savannas and pastures are generally pleasingly interspersed by thickets, treed watercourses (gallery forests in their most developed state) and many types of giant umbrella-shaped trees. One of these, the Guanacaste tree—the national tree of Costa Rica—is particularly attractive because of its huge trunk and great spreading crown. Ticos prize these trees for their beauty and utility in providing shade—one Guanacaste tree being sufficient "for an entire herd of cattle," according to many rancheros.

Guanacaste is rich in history and culturally important, a land where Ticos fought off invaders from Nicaragua three times between 1856 and 1955. Sites of these conflicts were centered around historic buildings in Santa Rosa National Park and more Ticos visit Santa Rosa because of its cultural importance than its ecological significance. It is their Alamo! Guanacaste is also the location of some of the most luxurious beach resorts in the country, mostly on the beautiful white sand beaches on the southwest coast of Peninsula de Nicoya. Although little of the Tico culture remains in some resorts, swimming pools are large, grounds are beautifully manicured and cuisine is excellent. There are also smaller establishments and some isolated beaches that are not too difficult to find; these are certainly worth the effort. Your tour guide book will give you all the information you need concerning beaches.

Despite the region's overall uniformity in sharing a pronounced dry season, substantial variations in climate and habitat exist within the Guanacaste region. In general, rainfall increases from north to south. The countryside

I bumped slowly along the rough dirt road as the light began to define leafless trees, savannas and the occasional cactus. I had to baby the low-clearance car over and around jagged rocks and boulders (they had once before ruptured a foolishly exposed fuel line). **A Thicket Tinamou** walked slowly across the road, became aware of me and scampered up the road embankment, bright orange legs flashing, propelling its football-shaped body into the underbrush. Santa Rosa National Park gets blazing hot during the dry season, but early morning hours are pleasant. It's a time for nocturnal animals to find a cozy hideaway, shelter from the coming light and heat. It's also a time for foraging, especially for birds. I was heading for the river bottom country, near Playa Naranjo, where the multi-hued greens of the gallery forest along the watercourses contrast with the bare white-gray limbs of the forest on hillsides and upper slopes. I parked the car and walked down the deeply shadowed dry riverbed of Río Poza Salada, thankful when the way was made easier as gravel and sand replaced boulders and cobbles in the streambed. I studied **White-lored Gnatcatchers** and **Rufous-naped Wrens** as they foraged in low thickets and also saw a few **Yellow Warblers** and **Yellow-throated Vireos** higher in the trees.

Down the broadened riverbed of the Río Nispersal, having passed the mouth of the Río Poza Salada, a flock of **White-crowned Parrots** landed and started foraging in nearby low trees along the north side of the river. Their brilliant red eye-rings, blue crowns, white foreheads and bright yellow beaks were a marvel as they climbed and fluttered through the treetops interspersed with startlingly red flowers. The lighting was ideal as the sun shone full upon them and a backdrop of blue sky completed an enchantingly beautiful picture.

between Chomes and Tárcoles is viewed as a transition zone that merges into the wetter, humid lowlands of the southwest. Rainfall also increases with elevation. Incongruously, the Guanacaste region also contains significant wetlands, relatively rare in Costa Rica owing to the country's overall rugged terrain. Important marshes and lakes are protected in Caño Negro National Wildlife Refuge, 9,969 hectares (24,623 acres), and Palo Verde National Park, 13,058 hectares (32,253 acres). Fortunately, the seasonal cycle is such that rains recharge wetlands in time for use by northern shorebirds and waterfowl. Hence, birders may enjoy both resident and migrant water birds from about September to March or April.

Lastly, although Costa Rica is not noted for large numbers or unique species of oceanic seabirds, the Golfo de Nicoya is by far the best place in the country to see petrels and shearwaters. Farms, ranches, marshes, large temporary lakes, nearshore marine waters and beaches all present good birding opportunities in the Guanacaste region, in addition to Central America's largest remaining dry tropical forest, protected by Santa Rosa National Park.

TRAVEL

Travel to the Guanacaste area from San José is quick and easy. At least eight Liberia-bound buses (Pulmitan 222-1650) leave San José daily from C14, A1 & 3. The trip takes a little more than four hours. An alternative route is via Puntarenas and ferrying to the Peninsula de Nicoya. Puntarenas buses (Empresarios 222-0064) leave San José nearly hourly from C12, A9 and arrive in about two hours. In Puntarenas, a bus to the ferry terminal (661-1069) runs along Avenida Central but for a dollar or so a taxi is more convenient. There are usually three morning and two afternoon sailings to Playa Naranjo during the busy season. There are also at least two sailings of a car and passenger ferry to the town of Paquera on the extreme southeastern tip of the peninsula and a new ferry service to Tambor has been initiated. Because ferry service to the Nicoya seems to be in a constant state of flux, check current schedules beforehand.

TROPICAL BIRD SPECIALTIES OF
THE NORTHWEST LOWLANDS

When you're birding in Costa Rica's Northwestern Lowlands, you will have a good opportunity to see a number of specialties, in addition to numerous birds that reach their southern limit of distribution in the region. The latter include North American water birds, doves, wrens, orioles, blackbirds and sparrows. Some are quite rare in Costa Rica or have restricted distribution. Within the country, 47 species are found only in the northwest (see Group 10 in Appendix I). Of these, the following 18 are considered fairly common tropical specialties which you have a good chance of seeing.

Thicket Tinamou	Brown-crested Flycatcher
Plain Chachalaca	White-throated Magpie-jay
Double-striped Thick-knee	Rufous-naped Wren
White-fronted Parrot	White-lored Gnatcatcher
Yellow-naped Parrot	Mangrove Vireo
Green-breasted Mango	Streaked-backed Oriole
Black-headed Trogon	Scrub Euphonia
Turquoise-browed Motmot	Yellow-throated Euphonia
Rose-throated Becard	Striped-headed Sparrow

A further eight common tropical specialties are restricted to the Valle Central and the Guanacaste lowlands:

Spotted-bellied Bobwhite	Cinnamon Hummingbird
Orange-fronted Parakeet	Plain-capped Starthroat
Pacific Screech-owl	Long-tailed Manakin
Steely-vented Hummingbird	Banded Wren

As if the above weren't enough, an additional 41 species (see Group 9 in the Appendix I) are restricted to the west. Although many of these species are rather common shorebirds, raptors, flycatchers, wrens and warblers which have broad distributions, sometimes ranging to North America in the summer, the following eight species are considered common tropical specialties to western Costa Rica. You also have a fairly good chance of spotting at least some of these species with a few days of birding in this region.

Lesser Yellow-headed Vulture	Rufous-and-white Wren
Plain-breasted Ground-dove	Mangrove Warbler
Striped Owl	Gray-headed Tanager
Panama Flycatcher	Ruddy-breasted Seedeater

PUNTARENAS AND PUNTARENAS FERRIES

If you are in Puntarenas for the night waiting for the morning ferry to the Nicoya Peninsula or otherwise, you should see some of the more common water-related birds. If you walk or drive along the river side of town, you are sure to see **Laughing Gulls**, **Royal Terns**, **Brown Pelicans** perching on boats (and making quite a mess of them) and scores of **Magnificent Frigatebirds** wheeling overhead. In the evening, flights of **White Ibis**, **Whimbrels** and the occasional **Willet** and **Olivaceous Cormorant** whiz down the far side of the river. It should also be a good area for shorebird migrations (August–October and March–May), but I've never had the chance to bird there at the proper time. There are more uncommon terns and gulls in the area, but most can be more easily seen in North America.

Taking the ferry from Puntarenas to the Nicoya Peninsula will give you a chance to study hosts of **Laughing Gulls** in all stages of development, and to scan for more uncommon seabirds such as **Franklin's Gull**, **Caspian Tern**, **Least Storm Petrel**, **Leach's Storm Petrel**, **Black Storm Petrel**, **Audubon's Shearwater** and the more common **Brown Booby**.

LIST OF BIRDS SIGHTED IN PUNTARENAS AREA
(a=abundant; c=common; u=uncommon; s=scarce; r=rare)

Species	Jan-Mar	Apr-Jun	Jul-Sep	Species	Jan-Mar	Apr-Jun	Jul-Sep
Brown Pelican	a			Whimbrel	a		
Olivaceous Cormorant	u			Willet	c		
Magnificent Frigatebird	c			Laughing Gull	a		
White Ibis	c			Royal Tern	c		
Turkey Vulture	a			Great Kiskadee	c		
Black Vulture	c			Great-tailed Grackle	a		

CURÚ HACIENDA AND WILDLIFE REFUGE

On most maps of Costa Rica, Curú Hacienda and Wildlife Refuge is a small dot on the coast of the eastern tip of the Nicoya Peninsula. Although Curú is relatively small, it is noteworthy because of bird watching and sustainable development and has an extremely interesting history, dating back to 1933 when Federico Schutt settled the area. Today, 84 hectares (207 acres), or five percent of the holdings of the Schutt family is a unique, privately owned and managed National Wildlife Refuge, recognized by the Government of Costa Rica. A further 70 percent, 1,100 hectares (2,717 acres), is protected forest, and 312 hectares (770 acres), 20 percent, is devoted to agriculture and cattle production.

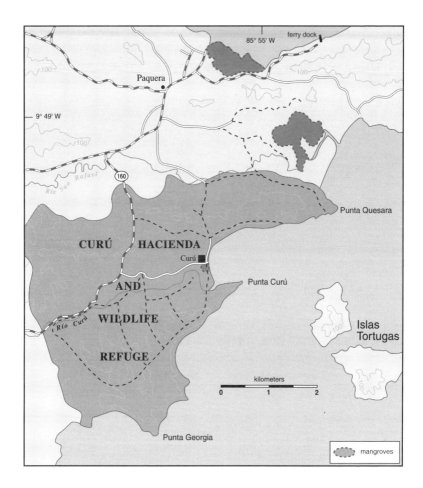

The far-sighted Schutt family seems to have been using their land for many years in a combination of conservation, tourism, farming, ranching and habitat enhancement practices that seem to fit the "modern" concept of sustainable development with very strong flavorings of biodiversity, research and innovation. It is a real living and breathing model that much of the rest of the world might look at with envy.

For birders, the result of the above effort is an alternative to national parks, which cost more to visit and generally have fewer developed trails and less infrastructure. It's also a great place to bird on the Nicoya because of the diverse habitats, including beaches, rocky headlands, mangrove swamps, dry and wet forested areas, pastures, orchards and stream bottoms. The family has also made special efforts to plant trees and shrubs, which provide food and shelter for wildlife.

LIST OF BIRDS SIGHTED IN CURÚ HACIENDA AND WILDLIFE REFUGE AREA

(a=abundant; c=common; u=uncommon; s=scarce; r=rare)

Species	Jan-Mar	Apr-Jun	Jul-Sep	Species	Jan-Mar	Apr-Jun	Jul-Sep
American White Pelican	c			Lineated Woodpecker	c		
Magnificent Frigatebird	c			Pale-billed Woodpecker	c		
Little Blue Heron	c			Ruddy Woodcreeper	s		
Great Egret	c			Olivaceous Woodcreeper	s		
Wood Stork	u			Streaked-headed Woodcreeper	c?		
Turkey Vulture	a			Barred Antshrike	u		
Black Vulture	a			Rose-throated Becard	s		
Common Black-hawk	u			Long-tailed Manakin	a		
Roadside Hawk	u			Scissor-tailed Flycatcher	s		
Crested Caracara	u			Tropical Kingbird	u		
Plain Chachalaca	c			Streaked Flycatcher	a		
Double-striped Thick-knee	u			Social Flycatcher	s		
Spotted Sandpiper	u			Great Kiskadee	a		
Red-billed Pigeon	c			Great-crested Flycatcher	c		
Common Ground-dove	c			Dusky-capped Flycatcher	s		
Inca Dove	a			Common Tody-flycatcher	s		
White-tipped Dove	a			Northern Rough-winged Swallow	c		
Orange-fronted Parakeet	c			White-throated Magpie-jay	a		
Orange-chinned Parakeet	c			Rufous-naped Wren	a		
White-fronted Parrot	c			Rufous-and-white Wren	a		
Yellow-naped Parrot	r			Tropical Gnatcatcher	u		
Squirrel Cuckoo	c			Yellow-throated Vireo	u		
Groove-billed Ani	c			Black-and-white Warbler	u		
Lesser Nighthawk	u			Prothonotary Warbler	s		
Little Hermit	u			Yellow Warbler	u		
Cinnamon Hummingbird	u			Chestnut-sided Warbler	u		
Black-headed Trogon	c			Northern Waterthrush	s		
Violaceous Trogon	s			Mourning Warbler	s		
Ringed Kingfisher	c			Rufous-capped Warbler	s		
Amazon Kingfisher	c			Great-tailed Grackle	c		
Green Kingfisher	c			Northern (Baltimore) Oriole	u		
American Pygmy Kingfisher	r			Red-legged Honeycreeper	u		
Turquoise-browed Motmot	c			Gray-headed Tanager	c		
Blue-crowned Motmot	c			Blue-black Grosbeak	s		
Hoffmann's Woodpecker	a			Blue-black Grassquit	u		

NW LOWLANDS

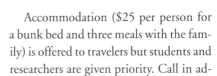

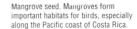

Accommodation ($25 per person for a bunk bed and three meals with the family) is offered to travelers but students and researchers are given priority. Call in advance (661-2392) even for a day visit, which costs $5. If you stay at Curú, don't expect gleaming porcelain, air conditioning or even a fan for that matter. There is a generator for electricity but it is sometimes down for repairs and the area where the main house is located is a rather ramshackle collection of frame houses and sheds with old and new farm equipment scattered about. Its first appearance may turn you off, but get out on the trails and enthusiasm will wax. If you don't want to rough it at Curú, stay at Ginana Restaurante y Cabinas (661-1444) in the pleasant town of Paquera, 5 kilometers (3 miles) to the north for $10 per person, including large clean rooms, private bath and fan. Their restaurant is excellent and very reasonably priced. There is also a camping area in a mango orchard near Paquera ($2 per person, including showers and toilets), about .5 kilometers (.3 miles) west of town on the right side of the road to the ferry dock. It's operated by the same business that has the ice plant.

When you bird Curú, you will be given a very useful map, but try to talk Adalina Schutt into accompanying you if she is there. She grew up on the farm and is a keen naturalist with a great wealth of knowledge on virtually everything in the area. Her sharp eyes were invaluable and together we managed to see more than 70 species. **Long-tailed Manakins** are especially abundant in the region. Look for them in thickets and low undergrowth. They are difficult to spot, so scan for bits of black and sky blue, and listen for their low whining *waaaah* call or a high-pitched whistle—*weet*. **Blue-crowned Motmots** and **Turquoise-browed Motmots** are also very common at Curú. We came upon a nesting **Double-striped Thick-knee** in a seemingly bare pasture with very little vegetation. She left her fairly large black-spotted egg in its scrape as she lumbered off in a not-too-hurried manner. **Rufous-naped Wrens** and **Rufous-and-white Wrens** are also abundant. The latter species' especially beautiful song of trills and whistles is often heard while scanning the thickets for this shy bird.

The mangrove habitat of Curú, near the road adjacent to the house as you arrive and along the Toledo trail, harbors bird specialties, including **Mangrove Warblers**, **Mangrove Hummingbirds**, **Mangrove Vireos** and **Prothonotary Warblers**.

I had good sightings in wet primary forest along the Punta Blanca Trail and Finca de los Monos. **Gray-headed Tanagers** were fairly common; look for these tame birds on the ground or perched on low undergrowth. **Orange-chinned Parakeets**, **White-fronted Parrots** and **Orange-fronted Parakeets** were also common. I spotted a **Blue-black Grosbeak**, a **Rufous-capped Warbler** and a **Yellow-breasted Vireo** near a small pool in an otherwise dry streambed. I also saw **Black-headed Trogons**, **Violaceous Trogons**, **Striped-headed Woodcreepers**, **Olivaceous Woodcreepers** and **Ruddy Woodcreepers**; the latter two species are quite uncommon.

The rare **Yellow-naped Parrot** is also found in Curú. **Squirrel Cuckoos** are abundant and, although I didn't see any, we heard several **Striped Cuckoos**. More importantly, Adalina said she sees **Lesser Ground-cuckoos** commonly near the road on the approach to the house. The same birds are probably involved in the sightings. Frequenting this area over a few days could result in a sighting of this rare species.

My best sightings at Curú were **Cinnamon Hummingbirds**, a **Lesser Nighthawk**, a **Rose-throated Becard** and an **American Pygmy Kingfisher**.

LIBERIA

The town of Liberia is the center and economic hub of the Guanacaste region. It is a pleasant, well-developed mature community with more paved roads and sidewalks than many other Tico towns. Some magnificent trees line the roads, especially near the courthouse. Typical of ranching centers, the town is slower paced, less hectic and crowded than some other faster growing Costa Rican communities.

Hotels, motels and B&B establishments exist in all price ranges. I stayed at the so-so, low-cost Hotel Guanacaste (666-2287) for a few days and paid $12 for a very small room, private bathroom and fan. It's conveniently close to the bus station but, with little effort, you can probably find better. The upscale Las Espuelas (666-0144, air-conditioned rooms $55–60), 2 kilometers (1.25 miles) east of Liberia, is about the best there is in the area. Their restaurant is also air conditioned, serves good food and is reasonably priced. If you really want a hoot, stay at Hotel La Ronda (666-2799) next door to Las Espuelas (about $12 a night). It looked closed, but persistent calling roused a friendly caretaker who cleaned and furnished a room on the spot. The entire establishment is dilapidated but shows signs of a lively "previous life" with a large vacant

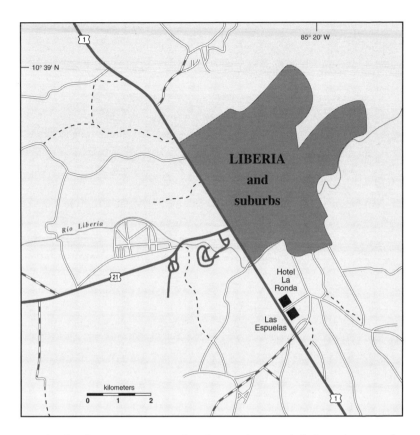

upstairs dancing area, empty swimming pool, grounds being taken over by surrounding vegetation and full-length mirrors beside each bed!

If you stay in the Liberia area, early morning walks are rewarding. For excellent light, walk north along the Interamerican Highway and turn off to the west (left) on one of the many side roads and trails at your first opportunity. **Orange-fronted Parakeets** are quite common in this area along with lesser numbers of **White-fronted Parrots**. The latter is especially striking. Both of these psittacids reach their southern limits of distribution in northwest Costa Rica. Beautiful **Turquoise-browed Motmots** are not uncommon. I saw one adult trying to feed a very large, fuzzy caterpillar to a juvenile. The adult had picture-perfect plumage, perhaps recently molted, with shining turquoise eyebrows and long, stalked tail feathers. Its rufous, green and black pattern stood out boldly in contrast to the juvenile, mostly a duller greenish blue. I also saw beautiful **White-winged Doves** with their black neck spot surrounded by pink, blue and orange pastels of their upper body, **Inca Doves, Plain-breasted Ground-doves, Hoffmann's Woodpeckers, Brown Jays** and **Black-headed Trogons**.

LIST OF BIRDS SIGHTED IN THE LIBERIA AREA
(a=abundant; c=common; u=uncommon; s=scarce; r=rare)

Species	Jan-Mar	Apr-Jun	Jul-Sep	Species	Jan-Mar	Apr-Jun	Jul-Sep
Turkey Vulture		a		Turquoise-browed Motmot		u	
Roadside Hawk		u		Hoffmann's Woodpecker		c	
Rock Dove		c		Tropical Kingbird		a	
Ruddy Ground-dove		u		Great Kiskadee		a	
Red-billed Pigeon		c		White-throated Magpie-jay		c	
White-winged Dove		u		Brown Jay		u	
Plain-breasted Ground-dove		s		Rufous-naped Wren		u	
Inca Dove		a		Great-tailed Grackle		a	
Orange-fronted Parakeet		c		Variable Seedeater		u	
White-fronted Parrot		c		Blue-black Grassquit		c	
Groove-billed Ani		a		Striped-headed Sparrow		u	
Black-headed Trogon		s		House Sparrow		c	

PALO VERDE NATIONAL PARK

Palo Verde is along the northeastern bank of the Tempisque River near its estuary in the Golfo de Nicoya. The park contains the most important wetlands in this area of Central America and is very important for concentrations of waterfowl, shorebirds and waders at the height of the dry season in January and February. Palo Verde is about the only place in Costa Rica to see **Jabirus**, **Glossy Ibises**, **Fulvous Whistling-ducks**, **Bay-winged Hawks** and North American waterfowl, including **American Wigeon**, **Northern Pintail** and **Cinnamon Teal**. Palo Verde also contains patches of dry tropical forest, where a variety of orioles, flycatchers, trogons and wrens occur.

The road to the park begins on the southeast side of Bagaces, a small town on the Interamerican Highway. There is a small sign at the turnoff, but watch closely, it's easily missed. Follow the signs to the park for about 24 kilometers (15 miles) and you're there. I saw hosts of **Scissor-tailed Flycatchers**, small numbers of **Plain-breasted Ground-doves** and other species along the road when I drove down. The road was passable (barely) for a car, and I had to get out several times to move large rocks. Parts of the drive could also get tricky during rains. Road works were in progress, so it may be improved by the time you get there. Palo Verde is difficult to access without a car, but taxis can be hired at Bagaces. I met one couple at the park who took a taxi from town for about $15, which was a real bargain considering the condition of the road.

Camping is permitted in three areas of the park, the most popular near the park headquarters, which also seems to be part of a working cattle ranch (somewhat disappointing in a national park!). This is also the only area with covered tenting areas, toilets, potable water and showers. The latter two are available

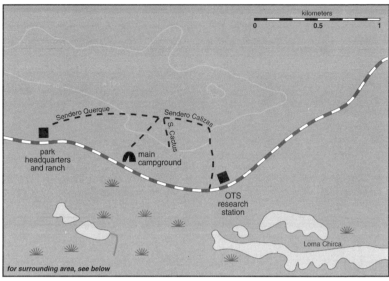

only at the park headquarters. Bring your own supplies here; there are no stores. If you make special arrangements (call 265-6696 or 240-9938), you can sometimes stay at the Organization of Tropical Studies research station for about $40, meals included. It's also sometimes possible to stay at the park headquarters for quite reasonable prices. Call 671-1062 or stop in at the park office in Bagaces to inquire about details.

Tours to the park are run by several companies operating out of Liberia, major towns on the Nicoya Peninsula and Cañas. Their one advantage is the boat transportation provided, so you are likely to see water-related species.

LIST OF BIRDS SIGHTED IN PALO VERDE AREA

(a=abundant; c=common; u=uncommon; s=scarce; r=rare)

Species	Jan-Mar	Apr-Jun	Jul-Sep	Species	Jan-Mar	Apr-Jun	Jul-Sep
Bare-throated Tiger-heron	c			Orange-fronted Parakeet	u		
Cattle Egret	a			Yellow-naped Parrot	u		
Little Blue Heron	a			Red-lored Parrot	s		
Great Egret	a			Squirrel Cuckoo	u		
Great Blue Heron	u			Groove-billed Ani	c		
Wood Stork	a			Blue-throated Goldentail	s		
Jabiru	s			Steely-vented Hummingbird	s		
Roseate Spoonbill	u			Black-headed Trogon	c		
Black-bellied Whistling-duck	c			Amazon Kingfisher	u		
Muscovy Duck	c			Hoffmann's Woodpecker	a		
Blue-winged Teal	c			Scissor-tailed Flycatcher	a		
Turkey Vulture	a			Tropical Kingbird	a		
Black Vulture	a			Great Kiskadee	c		
Common Black-hawk	c			Nutting's Flycatcher	s		
Gray Hawk	c			Great-crested Flycatcher	c		
Crested Caracara	u			Southern Rough-winged Swallow	c		
Yellow-headed Caracara	u			White-throated Magpie-jay	c		
Laughing Falcon	c			Rufous-naped Wren	c		
Northern Jacana	a			Banded Wren	s		
Mourning Dove	s			Yellow-throated Vireo	s		
Common Ground-dove	c			Yellow Warbler	s		
Plain-breasted Ground-dove	s			Northern (Baltimore) Oriole	c		
Inca Dove	a			Streaked-backed Oriole	c		
				Red-winged Blackbird	s		

If you don't take a tour, you're largely restricted to looking at most marshes from a distance and walking round the edges of the wetland area. However, like most day tours, travel is in the early morning and late afternoon, so the best birding times are more or less wasted. Consult your guide book for more details on organized tours.

One February morning, I birded the Sendero Cerros Calizos (Trail of the Limestone Hills), which takes off uphill near the main campground in a grove of mango trees. When I walked it early one morning, I quickly saw **Streaked-backed Orioles**, **Banded Wrens** and **Black-headed Trogons**. All three species are largely restricted to northwestern Costa Rica. The trail branches to the left in about .5 kilometers (.3 miles). The left-hand branch, Sendero Querque, arcs back and takes you behind the park administration building. The right-hand branch leads to two lookouts for broad vistas of the Tempisque River and marshlands.

The first branch, Sendero Cactus, is best for birding. From this vantage point, I was lucky enough to see a **Jabiru** flying over the marsh, along with numerous **Great Egrets** and **Wood Storks**. It's not uncommon to see lots of the latter soaring on the afternoon thermals. If you get to this area by mid-morning, it's best to backtrack to the Mango Grove Campground or continue on the Sendero Querque down to the park headquarters. If you continue eastward along Sendero Cerros Calizos you will go down the south face of the Cerro Guayacan, which is lightly treed and gets scorching hot even in the mid-morning sun.

One area not to miss is the spring that flows past the east side of the park headquarters building. Follow the cemented raceway upstream to the beginning of the spring. This is a favorite area for hummingbirds to drink and bathe. I saw dozens of **Steely-vented Hummingbirds** and a few **Blue-throated Goldentails**. **Yellow Warblers** and one vividly colored **Yellow-throated Vireo** also came for their morning ablutions.

Birding along the main road is also good because, in some areas, you can view the marsh area on one side and get a great view of the forest on the other. One evening, I birded about 300 meters (984 feet) east of the mango grove campground. **Blue-winged Teal**, **Black-bellied Whistling-ducks** and **Northern Jacana** were constantly flying by. Several flocks of **Muscovy Ducks** flew eastward, their white wing patches on dark bodies flashing in the evening sun. Looking in the other direction, I spotted **Orange-fronted Parakeets** and two quite uncommon **Yellow-naped Parrots**. Watch for the latter species as they fly by and land in the tops of the trees on the distant hillside. It's quite far away, but the lighting on the hillside is great in the evening and viewing is good with a spotting scope.

Closer to the road, **Hoffmann's Woodpeckers**, a **Crested Caracara**, **Red-winged Blackbirds**, **Northern Orioles**, **Streaked-backed Orioles** and **Rufous-naped Wrens** and flycatchers were visible. **Great-crested Flycatchers** are quite common, and I identified a **Nutting's Flycatcher** with some confidence as it regurgitated some insect bits and showed its orange mouth. Both species are quite tame and can be studied at length.

A road to the left of the park buildings leads to the Tempisque River. The road is barely passable for a car even when it's dry, so be careful if you are driving. Most of the road traverses flat river-bottom habitat where I saw few birds, perhaps owing to high winds when I was there, but the drive was worthwhile if only to see what I estimated to be 500–600 **Great Egrets** roosting on trees along the river, downstream of a park building. They looked like great globs of white cotton festooning the green vegetation. A few **Bare-throated Tiger-herons** were also mixed in with the egrets.

Gray Hawks and Yellow-headed Caracaras are quite common in this area, and I saw two **Common Black-hawks** along the road to the western camping area in the Catalina section of the park. One of my best experiences in Palo Verde was hearing a pair of **Laughing Falcons** giving a duet of their loud *wah-co, wah-co, wah-co* cries, which lasted for more than two minutes. Palo Verde and the surrounding area is about the only place in Costa Rica where you have a reasonable chance of seeing **Bay-winged Hawks**, which concentrate in the area to feed on water-associated birds.

In the southwest section of the park are trails through old-growth forest, savannas and wetlands. The mixture of habitats should be great for birds and a visit just to see the trees would be worthwhile. Palo Verde is also one of the better areas in Costa Rica to see other types of wildlife. Iguanas and howler and white-faced monkeys are everywhere; coatis (similar to a raccoon but with a long, flexible snout) and white-tailed deer are abundant. One morning a small band of collared peccaries (much like a pig with tusks) foraged through the camping area.

SANTA ROSA NATIONAL PARK

The entrance to Santa Rosa National Park is a few hundred meters west of the Interamerican Highway, about 37 kilometers (23 miles) north of Liberia. The most commonly visited portion of the park has a campground with potable water, showers and bathrooms at the end of a good 16 kilometer (10 mile) road. You can also eat with staff if you give them advance notice, but it's moderately expensive to do so. Visitors with no cars commonly take a bus from Liberia, get off at the park entrance beside the highway and hitchhike the rest of the way. Also near the campground are administrative buildings, accommodations for staff and a fort-like old ranch house around which some historic battles were fought.

Most of Santa Rosa is dry tropical forest where bird densities are quite low, especially in the dry season, from December to late April. But there are patches of beautiful gallery forest and some small mangrove areas near the beaches. Santa Rosa is the best place I know to see **Great Curassows** and **Crested Guans**. It's also a good place to look for the fairly rare **Elegant Trogon**, to study up on difficult-to-identify myiarchids, such as **Great-crested Flycatchers, Brown-**

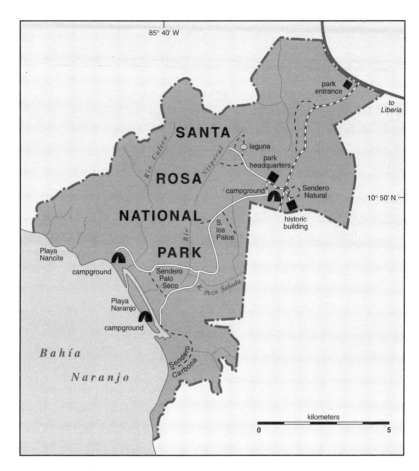

crested Flycatchers and Dusky-capped Flycatchers, and to search for rare cuckoos, including the **Yellow-billed Cuckoo, Mangrove Cuckoo** and **Lesser Ground-cuckoo.**

There is a cement trough filled with water near the main campground at Santa Rosa. If you are camping, try to get a spot near it or at least lounge nearby in midday. During the dry season, the water attracts many species of birds: **Hoffmann's Woodpeckers, White-throated Magpie-jays, White-tipped Doves, White-winged Doves, Inca Doves** and **Common Ground-doves.** A special treat was a small flock of **Crested Guans** that came to drink near sunset every day. These birds are fairly common only in parks in Costa Rica, because of deforestation and hunting.

About 2.5 kilometers (1.5 miles) from the campground down the road to Playa Naranjo is a trail, Sendero de los Patos, that takes off to the left and ends up at a look-out (*mirador*) slightly more than 1 kilometer (.6 miles) away. The trail winds through some dry forest with lots of bull's horn acacia trees. Watch out for the ants that live inside the thorns—they come out and sting things that touch the tree! Strangely enough, some birds, especially **Streaked-backed Orioles**, commonly hang their nests from these trees and the ants do not seem to bother them or their young.

The yellow blossoms and brown seed pods of Cortez trees bring bright relief to the dry tropical forest.

The mid-portion of the trail follows a streambed that usually retains some small pools of water, even in the dry season. The last third of the trail is along a slope with great views of the adjacent hillside and canyon, which are covered with gallery forest. I didn't see much except doves until I reached the lower area near the overlook. There I was rewarded with great views of **Streaked-backed Orioles**, **Scrub Euphonias** and **Plain-capped Starthroats**, all species that are specialties of northwestern Costa Rica. I also saw **Red-legged Honeycreepers** and a variety of flycatchers, including **Boat-billed Flycatchers**. When you're birding in Santa Rosa, give this area high priority. It's easy to get to, it's an easy walk with a great view at the end and I'm sure there are many more birds in the area than I saw.

The road from the campground to Playa Naranjo was barely passable by car during the dry seasons of 1995 and 1996, even though signs tell you it's not. There are *very* rough spots, but if you're a good driver and take it slowly, you shouldn't have many problems. As an alternative, try hitching a ride. Most people don't mind giving strangers a lift to the beach. The first 8 kilometers (5 miles) of the road are through dry forest and pasture reverting to forest. The road then descends a fairly steep slope for about 2 kilometers (1.2 miles) and then enters a beautiful mature gallery forest where most of the trees have leaves even during the dry season. This is in stark contrast to most of the leafless trees elsewhere. Walk down the road and along Sendero Palo Seco Estero Real for some excellent birding. **Great Curassows** are common in this area. I spotted three small groups in two days of birding in March. I also saw **Black-headed Trogons**, **Common Black-hawks**, **Squirrel Cuckoos**, **Pale-billed Woodpeckers**, **Great-crested Flycatchers** and **Brown-crested Flycatchers**.

LIST OF BIRDS SIGHTED IN SANTA ROSA AREA

(a=abundant; c=common; u=uncommon; s=scarce; r=rare)

Species	Jan-Mar	Apr-Jun	Jul-Sep
Thicket Tinamou	s		
Brown Pelican	u		
Magnificent Frigatebird	a		
Bare-throated Tiger-heron	c		
Green-backed Heron	u		
Snowy Egret	u		
Great Egret	c		
Great Blue Heron	u		
Wood Stork	c		
White Ibis	c		
Roseate Spoonbill	u		
Turkey Vulture	a		
Black Vulture	a		
Common Black-hawk	u		
Roadside Hawk	c		
Crested Caracara	u		
Crested Guan	c		
Great Curassow	c		
Spotted Sandpiper	u		
Red-billed Pigeon	s		
White-winged Dove	c		
Common Ground-dove	a		
Inca Dove	a		
White-tipped Dove	a		
Orange-chinned Parakeet	c		
White-fronted Parrot	c		
Yellow-naped Parrot	u		
Groove-billed Ani	c		
Striped Cuckoo	u		

Species	Jan-Mar	Apr-Jun	Jul-Sep
Common Pauraque	c		
Cinnamon Hummingbird	u		
Plain-capped Starthroat	u		
Ruby-throated Hummingbird	u		
Elegant Trogon	s		
Black-headed Trogon	c		
Ringed Kingfisher	u		
Green Kingfisher	u		
Hoffmann's Woodpecker	c		
Pale-billed Woodpecker	u		
Streaked-headed Woodcreeper	u		
Tropical Kingbird	u		
Boat-billed Flycatcher	u		
Great Kiskadee	c		
Brown-crested Flycatcher	c		
Great-crested Flycatcher	u		
White-throated Magpie-jay	a		
Rufous-naped Wren	c		
Banded Wren	u		
White-lored Gnatcatcher	c		
Yellow-throated Vireo	s		
Yellow Warbler	s		
Northern Waterthrush	s		
Northern (Baltimore) Oriole	u		
Streaked-backed Oriole	u		
Scrub Euphonia	s		
Red-legged Honeycreeper	s		

For a great early morning walk with the rising sun behind you, head down the bed of the Río Poza Salada from where the road crosses the river, and then down the bed of Río Nispersal to where the Sendero Palo Seco crosses the river. A left turn on the Sendero Palo Seco will take you back to the road. (Walk the Sendero Palo Seco from the road first so you can find where it crosses Río Nispersal. The trail crossing is not too obvious when you're coming down the riverbed and could be easily missed.) **Orange-chinned Parakeets** and **White-crowned Parrots** are fairly common along the river. The latter gave me especially beautiful views when a small flock perched on some low trees beside the riverbank to feed on some flowers. The morning sun vividly showed their blue crowns, red facial patches and white foreheads.

Yellow-naped Parrots also occur in the area. Watch for pairs flying overhead and try to see where they land. Their call is much lower and mellower than that of other parrots in the area. Low thickets along the river are good for **White-lored Gnatcatchers**, a species nearing its southern limit of distribution in northwest Costa Rica. Hummers were not abundant when I was there, but I did manage to see **Plain-capped Starthroats**, **Cinnamon Hummingbirds** and the good old North American standby, the **Ruby-throated Hummingbird**, which is quite uncommon in Costa Rica.

There were some isolated pools of water in the lower section of Río Nispersal. Flycatchers were common in these areas, as were a variety of water birds, including **Great Egrets**, **Snowy Egrets**, **Great Blue Herons** and even **Wood Storks** and a few **Roseate Spoonbills**. **Bare-throated Tiger-herons** were also quite tame and abundant. When I came upon a small flock of **Great Curassows** drinking from a pool, they "melted" into the surrounding underbrush instead of flying off when they detected me.

Another birding trail is the Sendero Natural, a short 1 kilometer (.6 mile) loop that begins at the hacienda. Most of it winds through dry forest, but a few patches of wetter terrain support larger trees and well-developed undergrowth. The trail also crosses a stream that winds through a short cave where a few bats can be seen entering and leaving. The streambed was dry when I was there in February, but it should attract more birds earlier in the dry season. There were not many birds in the area when I walked the trail early one morning—a few flycatchers, a **Banded Wren**, two **Crested Guans** still roosting in trees, a **Roadside Hawk** near the hacienda. However, my companion saw a quite rare **Elegant Trogon**, of which I only got a tantalizing glimpse as it flew through a patch of the second-growth forest.

Watch for **Thicket Tinamou** in Santa Rosa. They are quite common but most easily seen only in the very early morning.

COLORADO

Colorado is a small coastal town near the mouth of the Río Tempisque at the extreme north end of the Golfo de Nicoya. Although there is some good dry country birding in the vicinity, the region is also dotted with salinas, which are almost always adjacent to mangrove swamps. Salinas are areas where salt is made by evaporating sea water in a series of shallow ponds. The briny ponds are filled with multitudes of salt-loving crustaceans, which in turn attract a variety of water birds. Many salinas are scattered around flat regions adjacent to the Golfo de Nicoya and they should be high on the list of specialized habitats to bird in Costa Rica. Always ask permission to take a walk around the ponds because they are private property. I've never been refused this request and the owners or managers are usually very interested in what you are doing. They can also often tell you of special birds in the area and local movement patterns.

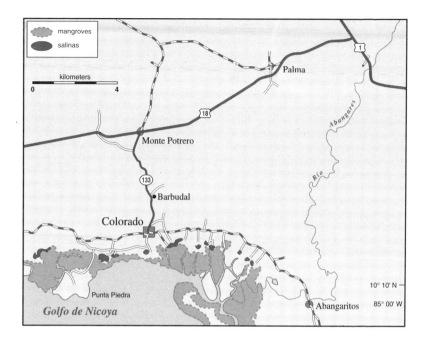

When I was in the Colorado area in early April, I was mainly interested in migrant shorebirds, but I saw other interesting species. A nice surprise was a small flock of **Spotted-breasted Orioles** feeding in a tree early one morning beside some farm buildings. Within Costa Rica, this species is restricted to the Guanacaste area and is much more difficult to find than the similarly restricted **Streaked-backed Oriole**. Another treat was a **Turquoise-browed Motmot** perched on a root beside its burrow along a road embankment. This colorful species is always a treat to see. **Black-headed Trogons**, **Rufous-naped Wrens**, **White-throated Magpie-jays** and **Squirrel Cuckoos** are also quite common in the region, along with other more common birds. I'm always a little surprised when I see an **Eastern Meadowlark**, as I did in this area, because it is a species I always associate with North America.

Nearly any road toward the coast will lead to a salina, including the main road through Colorado. While morning is the best time to look for mangrove species, many shorebirds come to salinas in the afternoon, primarily to rest and loaf. One day, I sat in the shade beneath some trees and let the birds come to me for a few hours. Several mixed flocks of **Western Sandpipers** and **Semipalmated Sandpipers** foraged in the area until they settled down to rest in early afternoon. Some of the Westerns were beginning to show the rufous of their breeding plumage in early April. At times it was possible to get both species in view with the spotting scope at once. Bill length of the two species is

LIST OF BIRDS SIGHTED IN COLORADO AREA

(a=abundant; c=common; u=uncommon; s=scarce; r=rare)

Species	Jan-Mar	Apr-Jun	Jul-Sep	Species	Jan-Mar	Apr-Jun	Jul-Sep
Olivaceous Cormorant		u		Sandwich Tern		u	
Magnificent Frigatebird		c		Rock Dove		c	
Bare-throated Tiger-heron		u		Common Ground-dove		u	
Green-backed Heron		u		Ruddy Ground-dove		a	
Little Blue Heron		u		Inca Dove		c	
Tricolored Heron		s		White-tipped Dove		c	
Snowy Egret		u		Squirrel Cuckoo		u	
Great Egret		c		Black-headed Trogon		u	
Wood Stork		c		Turquoise-browed Motmot		u	
White Ibis		c		Hoffmann's Woodpecker		c	
Common Black-hawk		u		Tropical Kingbird		a	
Crested Caracara		u		Great Kiskadee		a	
Black-necked Stilt		a		Great-crested Flycatcher		u	
Black-bellied Plover		a		Southern Rough-winged Swallow		c	
Semipalmated Plover		u		Mangrove Swallow		c	
Whimbrel		c		White-throated Magpie-jay		a	
Lesser Yellowlegs		u		Rufous-naped Wren		a	
Willet		c		Clay-colored Robin		c	
Spotted Sandpiper		u		Yellow Warbler		u	
Ruddy Turnstone		u		Great-tailed Grackle		a	
Short-billed Dowitcher		u		Spotted-breasted Oriole		u	
Western Sandpiper		a		Eastern Meadowlark		u	
Stilt Sandpiper		u		Blue-gray Tanager		c	
Laughing Gull		u		White-collared Seedeater		c	
Royal Tern		c		Striped-headed Sparrow		c	

noticeably different when they are side by side, but it's much more difficult to tell them apart as they dart about foraging.

Several flocks of **Black-bellied Plovers**, some also beginning to show their breeding colors, came in and promptly settled down to rest. A single **Ruddy Turnstone** was with one flock of **Black-bellied Plovers**, and a few **Semipalmated Plovers** walked about on the mud flats. There were also a few **Short-billed Dowitchers** lazily preening their feathers while the plovers slept. Nearly every salina seems to have at least 20 or 25 **Black-necked Stilts** permanently foraging in the ponds, along with a few **Lesser Yellowlegs** and **Spotted Sandpipers**. The stately **Black-necked Stilts** with their red legs and striking black and white pattern are in bold contrast to many of the other more drab shorebirds. I also saw a few **Stilt Sandpipers**, which seemed to tower above the other shorebirds on their long legs. Large flocks of **Royal Terns** also flew in and were joined by smaller numbers of **Sandwich Terns** to form a dense resting flock.

Other water birds such as **Wood Storks, White Ibis**, egrets and herons are also common around salinas. Some of the more uncommon ones to watch for are **Tricolored Herons, Bare-throated Tiger-herons, Olivaceous Cormorants** and **Reddish Egrets.** A host of other shorebirds winter or pass through the area on their way to their breeding grounds. Some of the more common ones to watch for are **Marbled Godwits, American Oystercatchers, Wilson's Phalaropes, Greater Yellowlegs, Sanderlings, Least Sandpipers** and **Red Knots.** Although Costa Rica is not world renowned for its shorebirds as it is for tropical species, it's still worthwhile to spend an afternoon or more birding salinas, especially from late March to early May when migrants are moving northward and beginning to show their more vivid plumages.

If you want to get to Colorado from San José, take the Interamerican Highway towards Liberia and 20 kilometers (12 miles) before Cañas, take Highway 18 towards the ferry that goes over the Tempisque. Proceed down Highway 18 for about 11 kilometers (7 miles), then take a left. Colorado is about 5 kilometers (3 miles) further along. If you don't have a car, this trip is more difficult but still possible. Any of the San José to Guanacaste buses will let you off along the Interamerican Highway. There are local buses from there between Juntas and Colorado.

Colorado is a small town with no tourist facilities. There is one rather dingy "hotel" next to a bar, called Calinar de Colorado (678-0141), where beds are about $5 per person. Cabinas de Raisal (no phone), located on a small farm about 2 kilometers (1.2 miles) east of Colorado, is said to have better accommodations for about $12 per person or $15 for two.

LOS CHILES

The town of Los Chiles is in north central Costa Rica, a few kilometers from the Nicaraguan border. Although the region was troubled during the strife in Nicaragua, life has returned to more peaceful times. This region is interesting for birders because it is on the eastern edge of the drier climatic zone that extends westward along the border and south into the Guanacaste region. A mixture of bird species characteristic of dry and wet climates is present in the area. The region also includes the large but temporary lake, Lago Caño Negro, which provides unique habitat for a number of species.

Two direct buses to Los Chiles from San José leave from A3, C.18 & 20 every day. More frequent buses for Los Chiles, nine a day, leave from Ciudad Quesada (San Carlos), so if the direct buses aren't convenient, get a bus from San José to Ciudad Quesada from the Coca Cola station and go on from there.

The Los Chiles area has inexpensive and moderately priced hotels, such as Hotel Jabiru. A nice place about 3 kilometers (2 miles) out in the country

south of town is Cuajipal Hotel y Restaurante (223-3030). It's a moderately priced, new motel-style small complex with a restaurant in a separate building. The good news is that it's located on a 200 hectare (500 acre) farm, which has fruit trees and swamps intermixed with bean fields, pastures and small patches of lowland forest. If you don't have a car it's a little inconvenient, but a taxi ride from Los Chiles only costs a few dollars. Waking up to the cool, quiet mists of the Caribbean lowlands is worth it and an early morning bird walk is at your doorstep.

I spotted 45 species in the area on a morning walk, including a **Black-collared Hawk**, which is quite rare in Costa Rica. These hawks are commonly seen in the Los Chiles–Lago Caño Negro area from December to April. Apparently local movements are involved but no one seems to know where the hawks go from May to November. I also saw **Black-throated Wrens** and **Hooded Warblers** foraging together in a small patch of second-growth forest which provided shade for cattle. The wrens were quite difficult to identify in the shady undergrowth, because of their constant movement and very inconspicuous white auricular streaks. (They acted more like antbirds than wrens.) The warblers, a fairly rare migrant and winter resident in Costa Rica, stood out like a neon sign with their bright yellow faces framed in black.

One evening, I walked to a brush pile in the bean field near the hotel, where I saw one **Yellow-olive Flycatcher**. Look for an eye-ring and a pale iris to distinguish it from the **Yellow-margined Flycatcher**. I was also pleasantly surprised to see a male **Indigo Bunting** and a pair of **Ruddy-breasted Seedeaters**. The latter species is very patchily distributed in Costa Rica and is found mainly in the Río Frío area and in a few areas in southwestern Costa Rica (e.g., Térraba

LIST OF BIRDS SIGHTED IN LOS CHILES AREA

(a=abundant; c=common; u=uncommon; s=scarce; r=rare)

Species	Jan-Mar	Apr-Jun	Jul-Sep	Species	Jan-Mar	Apr-Jun	Jul-Sep
Cattle Egret	a	a		Yellow-olive Flycatcher	s		
Little Blue Heron	c	c		Common Tody-flycatcher	u	u	
Great Egret	c	c		Northern Beardless-tyrannulet			r
Wood Stork	c	c		Yellow-bellied Elaenia	c	u	
Green Ibis	u			Mangrove Swallow	a	a	
Roseate Spoonbill	u			Black-throated Wren	u		
Blue-winged Teal	u			Clay-colored Robin	u	c	
Turkey Vulture	a	a		Black-and-white Warbler	u		
Black Vulture	a	a		Yellow Warbler	u		
Black-shouldered Kite	c	c		Northern Waterthrush	u		
Black-collared Hawk	c			Gray-crowned Yellowthroat	c		
Roadside Hawk	u			Hooded Warbler	s		
Crested Caracara	u	u		Bronzed Cowbird	u		
Northern Jacana	a	c		Great-tailed Grackle	a	c	
Rock Dove	a	c		Red-winged Blackbird	a		
Common Ground-dove	u	u		Eastern Meadowlark	c		
Inca Dove	c			Golden-hooded Tanager	c	u	
Orange-chinned Parakeet	c	c		Red-legged Honeycreeper	u	u	
White-crowned Parrot	c	u		Blue-gray Tanager	c	c	
Red-lored Parrot	u	s		Grayish Saltator	u	u	
Groove-billed Ani	a	a		Indigo Bunting	s		
Striped Cuckoo	u	u		White-collared Seedeater	a	a	
Lesser Nighthawk	c			Variable Seedeater	c	a	
Rufous-tailed Hummingbird	c	u		Ruddy-breasted Seedeater	u	c	
Lineated Woodpecker	u			Thick-billed Seed-finch	a		
Tropical Kingbird	a	a		Blue-black Grassquit	a	a	
White-ringed Flycatcher	c	c		Black-striped Sparrow	c	c	
Social Flycatcher	u	c		House Sparrow	u	u	
Great Kiskadee	a	a					
Tropical Pewee	c	s					

and Coto). **Indigo Buntings** are not all that commonly seen in Costa Rica, except when numerous birds are passing through during migrations. During their winter residence in the tropics, male **Indigo Buntings** are not the bright blue that people are accustomed to seeing during the North American summer. They are dressed more like females, but with slightly bluer shoulders and scattered blue feathers elsewhere.

On another very brief outing in May near Los Chiles, I saw a pair of diminutive **Northern Beardless-tyrannulets** in shrubs bordering an open cattle pasture. This species reaches the southern limit of its distribution in Costa Rica and can be quite difficult to find within the country.

Watch for **Lesser Nighthawks**, which are commonly seen feeding in the area at dusk.

RÍO FRÍO—CAÑO NEGRO WILDLIFE REFUGE

The Río Frío drains an extensive low marshy area south of Los Chiles and forms Lago Caño Negro between June and April. Because of its unique character, much of the area is protected by the 1,000 hectare (2,500 acre) Refugio Nacional de Vida Silvestre Caño Negro. Owing to its swampy nature, the area is renowned for its water birds, many of which you can see in the southern United States. But there are also special tropical birds that are easily seen in this area, including **Jabirus**, **Wood Storks**, **Muscovy Ducks** and **Great Potoos**. The only known breeding colony of **Nicaraguan Grackles** in Costa Rica is located near Lago Caño Negro.

Because of the popularity of the area, there are now boat tours up the Río Frío that start in the town of Los Chiles. One of the easiest ways to see the area is to join a day tour from the town of Fortuna (near the Arenal volcano) for a cost of about $40 per person. This price includes the drive to Los Chiles, a four- or five-hour boat trip up the Río Frío, a hot lunch somewhere along the river and return. Boats are canopied and have a capacity of about 20, although the one we were on was only half full. The guides on the boats are quite knowledgeable and keep each other informed about the locations of special birds and animals along the way.

Although the Río Frío winds through mostly farmland from Los Chiles to Caño Negro, most of the streambanks and some surrounding land are heavily vegetated and give the impression of wilderness. This impression is augmented by iguanas sunning on branches, turtles basking on logs and howling monkeys in the treetops. A great variety of birds becomes visible as each bend of the river is negotiated along with hundreds of caimans, reptiles similar to alligators and crocodiles, in the river and along the banks. Go if you can—it's well worth the effort, even though the tours take place from mid-morning to mid-afternoon.

When I took the trip in mid-June, Lago Caño Negro was just beginning to flood and none of the wintering ducks were present. I saw five species of herons, including **Boat-billed Herons** and **Bare-throated Tiger-herons**, and a number of **Wood Storks**, **Green Ibises** and **Purple Gallinules**. A **Gray-necked Wood-rail** was foraging in marsh grass across from our luncheon spot. On the way back to Los Chiles, I was very fortunate to see a **Sungrebe**, and a **Great Potoo** was sitting on a high branch beside the river. This tropical nocturnal owl-like bird normally perches with an upright stance. When disturbed, it raises its head so that its entire body is vertically oriented, more resembling the continuation of a dead limb than a bird. Other nice sightings included a **Black-headed Trogon** and a **Red-fronted Parrotlet**. The latter species is more commonly found in east slope foothills and was a very unusual sighting for the area. Although I didn't see any, **Nicaraguan Grackles** and **Lesser Yellow-headed**

LIST OF BIRDS SIGHTED ALONG
THE RÍO FRÍO AND IN THE LAGO CAÑO NEGRO AREA
(a=abundant; c=common; u=uncommon; s=scarce; r=rare; vr=very rare)

Species	Jan-Mar	Apr-Jun	Jul-Sep	Species	Jan-Mar	Apr-Jun	Jul-Sep
Olivaceous Cormorant	a			Yellow-headed Caracara	u		
Anhinga	a			Limpkin	s		
Bare-throated Tiger-heron	u			Gray-headed Chachalaca	s		
Black-crowned Night-heron	c			Gray-necked Wood-rail	s		
Yellow-crowned Night-heron	c			Purple Gallinule	u		
				Sungrebe	r		
Boat-billed Heron	s			Northern Jacana	c		
Green-backed Heron	c			Crimson-fronted Parakeet	u		
Little Blue Heron	c			Red-fronted Parrotlet	s		
Snowy Egret	c			Squirrel Cuckoo	u		
Great Egret	a			Great Potoo	s		
Green Ibis	u			Black-headed Trogon	u		
White Ibis	a			Ringed Kingfisher	c		
Roseate Spoonbill	u			Amazon Kingfisher	c		
Black-bellied Whistling-duck	u			Green-and-rufous Kingfisher	vr		
				Mangrove Swallow	c		
Roadside Hawk	u			Montezuma Oropendola	c		

Vultures are quite common in the Caño Negro area, the only region in Costa Rica where they regularly breed.

On another short boat ride on the Río Frío in May a few years later, I was lucky enough to see a **Green-and-rufous Kingfisher**, the rarest of kingfishers in Costa Rica, and my first **Limpkins** in the country.

If you stay in Los Chiles, you can hire a local guide with a smaller boat who should have flexible hours and can give personalized service. Oscar Rojas at Los Patates Restaurante (471-1297) is a good choice. His boat can hold up to 10 people, but he likes fewer. His rates are $15 per person for six people or more, or $25 per person for four people. Of course, he would be glad to take one or two people for about $100. Not a bad deal for a personal boat tour where you can set your own pace and objectives and have an expert guide.

Some of Oscar's good regular bird sightings include **Royal Flycatchers, Black-collared Hawks** (December to April), **Spotted-breasted Wrens, Bay Wrens, American Pygmy Kingfishers, Limpkins** (October to January), **White-collared Manakins, Prothonotary Warblers, Little Tinamous, Nicaraguan Grackles** and **Lesser Yellow-headed Vultures**. Of course, this list does not include a host of more common birds that you will surely see. While most of the above birds can be seen near Los Chiles or along the Río Frío, you have very little chance of seeing **Lesser Yellow-headed Vultures** unless you go to Lago Caño Negro. Oscar and other local guides know where they are.

THE SOUTHWESTERN LOWLANDS

The Red-crowned Woodpecker is found only in southwestern Costa Rica and western Panama.

The Southwestern Lowlands of Costa Rica are extremely diverse in topography, climate and vegetation and, of course, avifauna. The foothills of Cordillera de Talamanca form the northeastern boundary of this region and the Pacific Ocean laps its southwestern shore. Main geographic features are the Peninsula de Osa, Golfo Dulce, Valle del General and Valle de Coto Brus, while the major river system in the area is the Río Grande de Térraba, which drains the latter two valleys. A low mountain range, Fila Casteña, runs in a NW–SE direction to enclose the Valle de General and Valle de Coto Brus from the southwesterly direction.

Major communities in the region are the bustling, rapidly growing town of San Isidro in the Valle del General, the port city of Golfito, San Vito at the head of Valle de Coto Brus, and Quepos on the northern coast. Rice, bananas and palm oil are major crops in coastal flatlands, while pineapples predominate in the lower Valle del General. Coffee and sugarcane are favorite crops at higher elevations.

Wet rainforest once dominated this region, except in the somewhat drier sheltered interior valleys, where open savannas are present. These savannas have long been maintained by burning, perhaps even before the time of the first Spanish landings. Today, Carara Biological Refuge at 4,700 hectares (11,600

Birding Locations in the
Southwestern Lowlands of Costa Rica

- **9** Tárcoles
- **10** Tarcol Lodge
- **11** Carara Biological Reserve
- **12** Villa Lapas
- **13** Los Cusingos
- **14** Palmar Norte
- **15** Las Ventanas de Osa
- **16** Golfito
- **17** Esquinas Rainforest Lodge

acres), Golfito Wildlife Refuge, 1,309 hectares (3,300 acres) and, especially, the world-famous Corcovado National Park, 41,788 hectares (103,200 acres), protect tracts of relatively undisturbed jungle in lowland areas. The Mangrove Forest Reserve, 22,000 hectares (54,300 acres), also gives some protection to the largest mangrove forest in Costa Rica, which forms the northwestern side of Peninsula de Osa.

Dry, sunny weather prevails in this region from January to March and afternoon–evening showers (or downpours) are common thereafter. The wettest month is commonly October. Temperatures are quite warm and humidity increases to the southwest. The dry season (although still humid) early in the year followed by the more typical wetter months allows a unique assemblage of plants and animals to flourish in the region, especially on the Peninsula de Osa and in Corcovado National Park. Here, communities from North America overlap with those of South America to create an amazing array of plants and animals, said to be the most diverse in Central America.

Since the northern beaches of this area are little more than an hour's drive from San José, the more accessible ones (e.g., Playa Jaco), are busy and somewhat crowded, especially on weekends during the dry season. Several good surfing beaches are also in this vicinity (e.g., Playa Hermosa—which has an annual contest in August). All in all these areas are good places to go if you want to socialize, party and perhaps forget about the birds for a short time.

TRAVEL

The Interamerican Highway south from San José is the fastest way to get to the heart of southwestern Costa Rica. It passes through Cartago, goes over the northern portion of the Talamancas and descends to San Isidro. A more roundabout route is west out of San José to Quepos, Dominical and then east over a low range of mountains to San Isidro. A coastal "highway" between Dominical and the Cortés–Palmar Norte area has been under construction for several years. Last time I traveled the road it was passable for a passenger car, but if you plan to go this way, ask locals about road conditions before you set out, especially during rainy periods.

Bus travel from San José to major centers in southwest Costa Rica is fast and efficient. Quepos is served four times a day by Transportes Morales (223-5567); buses leave from the Coca-Cola terminal at C16, A1. Transportes Musoc (223-0686) at C16, A1 or TUASUR (222-9763), across the street from the Musoc office, both serve San Isidro with over 15 departures daily. Tracopa (221-4214 or 223-7685) buses go farther south—to Palmar Norte (six departures), Golfito (three departures), Ciudad Neily (five departures). Their terminal used to be at A18, C4, but they recently opened a new one near the Coca-

I crouched low following closely behind my guide, Augustino, as he made his way through the dense vegetation along Quebrada Negra near Esquinas Lodge. We sought the **Black-cheeked Ant-tanager**, a species that loves dense vegetation, especially near streams. With its dull gray plumage it can be difficult to spot, even with some light orange-red shading on its throat and chest to give it some contrasting colors. Even its brighter orange crown patch is usually at least partially concealed by the blackish-gray feathers around it, giving further confirmation that this bird really doesn't want to be seen. It is another feather in the birder's cap, another species on "The List" if one succeeds.

But the **Black-cheeked Ant-tanager** is extra special because of its extremely restricted distribution. It's only found in lowland forested areas around Golfo Dulce. That's it! Nowhere else in the world! So there I was, hot on the trail of **Black-cheeked Ant-tanagers** thanks to Augustino, who knows the areas they frequent. It was already after 9 a.m. and getting quite warm, even in complete shade. Sweat was beading my forehead as we rounded a bend in the trail, and Augustino stopped and pointed towards the top of a thicket a short distance away. "*Tangara*," he said. I moved closer to him to get a better angle but still could see nothing. Finally, I saw a slight movement and with some excitement raised my binoculars only to have it flutter away. Moving a few steps brought the bird into view at the same time as I was attacked by huge horseflies (*tabanids*). Yes, I did manage to get a brief look at the bird, and it was a **Black-cheeked Ant-tanager**—a dingy, nondescript female with only faint orangey-pink coloration about the throat. So with parts of me on fire from insect bites and salty sweat dripping into my eyes, I mentally added the bird to "The List" and we headed towards the lodge for a late breakfast. Isn't birding fun?

Cola terminal area. From San José, it takes about three hours to get to San Isidro, six hours to Palmar Norte, eight hours to Golfito and seven hours to Neily.

TROPICAL BIRD SPECIALTIES OF THE SOUTHWEST LOWLANDS

Within Costa Rica, 39 species of birds (see Appendix I, Group11) are restricted to the Southwest Lowlands; 15 of these are considered common tropical specialties. If possible, review their characteristics before you go birding because you have a very good chance of seeing them.

Yellow-headed Caracara	Red-crowned Woodpecker
Smooth-billed Ani	Black-hooded Antshrike
Band-rumped Swift	Orange-collared Manakin
Beryl-crowned Hummingbird	Riverside Wren
White-tailed Emerald	Red-breasted Blackbird
Baird's Trogon	Spotted-crowned Euphonia
Fiery-billed Aracari	Streaked Saltator
Golden-naped Woodpecker	

In addition, five common tropical species are restricted to western Costa Rica and are easily seen in southwestern Costa Rica.

Scarlet Macaw	Rufous-breasted Wren
Fork-tailed Flycatcher	Ruddy-breasted Seedeater
Panama Flycatcher	

TÁRCOLES

The Tárcoles region, nearly centrally located on the west coast of Costa Rica, is great for birding. It's in an area of overlap between dry climatic conditions to the north and the more humid, wet areas to the southwest; hence, a mixture of birds typical of both regions is found in the area. For example, it's not at all uncommon to observe **White-throated Magpie-jays, Rufous-naped Wrens, Hoffmann's Woodpeckers** and **Rose-throated Becards**—dry country species—and **Fiery-billed Aracaris, Riverside Wrens, Black-bellied Wrens** and **Black-headed Antshrikes** all within the same general region. Carara Biological Reserve is also near the small town of Tárcoles. Because the surrounding countryside is largely deforested, this lowland forest reserve serves as a very important sanctuary and reservoir for countless species of plants and animals, not just birds. This area is also very accessible—only a few hours from San José by car or bus. Finally, it's one of the few areas in Costa Rica where you are nearly assured of seeing **Scarlet Macaws**, given a day or so of serious birding.

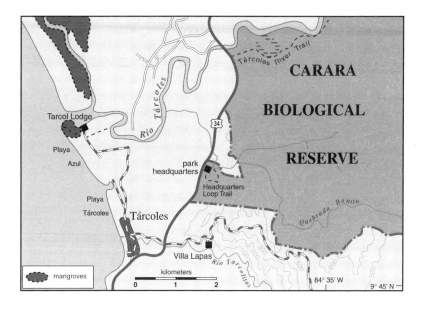

To get to the small town of Tárcoles, take the main highway west from San José and proceed southwest through Atenas, San Mateo and Orotina. Tárcoles is on the coast, just south of the estuary of the Río Tárcoles. If you're busing, any bus for Jaco, Quepos or Manuel Antonio will let you off at Tárcoles. The buses leave every hour or so from the main Coca-Cola terminal. (These destinations are very popular with tourists and Ticos, and buses can be very crowded on weekends and holidays.) Ask the bus driver to stop at the northern-most Tárcoles bus stop—the one called Playa Azul. Otherwise, you will be let off at another stop about 1 kilometer (.6 miles) south and you will have to backtrack to accommodations. From the Playa Azul bus stop, the northern part of Tárcoles is less than 1 kilometer (.6 miles) down the gravel road.

There are several places to stay and eat in and around Tárcoles. Cabinas Carara (661-0455) is moderately priced. Rooms are clean with fans and one air-conditioned room is available. Across the street is the best eating in town, Guaria Restaurante, which also rents some low-cost rooms. Things in the Tárcoles area tend to be a little overpriced, perhaps because of the popularity of nearby areas—Jaco, Carara and Manuel Antonio. The town of Tárcoles itself and the adjacent areas are quiet and some beachfront developments appear to be old, left behind as development moved down the coast to the more popular beaches near Jaco and southwards. One aesthetic drawback to the area is that the Tárcoles River, which drains San José and most of the rest of the Central Valley, empties its extremely polluted waters into the Pacific in this area, contaminating nearby waters, beaches and tide flats near the estuary.

LIST OF BIRDS SIGHTED IN TÁRCOLES AREA

(a=abundant; c=common; u=uncommon; s=scarce; r=rare)

Species	Jan-Mar	Apr-Jun	Jul-Sep
Brown Pelican	c	c	
Olivaceous Cormorant	c		
Anhinga	c		
Magnificent Frigatebird	a	a	
Yellow-crowned Night-heron	c		
Boat-billed Heron			s
Green-backed Heron		a	
Little Blue Heron	c		
Tricolored Heron	r		
Snowy Egret	c	c	
Great Egret	a	c	
Great Blue Heron	u		
Wood Stork	a		
White Ibis	a	c	
Roseate Spoonbill	c		
Turkey Vulture	a		
Osprey	u		
Gray Hawk	u		
Roadside Hawk			u
Crested Caracara	u	c	
Yellow-headed Caracara	u		
Northern Jacana	u	c	
American Oystercatcher	c		
Semipalmated Plover	c		
Whimbrel	c		
Willet	c		
Spotted Sandpiper	a	c	
Ruddy Turnstone	u		
Least Sandpiper	a		
Laughing Gull	a		
Least Tern	u		
Royal Tern	c		
Black Skimmer	c		
Red-billed Pigeon			u
Short-billed Pigeon			c
Ruddy Ground-dove			c
Inca Dove			c
White-tipped Dove	u	c	
Scarlet Macaw	c	u	
Orange-chinned Parakeet			c
White-crowned Parrot			c
White-fronted Parrot	c		
Yellow-naped Parrot		s	
Squirrel Cuckoo	r	u	
Groove-billed Ani			c

Species	Jan-Mar	Apr-Jun	Jul-Sep
Lesser Nighthawk		c	
Common Pauraque		c	
Scaly-breasted Hummingbird			c
Rufous-tailed Hummingbird			c
Violaceous Trogon			u
Ringed Kingfisher			c
American Pygmy Kingfisher		r	s
Hoffmann's Woodpecker	u	c	
Streaked-headed Woodcreeper	c	c	
Buff-throated Foliage-gleaner			u
Barred Antshrike	u	a	
Rose-throated Becard			s
Tropical Kingbird			a
Piratic Flycatcher	r	u	
Streaked Flycatcher	c		
Gray-capped Flycatcher			u
Social Flycatcher	c	c	
Great Kiskadee	c	a	
Panama Flycatcher			c
Great-crested Flycatcher			s
Slate-headed Tody-flycatcher			s
Yellow-bellied Elaenia			s
Mistletoe Tyrannulet			s
Barn Swallow	c		c
Northern Rough-winged Swallow	a	c	
Mangrove Swallow	a		
White-throated Magpie-jay	r		u
Brown Jay	u		
Rufous-naped Wren	c	a	
Clay-colored Robin	a	a	
Tropical Gnatcatcher			u
Mangrove Vireo	r		u
Yellow-throated Vireo			c
Golden-winged Warbler			s
Tennessee Warbler			u
Yellow Warbler	u	a	
Northern Waterthrush			u
Great-tailed Grackle	u		c
Northern (Baltimore) Oriole			c
Yellow-crowned Euphonia			u
Red-legged Honeycreeper	u		u

SW LOWLANDS

Good to excellent birding can be had from the town of Tárcoles, along the roads that lead north near the coast through farmland, second growth and orchards. Many paths branch off through farms, where permission should be obtained before entry.

About 100 meters (325 feet) north of the Tárcoles Guard Station, the main road crosses a small slough with one small clump of rather forlorn-looking mangroves on the seaward side. Peer closely into the dense root-like supports and you may see a **Boat-billed Heron,** which slumbers here throughout the day. An acquaintance also saw two **Ferruginous Pygmy Owls** going into their burrow in an old palm trunk and an **Olivaceous Piculet** in the same area. **White-throated Magpie-jays, Squirrel Cuckoos, Yellow-crowned Euphonias** and psittacids, **Orange-chinned Parakeets, White-crowned Parrots** and even **Scarlet Macaws** are easily seen along the main road. **Crested Caracaras** are common near beaches, as are **Magnificent Frigatebirds** and **Brown Pelicans.**

Many smaller, more obscure birds can also be seen in this area. There is a great birding trail a few hundred meters before you get to Tarcol Lodge directly across from the school playground. It winds through a small grove of huge mango trees, scrub and mixed pasture, past some mangroves, and ends on the grassy banks of the Río Tárcoles. I walked it one March morning and saw **Mangrove Vireos, Piratic Flycatchers, Streaked Flycatchers, Barn Swallows** and hosts of **Mangrove Swallows.** I was also lucky enough to see an **American Pygmy Kingfisher** perched on a low twig above a small backwater. It was quite tame and everyone in the group I was with had a good chance to study it. Although this species is fairly widely distributed (South Mexico to Brazil) it is quite uncommon in Costa Rica. **Painted Buntings** are also a regular feature of this area.

On another visit to the same area later in the year, I sat in the mangroves for an hour or so enjoying the isolation and relative coolness. Small gray shadows flickering through the mangrove foliage usually turned out to be **Panama Flycatchers.** Several **Rose-throated Becards** passed through along with **Streaked-headed Woodcreepers** and a few **Buff-throated Foliage-gleaners.** A **Great Kiskadee** made several trips through the area with nesting material and **Scaly-breasted Hummingbirds** perched on nearby twigs.

Out in the more open scrub, flycatchers abounded. The more uncommon species were **Mistletoe Tyrannulets, Piratic Flycatchers, Yellow-bellied Elaenias, Great-crested Flycatchers** and **Slate-headed Tody Flycatchers.** Also in evidence were **Mangrove Vireos, Yellow-throated Vireos** and a few beautiful **Golden-winged Warblers**. Unlike in many other areas, birds seemed to be very active in this region from about 3 to 5 p.m., as well as in early morning.

Shorebirds and water-associated birds are plentiful in this area as well. You can see them where the road ends at the Tárcoles estuary or, better yet, stay at the Tarcol Lodge.

TARCOL LODGE

The Tarcol Lodge is a ramshackle two-storey house on the estuary of the Río Tárcoles. At high tide, the water is lapping at the foundations and expanses of mud flats teem with life at low tide. The managers of the lodge, Lisa and Bryon, are keen birders and, with the help of guests and guides, have compiled a bird list of the region of over 400 species. Normal rates are about $100 per day (private room with shared bathrooms) for an all-inclusive package including transport to and from San José, one trip to Carara Biological Reserve and a boat trip on the estuary. (Evening meals are almost exclusively seafood and are wonderful!) If you just show up at the lodge, as I did, you may get lower rates.

To get to the lodge, go through the town of Tárcoles and head north for about 4 kilometers (2.5 miles). The lodge is at the very end of the road, just past Playa Azul. It's quite a hike from the bus stop on the highway, about 5 kilometers (3 miles), but there are a few *sodas* (restaurants) along the way where you can stop, rest and bird. Ask around in Tárcoles for a taxi if you're really tired, or traveling heavy.

Itabos are common garden trees used as nesting sites by tanagers and other birds.

LIST OF BIRDS SIGHTED IN TARCOL LODGE AREA
(a=abundant; c=common; u=uncommon; s=scarce; r=rare)

Species	Jan-Mar	Apr-Jun	Jul-Sep	Species	Jan-Mar	Apr-Jun	Jul-Sep
Brown Pelican	c			White-tipped Dove	u		
Olivaceous Cormorant	c			Scarlet Macaw	c		
Anhinga	c			White-fronted Parrot	u		
Magnificent Frigatebird	a			Squirrel Cuckoo	s		
Yellow-crowned Night-heron	c			American Pygmy Kingfisher	r		
Little Blue Heron	c			Hoffmann's Woodpecker	u		
Tricolored Heron	r			Streaked-headed Woodcreeper	c		
Snowy Egret	c			Barred Antshrike	u		
Great Egret	a			Piratic Flycatcher	r		
Great Blue Heron	u			Streaked Flycatcher	r		
Wood Stork	a			Social Flycatcher	c		
White Ibis	a			Great Kiskadee	c		
Roseate Spoonbill	c			Barn Swallow	c		
Turkey Vulture	a			Northern Rough-winged Swallow	a		
Osprey	u			Mangrove Swallow	a		
Gray Hawk	u			White-throated Magpie-jay	r		
Crested Caracara	u			Brown Jay	u		
Yellow-headed Caracara	u			Rufous-naped Wren	c		
Northern Jacana	u			Clay-colored Robin	a		
American Oystercatcher	c			Mangrove Vireo	r		
Semipalmated Plover	c			Yellow Warbler	u		
Whimbrel	c			Great-tailed Grackle	u		
Willet	c			Red-legged Honeycreeper	u		
Spotted Sandpiper	a			Blue-gray Tanager	c		
Ruddy Turnstone	u			Hepatic Tanager	r		
Least Sandpiper	a			Variable Seedeater	c		
Laughing Gull	a			Blue-black Grassquit	c		
Least Tern	u			Black-striped Sparrow	c		
Royal Tern	c						
Black Skimmer	c						

I sighted over 50 species in a lazy day of birding, mostly from the deck of the lodge, without really trying. Meanwhile, a "keener" rushed around and saw over 125 species! When I was there in March, **Least Sandpipers** (look for their yellowish legs), **Whimbrels** and **Willets** were common, while **American Oystercatchers, Semipalmated Plovers, Ruddy Turnstones** and **Black-bellied Plovers** were also present. The latter were just beginning to molt and showed a few dark breast feathers.

Herons and other large, colorful water birds are common. In March, the **Tricolored Herons** were especially beautiful with newly molted breeding plumage of long white feathers along the nape of the neck. **Great Egrets** and **Little**

Blue Herons were everywhere and were fun to watch as they would occasionally stalk prey with unbelievable concentration. **Wood Storks, Black Skimmers** and **Royal Terns** were also common.

It's not unusual to see **Ospreys** catch fish in the estuary and sightings of **Crested Caracaras** and **Yellow-headed Caracaras** are daily occurrences. **Scarlet Macaws** are usually seen in the evenings as they fly to their roosts across the river. It's also common to see 5–6 meter (15–20 foot) long alligators basking along the riverbank. A tour specializes in feeding these monsters—I haven't gone, but the pictures I've seen look quite exciting!

Management at Tarcol Lodge caters especially to birders and they make it their business to know the locations of many rare birds and common specialties of the region. If you stay here and bird with them, you have a good chance of seeing **Painted Buntings, Mangrove Warblers, Peregrine Falcons, Plumbeous Kites, Green-breasted Mangos, Blue-throated Goldentails, Tawny-winged Woodcreepers, Slaty Spinetails, Cinnamon Becards, Brown-crested Flycatchers, Yellow-bellied Flycatchers, Yellow-olive Flycatchers, Scrub Flycatchers, Ochre-bellied Flycatchers, Rufous-browed Peppershrikes** and **Scrub Greenlets.**

CARARA BIOLOGICAL RESERVE

Carara Biological Reserve is a few kilometers from the town of Tárcoles. Its 4,700 hectares (11,600 acres) is mostly primary forest on the coastal shelf and in the low foothills of the Fila Negra. Although the reserve is sizable, there are only two public trails, one quite short. That, combined with relatively heavy use, can make the park seem quite crowded. Tour buses usually start arriving about 8:30 or 9 a.m. so, if you get an early start, it's possible to get a few quiet hours in. Gates don't officially open until 7 a.m. at the main entrance (a sign says 8 a.m. at the secondary entrance), but I've never had any trouble going in early and paying on the way out.

The best birding trail, the Vigilancia Trail (Tárcoles River Trail), is north of the reserve headquarters at a secondary entrance, near the highway bridge over the Tárcoles River. It winds through primary jungle, second growth, thick stands of heliconias, marshes and open areas on the banks of the Río Tárcoles to end about 4.5 kilometers (2.75 miles) after crossing the Río Carara (possible only during the dry season). The Headquarters Loop Trail is a 3 kilometer (2 mile) loop through well-developed primary forest. Birding is more difficult here and can sometimes be quite impossible because of constant traffic on the trail.

In March, **Scarlet Macaws** screeched overhead in trees along the Vigilancia Trail every morning I birded in the park. I was also rewarded with views of a beautifully patterned **Double-toothed Kite** and two **Mealy Parrots**, high in

LIST OF BIRDS SIGHTED IN THE CARARA AREA
(a=abundant; c=common; u=uncommon; s=scarce; r=rare)

Species	Jan-Mar Apr-Jun Jul-Sep
Cattle Egret	u
Little Blue Heron	c
Great Egret	c
White Ibis	c
Turkey Vulture	c
Black Vulture	c
Double-toothed Kite	s
Northern Jacana	c
Ruddy Ground-dove	c
Blue Ground-dove	u
Scarlet Macaw	c
Mealy Parrot	u
Squirrel Cuckoo	c
Long-tailed Hermit	c
Scaly-breasted Hummingbird	a
Baird's Trogon	s
Black-headed Trogon	u
Violaceous Trogon	c
White-whiskered Puffbird	r
Lineated Woodpecker	c
Pale-billed Woodpecker	c
Wedge-billed Woodcreeper	u
Streaked-headed Woodcreeper	c
Plain Xenops	c
Barred Antshrike	a
Black-hooded Antshrike	c

Species	Jan-Mar Apr-Jun Jul-Sep
Slaty Antwren	u
Dot-winged Antwren	s
Dusky Antbird	u
Chestnut-backed Antbird	c
White-winged Becard	u
Orange-collared Manakin	a
Tropical Kingbird	c
Piratic Flycatcher	u
Sulphur-bellied Flycatcher	s
Streaked Flycatcher	a
Great Kiskadee	c
Nutting's Flycatcher	u
Dusky-capped Flycatcher	u
Slate-headed Tody-flycatcher	c
Northern Rough-winged Swallow	c
Mangrove Swallow	a
Rufous-naped Wren	c
Philadelphia Vireo	u
Black-and-white Warbler	u
Tennessee Warbler	u
Northern Waterthrush	u
Northern (Baltimore) Oriole	c
Red-legged Honeycreeper	u
Scarlet-rumped Tanager	u
Buff-throated Saltator	u
Blue-black Grosbeak	u

the canopy. Another party saw a **Crane Hawk** in the same area. **Scaly-breasted Hummingbirds** were very common and their habit of sitting for longer periods of time than other hummers makes them fairly easy to observe. Antbirds were especially abundant and tame in the undergrowth beside the trail. **Chestnut-backed Antbirds** and **Black-hooded Antshrikes** were common, as were **Barred Antshrikes**. The crests of the females of the latter species seemed to be especially prominent as they moved about in great excitement. Beautifully patterned **Dot-winged Antwrens** were present, along with the more subdued **Dusky Antbirds**. An acquaintance saw two **Black-faced Antthrushes** foraging on the ground along Headquarters Trail.

An active lek (courtship area) of **Orange-collared Manakins** was present about .2 kilometers (.1 miles) along the Vigilancia Trail in late March. A well-beaten path to the right marked its location and frequent snaps made us aware

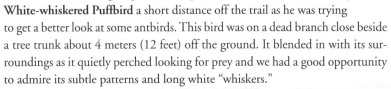

The fruit of the cashew tree, common around houses in Costa Rica, is eaten by a variety of birds. The pod containing the nut hangs down below the fruit. It must be roasted before it is opened to neutralize a highly corrosive sticky resin that surrounds the nut.

of its presence as well. There were at least five or six males present—all ricocheting off branches and snapping their wings in seemingly random movements within a meter or so of the ground. The bright orange and black patterns were accentuated as they puffed their feathers out, some in full sunlight, some shaded by overhead leaves.

Plain Xenops were also fairly plentiful. They occasionally flew across the path and once in a while, one would alight in a vine tangle and forage for food, often upside-down. A keen birding acquaintance spotted a **White-whiskered Puffbird** a short distance off the trail as he was trying to get a better look at some antbirds. This bird was on a dead branch close beside a tree trunk about 4 meters (12 feet) off the ground. It blended in with its surroundings as it quietly perched looking for prey and we had a good opportunity to admire its subtle patterns and long white "whiskers."

Flycatchers are abundant, especially in more open areas along the trails in Carara. **Piratic Flycatchers** and **Slate-headed Tody-flycatchers** are more common here than in many other regions of Costa Rica. Watch for the rather long, flattened beak of the latter species and the very small, quite unflycatcher-like beak of the former. Both **Streaked Flycatchers** and **Sulphur-bellied Flycatchers** were present, as were **Northern Waterthrushes** and **Louisiana Waterthrushes**. Other migrants such as **Black-and-white Warblers**, **Philadelphia Vireos** and **Tennessee Warblers** were also common. I was also treated to the sight of a lovely pair of **Blue-black Grosbeaks** as they perched near me on the roots of a fallen tree.

Trogons are quite common in Carara and adjacent regions. Again, a mixture of dry country species, such as the **Black-headed Trogon** and wet country varieties such as **Baird's Trogon** are present, along with less specialized species, including **Slaty-headed Trogon**, **Black-throated Trogon** and **Violaceous Trogon**.

Birding in Carara will uncover different species on a daily basis for months on end. Among the other more common park specialties are **Little Tinamous**, **Ruddy Quail-doves**, **Brown-hooded Parrots**, **White-collared Swifts**, **Band-rumped Swifts**, **Blue-throated Goldentails**, **Purple-crowned Fairies**, **Rufous-tailed Jacamars**, **Olivaceous Piculets**, **Buff-throated Woodcreepers**, **Black-faced Antthrushes**, **Spectacled Antpittas**, **White-winged Becards**, **Yellow-bellied Fly-**

catchers, Royal Flycatchers, Stub-tailed Spadebills, Golden-crowned Spadebills, Yellow-olive Flycatchers, Ochre-bellied Flycatchers, Black-bellied Wrens, Rufous-breasted Wrens, Long-billed Gnatwrens, Green Shrike vireos, Tawny-crowned Greenlets, Lesser Greenlets, Thick-billed Euphonias and Gray-headed Tanagers.

VILLA LAPAS HOTEL

Villa Lapas Hotel (288-1677) is in the countryside about .5 kilometers (.3 miles) north of the highway near Tárcoles. This upscale resort has a small pool, manicured grounds, a good, reasonably priced restaurant and clean, spacious rooms with fans or air conditioning and private bath (about $75 a night). The grounds are extensive and include 4–5 kilometers (3 miles) of good, gentle trails that wind along a small stream above the resort. The resort is actually an old farm, where pasture land is being allowed to revert to native vegetation. Although most trees and shrubs are still fairly small on the slopes, the valley floor is lined with large trees, present from the time the land was actively farmed. Bird feeders are maintained around the lodge, especially near the restaurant, where birding can be quite good. If you're not staying at the hotel but at least eat in the restaurant, you can probably get permission to walk the trails if you ask the management.

If you're busing to the hotel from San José, ask the driver to let you off at the northernmost Tárcoles bus stop, the one called Playa Azul. From the stop, Villa Lapas is a short .5 kilometer (.3 mile) walk, which could seem long if you have a lot of luggage. Travel light! If the hotel knows you are coming, I'm sure they would meet the bus.

On one morning of birding on the trails at Villa Lapas I got a number of good species: **Blue Ground-doves**, a beautiful male **Black-crowned Tityra**, several **Chestnut-backed Antbirds**, **Streaked-headed Woodcreepers** and a **Buff-throated Foliage-gleaner**. In addition, I came across an **Orange-billed Sparrow** hopping about low in a thicket, and a **Streaked Flycatcher** near the restaurant. I was also treated to four truly beautiful **Scarlet Macaws** feeding in a low tree on a slope beside the trail. In this area, macaws make routine feeding forays to the hills in the vicinity of Villa Lapas from their roosts near the Río Tárcoles estuary. A walk along the road north of the resort yielded **Rufous-and-white Wrens**, **Rufous-naped Wrens**, **Squirrel Cuckoos**, **Hepatic Tanagers**, and **Gray-capped Flycatchers**, in addition to other more common species.

Later in the year, I was very pleasantly surprised to see a **White Hawk** perched on a snag in an upstream valley visible from the main restaurant. I also heard a pair of **Laughing Falcons** giving their loud *guaco* calls for what seemed like minutes on end and **Scarlet Macaws** were commonly seen flying overhead,

LIST OF BIRDS SIGHTED IN THE VILLA LAPAS AREA

(a=abundant; c=common; u=uncommon; s=scarce; r=rare)

Species	Jan-Mar	Apr-Jun	Jul-Sep
Little Blue Heron		u	
White Ibis	c	c	
Turkey Vulture	a	c	
Black Vulture	c	c	
White Hawk		r	
Laughing Falcon		u	
Ruddy Ground-dove	a		
Blue Ground-dove	u	u	
White-tipped Dove	c	c	
Scarlet Macaw	u	c	
Squirrel Cuckoo		u	
Groove-billed Ani	c		
Common Pauraque		u	
Rufous-tailed Hummingbird		c	
Slaty-tailed Trogon		c	
Baird's Trogon		u	
Ringed Kingfisher		c	
Belted Kingfisher	u		
Amazon Kingfisher	u	c	
Blue-crowned Motmot		u	
Fiery-billed Aracari		u	
Chestnut-mandibled Toucan		u	
Hoffmann's Woodpecker		u	
Pale-billed Woodpecker		u	
Streaked-headed Woodcreeper	c	u	
Buff-throated Foliage-gleaner	c	u	
Chestnut-backed Antbird	u	c	
Rose-throated Becard		r	
Black-crowned Tityra	s		
Tropical Kingbird	a	c	
Boat-billed Flycatcher	u	u	
Bright-rumped Attila		r	
Streaked Flycatcher	u	c	
Gray-capped Flycatcher	s		
Social Flycatcher	a	c	
Great Kiskadee	a	a	
Yellow-olive Flycatcher		u	
Common Tody-flycatcher	c		
Northern Bentbill		r	
Yellow-bellied Elaenia		u	
Northern Rough-winged Swallow			c
Rufous-naped Wren	c	c	
Rufous-and-white Wren	u		
House Wren	a		
Clay-colored Robin			c
Tennessee Warbler			u
Yellow Warbler			c
Northern Waterthrush			u
Great-tailed Grackle			c
Northern (Baltimore) Oriole			c
Red-legged Honeycreeper		u	
Blue-gray Tanager	a	c	
Hepatic Tanager		u	
Buff-throated Saltator	u		
Orange-billed Sparrow			u

especially in the morning. **Slaty-tailed Trogons** were common, and a few **Baird's Trogons** were present along the trails upstream of the lodge. The bellies of these birds were much more orange than in the illustrations of this species in Stiles and Skutch (1989). A few **Chestnut-mandibled Toucans, Blue-crowned Motmots** and **Fiery-billed Aracaris** were present on a daily basis, as were **Streaked Flycatchers, Chestnut-backed Antbirds** and **Red-legged Honeycreepers.** More uncommon birds in the area were **Rose-throated Becards, Bright-rumped Attilas, Yellow-olive Flycatchers, Yellow-bellied Elaenias** and tiny **Northern Bentbills.** Look for the latter species in trail-side thickets, usually close to the ground. They are quite tame, but difficult to spot.

FINCA LOS CUSINGOS

Cusingos is the Tico name for the aracari and Finca Los Cusingos is a farm named especially for the **Fiery-Billed Aracari**, which was once common in the region. Until recently, this land, about 100 hectares (250 acres), was the farm of world-renowned scientist, naturalist and philosopher Alexander Skutch—co-author of what should be your constant companion, *A Guide to the Birds of Costa Rica,* and author of numerous other books and scientific publications.

For some extremely interesting reading, pick up a copy of *A Naturalist in Costa Rica* by Skutch, published by the University of Florida Press. His accounts of Costa Rica in the 1930s and 1940s are priceless. Narratives of his adventures and accounts of tropical biology, with heavy emphasis on birds, are deeply informative, especially when read while traveling in Costa Rica.

Dr. Skutch, still active at 91 when I had the pleasure of talking and birding with him, recently endowed most of the acreage of Finca Los Cusingos to the Organization of Tropical Studies. This act protects Los Cusingos and the area is now used by naturalists, scientists and, of course, birders from all over the world. Access to the "farm" should be arranged in advance by calling OTS (265-6696 or 240-9938). The daily fee of $8 goes towards such expenses as a full-time guard, fencing and trail maintenance. A total of 277 species of birds have been recorded on the property by Dr. Skutch himself, although he believes there are now somewhat fewer species because of the extensive deforestation of most of the Valle del General. Although much of the land was cleared cattle pasture when Dr. Skutch acquired it in 1941, it is now mostly covered by maturing second growth.

Los Cusingos is somewhat difficult to access, but it's well worth the effort, especially when you consider the cultural value of the area. Skutch is a living legend and if you're lucky enough to meet him and perhaps bird with him, the memory will last through the years. The easiest way to get to Los Cusingos is by taxi from San Isidro—most of the taxi drivers know where the farm is and will take you there for about $10. Have them drop you off at the gate and walk the .5 kilometers (.3 miles) or so to the house. It is possible to get to Los Cusingos by taking the bus to Quizarra, but buses are infrequent. Buses leave from the market area in San Isidro. Ask about daily schedules if you have no other way to get there. If you're driving, take the Interamerican Highway south from San Isidro and turn left on a paved road toward Chiles. Bear right across the bridge over Río General, bear right and pass through Hermosa. Then bear left on a dirt road that has signs showing the way to Quizarra. Approximately 2 kilometers (1.25 miles) later, bear right (the left fork goes to Santa Elena) and continue for 1 kilometer (.6 miles). You will come to the top of a ridge with a beautiful view of the San Isidro valley with a small cemetery on the

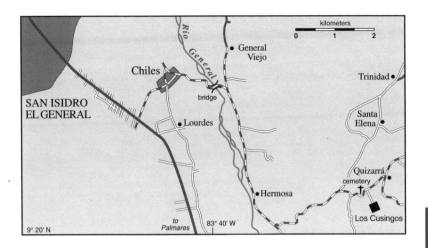

right. As you descend the other side of the ridge, you will come to a barbed wire gate on the right with a sign, "*Carros No!*" which means "No Guns!" Leave your car here or get dropped off and walk along the road for about .5 kilometers (.3 miles) and you're there! Sound complicated? It is! The best way to negotiate the roads in Costa Rica is to plan on getting lost, or at least accept the inevitable. Ask for directions along the way frequently. Local people are glad to help you out.

The first day we birded at Los Cusingos, I spotted a juvenile **Roadside Hawk** raking at leaves in a tall tree near the house, quite an unusual behavior pattern since the hawk appeared to be eating leaves! When I described this behavior to Dr. Skutch, he said the hawk was probably eating grasshoppers. A plague of them, the likes of which he had never seen, was then in the process of defoliating several trees in the area. A few hours of birding (mostly sitting) along a trail below the main residence yielded **Green Honeycreepers, Red-legged Honeycreepers** and **Speckled Tanagers**, the latter being one of the most beautifully patterned birds I have ever seen—all in all quite a spectacular assemblage of brightly colored birds.

In a more forested portion of the trail, a **Red-capped Manakin** obligingly perched briefly on a nearby twig. Birding from the porch with Dr. Skutch yielded similar species, in addition to **Golden-hooded Tanagers, Gray-chested Doves, Masked Tityras** and **Black-crowned Tityras**, while **White-collared Swifts, Chestnut-collared Swifts** and **Band-rumped Swifts** wheeled overhead. We also heard, but did not see, the cackling cry of one of Skutch's favorite birds, the **Laughing Falcon**, which preys almost exclusively on snakes.

Any of the roads and trails in the vicinity of Finca Los Cusingos also offer excellent birding opportunities. Early one morning while walking to Los

LIST OF BIRDS SIGHTED IN THE LOS CUSINGOS AREA
(a=abundant; c=common; u=uncommon; s=scarce; r=rare)

Species	Jan-Mar	Apr-Jun	Jul-Sep	Species	Jan-Mar	Apr-Jun	Jul-Sep
Turkey Vulture		a		Tropical Kingbird		a	
Black Vulture		a		Social Flycatcher		a	
Roadside Hawk		u		Tropical Pewee		c	
Laughing Falcon		u		Yellow-olive Flycatcher		u	
White-tipped Dove		c		Common Tody-flycatcher		c	
Gray-chested Dove		u		Bananaquit		c	
Chestnut-collared Swift		u		Speckled Tanager		u	
White-collared Swift		u		Golden-hooded Tanager		c	
Band-rumped Swift		c		Bay-headed Tanager		s	
White-crested Coquette		s		Green Honeycreeper		u	
Rufous-tailed Hummingbird		c		Red-legged Honeycreeper		u	
Purple-crowned Fairy		u		Blue-gray Tanager		c	
Violaceous Trogon		u		Scarlet-rumped Tanager		c	
Masked Tityra		c		White-lined Tanager		s	
Black-crowned Tityra		r		Buff-throated Saltator		u	
Red-capped Manakin		u		Variable Seedeater		c	

Cusingos, I spotted **Squirrel Cuckoos**, a **Violaceous Trogon, Tropical Pewees**, a **Yellow-olive Flycatcher, Bay-headed Tanagers** and **White-lined Tanagers** in addition to the more common flycatchers, tanagers and seedeaters.

Later in the day while resting in a grove of long-leaf conifers which provided shade for a coffee plantation, I was graced by the presence of two species of hummingbirds. I finally got a good view of a male **White-crested Coquette**. This species is largely restricted to southwestern Costa Rica and western Panama and is quite uncommon; however, you have a good chance of seeing it in the San Isidro area. This little hummingbird, less than 7 centimeters (3 inches) long, is decorated with a white crest and green cheek tufts, which extend like small barbs behind the neck. I had, for several days previously and in different areas, seen small hummers with rufous and white markings, but was unable to identify them because of their constant darting movements. Although this male was some distance off, it sat on a bare twig for a minute or so, giving me an opportunity to study it in good light at moderate magnification, and it was quite satisfying to finally make the identification.

A short time later, a female of the same species hovered above me only a few feet away. Its white rump band, rufous belly and white throat were positive identifying characteristics. About half an hour later, a male **Purple-crowned Fairy** darted, hovered and finally sat for a few moments on a bare branch about 1 meter (3 feet) off the ground. This species normally pierces flowers at the base to access their nectar. In doing so, it often hovers head-down with its completely white underside exposed. In this position it gives the impression of a butterfly rather than a bird. At other times, I've noticed it hovering with its tail arched over its back—quite an aerial acrobat!

Other interesting species common at Los Cusingos or nearby include **Little Tinamou, Barred Forest-falcon, Scaled Pigeon, Brown-headed Parrot, Violet-headed Hummingbird, Snowy-breasted Hummingbird, Long-billed Starthroat, Baird's Trogon, Collared Trogon, Olivaceous Piculet, Tawny-winged Woodcreeper, Buff-throated Woodcreeper, Pale-breasted Spine-tail, Scaly-throated Leaftosser, Russet Antshrike, Plain Antvireo, Slaty Antwren, Bare-crowned Antbird, Black-faced Antthrush, Bicolored Antbird, Streak-chested Antpitta, Spectacled Antpitta, White-winged Becard, Yellow-bellied Flycatcher, Royal Flycatcher, Eye-ringed Flatbill, Northern Bentbill, Yellow Tyrannulet, Lesser Elaenia, Southern Beardless-tyrannulet, Ochre-bellied Flycatcher, Rufous-breasted Wren, White-breasted Wood-wren, Nightingale Wren, Green Shrike-vireo, Tawny-crowned Greenlet, Shining Honeycreeper, Kentucky Warbler, American Redstart, Rose-breasted Thrush-tanager, White-vented Euphonia, Red-crowned Ant-tanager** and **Yellow-bellied Seedeater.**

PALMAR NORTE

Palmar Norte is a small town in southwestern Costa Rica, about 80 kilometers (50 miles) northwest of Golfito. It lies a few meters above sea level on the banks of the Río Térraba just before the river drains into the largest mangrove forest in Costa Rica. Bananas are a principal crop in lowland areas, along with smaller amounts of rice, vegetables and fruits. A relatively low coastal range of mountains nearby, Fila Costeña, gives you the opportunity to bird at elevations of slightly over 1,000 meters (3,300 feet). Thus the mangrove forests, beaches, tide flats, river bottom lands, farms and patches of remaining lowland rainforest present a wide variety of habitats for birds in the region.

Palmar Norte itself serves as a transportation hub for the area. Local people may stop there but most tourists pass through on their way to other places. Hence, the town is typical Tico, with a collection of *pulperias* (general stores), clothing and grocery stores and a few hotels. If you stay in town, try the Hotel Amarilla (784-6251) near the soccer field on the south side of town. It has economical, air-conditioned rooms and is clean and quiet. If you have just arrived in southwestern Costa Rica, the air conditioning may give you a chance to adjust to the hot humid weather typical of the region. The Tracopa bus station is four blocks down the street and you can generally find taxis in that area. There is the normal complement of Tico restaurants in town serving adequate but not memorable meals. Good Chinese food is available at the Chang Yeng Restaurant along the highway.

LIST OF BIRDS SIGHTED IN THE PALMAR NORTE AREA

(a=abundant; c=common; u=uncommon; s=scarce; r=rare)

Species	Jan-Mar	Apr-Jun	Jul-Sep	Species	Jan-Mar	Apr-Jun	Jul-Sep
Cattle Egret	a			Tropical Pewee	c		
Yellow-headed Caracara	u			Common Tody-flycatcher	s		
Pale-vented Pigeon	c			Riverside Wren	s		
Short Billed Pigeon	c			Black-bellied Wren	?		
Ruddy Ground-dove	c			House Wren	a		
White-tipped Dove	c			Clay-colored Robin	c		
Crimson-fronted Parakeet	c			Tropical Gnatcatcher	u		
Groove-billed Ani	c			Tennessee Warbler	c		
Crested Owl	r			Yellow Warbler	c		
Purple-crowned Fairy	s			Great-tailed Grackle	a		
Fiery-billed Aracari	c			Northern (Baltimore) Oriole	c		
Red-crowned Woodpecker	c			Yellow-crowned Euphonia	u		
Barred Antshrike	s			Golden-hooded Tanager	u		
Plain Antvireo	r			Red-legged Honeycreeper	u		
Masked Tityra	c			Blue Dacnis	u		
Black-crowned Tityra	s			Blue-gray Tanager	c		
Red-capped Manakin	s			Palm Tanager	c		
Tropical Kingbird	a			Scarlet-rumped Tanager	c		
Streaked Flycatcher	c			Yellow-faced Grassquit	c		
Gray-capped Flycatcher	s			Variable Seedeater	c		
Social Flycatcher	a			Blue-black Grassquit	c		
Great Kiskadee	a			Black-striped Sparrow	u		

A good birding walk starts with a right turn on the highway as you're entering the town from the east. The road to take is directly opposite the sign for Cabinas Tico Aleman (the same sign advertises Derby cigarettes). Walk up the road through a housing development, past Escuela Alemania and bear left across a small cement bridge as the main road makes a sharp right-hand turn. (A $2 taxi ride will also get you through town to the foot of the hill.) Follow the dirt road, which passes through a watershed that is protected for the Palmar Norte water supply. The upper part of the trail is nicely forested. A steep trail crosses the stream and winds up the slope to a farmer's dwelling about 300 meters (1,000 feet) up on the hillside.

An evening walk in January along the path yielded **Streaked Flycatchers**, brightly colored **Yellow-crowned Euphonias** and a **Purple-crowned Fairy**. Some leafless trees on the right were especially good about an hour before sunset for **Blue Dacnis**, **Red-legged Honeycreepers**, **Yellow Warblers**, **Tennessee Warblers** and **Tropical Gnatcatchers**. Also look for **Barred Antshrikes** and **Riverside Wrens** in the thickets beside the road. One morning in the upper forested

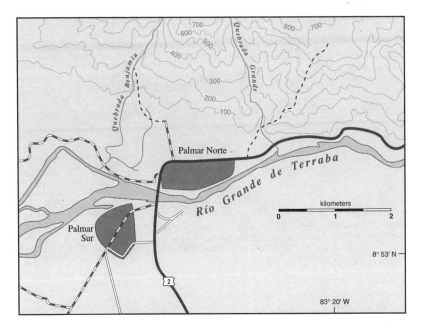

part of the track, I spotted a beautiful male **Red-capped Manakin** and a **Plain Antvireo**, quite a rare bird for the area. I was also lucky enough to come across a very tame **Crested Owl** on the ground beside the stream.

On another trip near Palmar Norte, I was driving north of town when I saw a hawk pounce into the grass from an overhanging limb near the road. Moments later, it flew back to its perch carrying a fair-sized snake in its talons. I recognized it as a **Laughing Falcon** (see illustration, page 78) by its broad, dark brown mask.

Other common birds in the area are **Yellow-headed Caracaras, Pale-vented Pigeons, Crimson-fronted Parakeets, Golden-hooded Tanagers, Fiery-billed Aracaris, Chestnut-mandibled Toucans, Black-crowned Tityras** and **Red-crowned Woodpeckers**. All in all, this is quite a productive area.

LAS VENTANAS DE OSA

If you want to bird southwestern Costa Rica in the lap of luxury, this is the spot for you. Las Ventanas de Osa is about 40 kilometers (25 miles) northwest of Palmar Norte on the shores of the Pacific Ocean. This jungle lodge was built in the late 1970s when access to the area was by four-wheel drive and then only in the dry season because several rivers had to be forded. The owner managed the facility as his own semi-private retreat and really didn't care if he had customers or not. Tender loving care shows everywhere on the approximately 5 hectares

Laughing Falcons subsist primarily on snakes.

(12 acres) of manicured gardens surrounding the swimming pool and two guest lodges, which sit about 150 meters (500 feet) above the nearby Pacific.

In addition, about 50 hectares (125 acres) of primary jungle surround the facility, which abounds with white-faced monkeys, howler monkeys, agoutis, (a rodent related to the guinea pig and about as big as a rabbit), sloths and a variety of other wildlife.

Southwestern Costa Rica specialties are common in the immediate vicinity of the lodge, including **Yellow-headed Caracaras, Golden-naped Woodpeckers, Red-crowned Woodpeckers, Fiery-billed Aracaris, Orange-collared Manakins, Black-hooded Antshrikes** and **Riverside Wrens.** Since its inception, this lodge has catered to birders and now boasts a bird list of over 430 species recorded in the general area. Its resident manager, Gabriel Sanchez, is an expert birder and will guide if desired.

Standard rates are about $100 per day per person for an all-inclusive package with transportation from and back to your hotel in San José. All meals and beverages, including alcohol, are included, along with international cuisine plus wine with meals, daily laundry service and guided excursions to surrounding areas and along private trails. A good quality 20 X to 60 X spotting scope is also available for guest use. In the summer of 1995 there was talk of offering a lower cost alternative and also of offering guided tours to non-guests for a nominal cost. Despite what some recent travel guides say, this is no longer a private lodge open only to club members. Everyone is welcome. If you are interested, contacts are *Costa Rica*–Gabriel Sanchez 506-236-5926; *Canada*–Bill Ross, 403-768-2212. There are two other lower cost hotels in the area, the Posada del Playa

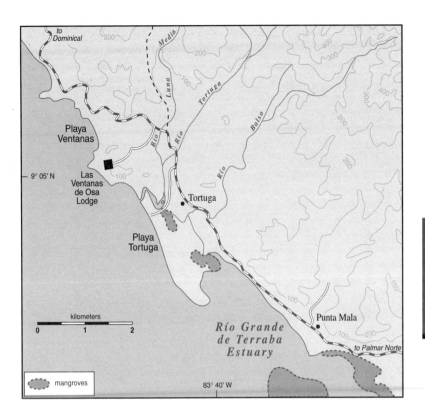

de Tortuga and Hotel Paraiso del Pacifico. Both are good value but neither has private acreages and both are in heavily disturbed areas.

It's possible to get to Las Ventanas by the local bus from Cortés which goes north along the coast. The drivers know where the turn-off to Las Ventanas is, but you will have to walk the kilometer (.6 miles) or so to the lodge. Because of highway improvements in the area in the last few years, bus schedules and routes have been changing. Check for the latest information in Cortés or Palmar Norte. If you are driving to the area yourself, the fastest way, as of late 1995, is to drive the Pan-American Highway south to Palmar Norte. From there, turn off on the road to Cortés and continue on to Playa Tortuga. The turn-off to Las Ventanas is a left turn .5 kilometers (.3 miles) north of Río Media Luna; it is *unmarked* (as of late 1995) and is difficult to find.

The coastal "highway" between Dominical and Palmar Norte has been under construction for years and until recently has been impassable for normal cars. Things are improving. Heavy trucks were using the road in early 1995 and the last time I traveled it (mid-1995) it was okay for all types of traffic.

LIST OF BIRDS SIGHTED IN LAS VENTANAS DE OSA LODGE AREA

(a=abundant; c=common; u=uncommon; s=scarce; r=rare; vr=very rare)

Species	Jan-Mar	Apr-Jun	Jul-Sep
Great Tinamou		s	s
Brown Pelican		u	
Olivaceous Cormorant		u	
Anhinga		u	
Magnificent Frigatebird	a	a	
Cattle Egret	c	c	
Green-backed Heron		u	c
Little Blue Heron	u	c	c
Tricolored Heron		u	
Reddish Egret		r	
Snowy Egret	u	u	
Great Egret	c	c	
Wood Stork		u	
White Ibis		c	
Roseate Spoonbill		u	
Black-bellied Whistling-duck		u	u
Turkey Vulture	a	a	a
Black Vulture	a	a	
King Vulture		r	s
Osprey		u	
American Swallow-tailed Kite	u		u
Black-shouldered Kite			u
Gray Hawk			u
Roadside Hawk			c
Ornate Hawk-eagle		vr	
Yellow-headed Caracara	u		c
Laughing Falcon		r	u
Bat Falcon		u	c
Gray-headed Chachalaca		u	u
Northern Jacana		c	
American Oystercatcher	s		
Semipalmated Plover		u	
Whimbrel		c	
Willet		u	
Spotted Sandpiper		u	s
Sanderling		u	
Rock Dove		u	
Pale-vented Pigeon			s
Short Billed Pigeon		u	

Species	Jan-Mar	Apr-Jun	Jul-Sep
Ruddy Ground-dove		u	
Blue Ground-dove			c
White-tipped Dove	c	c	a
Ruddy Quail-dove		r	
Orange-chinned Parakeet	c	c	
White-crowned Parrot			c
Red-lored Parrot	c	c	
Smooth-billed Ani		u	
Spectacled Owl		r	
Black-and-white Owl	c	c	c
Common Pauraque		c	
Band-tailed Barbthroat			u
Long-tailed Hermit			c
Scaly-breasted Hummingbird			s
Snowy-bellied Hummingbird		u	
Purple-crowned Fairy		u	
Slaty-tailed Trogon	r		u
Ringed Kingfisher		u	u
Belted Kingfisher	c	c	
Amazon Kingfisher		u	c
Green Kingfisher		c	
Blue-crowned Motmot		s	
White-necked Puffbird			r
Fiery-billed Aracari	a	a	a
Chestnut-mandibled Toucan		a	c
Golden-naped Woodpecker	a	a	a
Red-crowned Woodpecker	u	c	u
Lineated Woodpecker	u	u	u
Pale-billed Woodpecker		r	r
Streaked-headed Woodcreeper		c	
Plain Xenops			r
Black-hooded Antshrike	c	c	c
Chestnut-backed Antbird	c	c	c
Masked Tityra	c	c	c
Black-crowned Tityra			s
Red-capped Manakin			u
Blue-crowned Manakin			u

Species	Jan-Mar	Apr-Jun	Jul-Sep
Tropical Kingbird	a	a	a
White-ringed Flycatcher			s
Boat-billed Flycatcher	r		
Streaked Flycatcher	u		
Gray-capped Flycatcher		r	u
Social Flycatcher	a	a	c
Great Kiskadee	a	a	c
Barn Swallow		u	
Southern Rough-winged Swallow		u	
Northern Rough-winged Swallow		c	
Mangrove Swallow		u	u
Riverside Wren			c
House Wren	c	c	u
Clay-colored Robin	a	a	
Swainson's Thrush		r	
Long-billed Gnatwren			s
Bananaquit		u	
Yellow Warbler			c
Chestnut-sided Warbler	u	u	
Yellow-billed Cacique		r	

Species	Jan-Mar	Apr-Jun	Jul-Sep
Great-tailed Grackle		u	
Northern (Baltimore) Oriole		u	
Thick-billed Euphonia		u	
Spotted-crowned Euphonia		r	
Golden-hooded Tanager	u	u	u
Red-legged Honeycreeper	c	c	
Blue Dacnis	r		u
Blue-gray Tanager	a	a	c
Palm Tanager		c	
Scarlet-rumped Tanager	a	a	a
Summer Tanager	r		
Gray-headed Tanager			r
Buff-throated Saltator		u	s
Yellow-faced Grassquit		u	
White-collared Seedeater		u	
Variable Seedeater	c	c	c
Thick-billed Seed-finch	r		
Blue-black Grassquit	s		
Black-striped Sparrow			u

Birding from the grounds surrounding the main lodge deck is great in the morning from about 5:30 to 8 a.m., although there is some activity throughout the day. The early morning sunlight on the southwest side of the lodge shows the vivid coloration of many birds to great advantage. One morning in early April the birds were especially active in the lightning-killed trees to the southwest. While the vultures were still roosting, awaiting development of rising air currents, a **Chestnut-billed Toucan** arrived and trilled until joined by a few other members of the flock. Their gaudy blue feet, red crissum, yellow throat and red breast band were straight out of a comic book, while the subtler colors and striations on their bills and bluish-yellow facial patterns were also clearly visible in the morning sunlight. They hopped about peering into crevices and holes and were especially interested in pillaging a nest of **Masked Tityras**. They were unsuccessful, but did manage to pull a few bits of dead bark and wood from around the cavity while being harried by the parents.

    Red-lored Parrots raucously descended into an adjacent tree, and since they were nearly at eye level and the lighting was optimal, I could see their bluish crown and the fine black edgings of their nape feathers. They didn't get on well with the toucans and soon left. A few **Fiery-billed Aracaris** perched briefly before also going to more interesting places, while three newly fledged **Blue-gray Tanagers** sat calmly in the top of a dead tree and watched all the activity. A family of **Red-crowned Woodpeckers** was also about. Their newly fledged young should have been thankful to have been reared successfully in the midst of all the toucans.

Early the next morning, I watched a **Bat Falcon** pluck feathers from its breakfast while perched on a high dead branch to the southeast of the lodge. The night before, a pair were perched in the open in the same tree, seemingly oblivious to a fairly heavy rain that was drenching them. According to Gabriel Sanchez, although they disappear occasionally for a few weeks, the pair seem to have made the area their home. These speedsters often prey on bats, swallows and swifts, which they snatch in mid-air. Their lightning-fast flights keep other birds watchful, and they are truly astonishing to watch.

After breakfast, I was treated to the sight of a magnificent **King Vulture** that obligingly perched on a nearby tree on the west side of the lodge. Its huge black and white contrasting body was impressive, but with a good view through the spotting scope I could see the curiously wattled face, painted with bright shades of yellow and orange mixed in with softer blue. It surveyed the lodge for a few minutes before giving a few flaps and gliding away. Later in the day, I was at the nearby Playa Ventanas with Gabriel and found a group of **Turkey** and **Black Vultures** feeding on a dead white-faced monkey, whose body was in some rocks beneath a high vegetated cliff (cause of death unknown, but monkeys do occasionally miss their dare-devil leaps!). Two **King Vultures** magically appeared—I think they had been roosting in nearby overhead trees. They didn't really join the fray, but shouldered their cousins aside, took a few tasty morsels, appeared to be satisfied and flew off.

Las Ventanas is also good for **Riverside Wrens**. Look for these Costa Rican specialties along the road at the top of the hill near the lodge. They are the only wren whose entire underside is barred. Live birds are much prettier than any illustration I've seen. The far end of the road in the hollow near the highway is good for **Red-capped Manakins** and **Blue-crowned Manakins**. They respond to calling but won't stay put for long. Cement benches along the Pipeline Trail (ask for directions at the lodge or get a guide to take you there) indicate a lekking area for **Orange-collared Manakins**. While I was there, I didn't see the manakins, but did see some newly fledged **Long-billed Gnatwrens**. They were especially tame and hopped about in the low underbrush for some time.

Black-hooded Antshrikes and **Chestnut-backed Antbirds** are very common. You are sure to see them while walking any of the jungle trails. Both species are quite restricted in distribution and the former is only found in southwestern Costa Rica and western Panama. Other birds of note at Las Ventanas are **Great Tinamous** (very early morning along trails), **Ruddy Quail-doves** (along road near highway), **White-necked Puffbirds** (in trees near lodge) and **Pale-billed Woodpeckers** (in heavy forest). Also note that **Black-and-white Owls** perch on the flagpole near the swimming pool every night!

There is great birding near Las Ventanas in the river bottom of the Río Media Luna and in the estuary of the Río Térraba. The former is good for flycatchers, ibises, jacanas and herons, the latter for shorebirds and ducks. Both areas are good for raptors.

One remarkable day in June, a friend and I spotted a pair of **Spectacled Owls** in heavy forest when walking the Pipeline Trail. Both flew from a perch as we approached. One, fortunately, landed on a nearby branch and, although its back was toward us, it swiveled its neck to look back at us, giving us time to admire its great, dark-brown head and yellow eyes, partially encircled with white. On the same day we were also privileged to spot an immature **Ornate Hawk-eagle** on the grounds at Las Ventanas. It was settling down to roost for the night in a large tree between the ocean cliffs and the main lodge. Although it did not have the black and white barring of the adult and had only a few rufous neck feathers, it did have large black feathers extending from the head, from whence it derives its name. These fluttered in the breeze or drooped jauntily when the bird deemed to lower its head, perhaps to get a better look at us. The next morning, it was in a nearby tree and we had another chance to view this magnificent bird before it flew off to begin its daily routine.

GOLFITO

Birding around Golfito, less than 40 kilometers (25 miles) from the Panama border in the southwest lowlands of Costa Rica, can be very good, because the area contains many specialties that are relatively easy to see, and the lowland forest, much of it primary, is surprisingly accessible. The town of Golfito is strung out over several kilometers on a relatively flat but very narrow shoreline, which then abruptly rises to over 500 meters (1,600 feet). Because of a shortage of flat land, there is also a shortage of roads, and the main highway bears all motor, bus, motorcycle and foot traffic. Be careful if you are driving. There are also some confusing one-way streets. Most travel guides have a street map of Golfito, which you will find useful.

There are myriad hotels and *cabinas* and a few resort marinas in Golfito in all price ranges. But if you want some peace and quiet, try Cabinas Purruja in the "small town" of Purruja, about 5.5 kilometers (3.5 miles) southwest of Golfito. This low-priced establishment is a real bargain with large, very clean rooms with fans and private bath, set on about 3 hectares (7.5 acres) of garden with adjacent countryside. I saw a **Piratic Flycatcher** on the grounds one morning, and a **Social Flycatcher** was feeding her nestlings in a palm tree nearby. **Piratic Flycatchers** are interesting because they are one of the relatively few species that comes

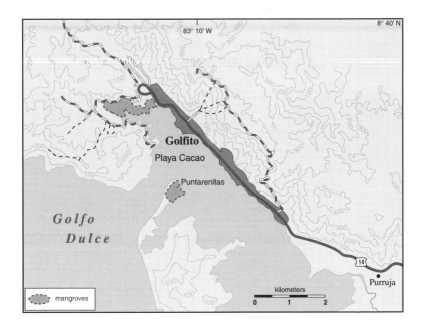

north to Costa Rica to breed and raise their young. They then return to South America. A few hours of birding near the *cabinas* is bound to yield other species.

Someone with foresight managed to get most of the watershed that affects the town of Golfito into protected status, and primary rainforest now surrounds the town. As a result, Golfito has not suffered the disastrous mud- and landslides owing to deforestation and "development" that are common events in other towns in Costa Rica. Today, this area is officially known as Golfito Refugio Nacional de Fauna Silvestre, and it consists of 1,309 hectares (3,233 acres). This gem surrounding the town makes the region memorable. In addition, while much of the refuge is very steep and rugged, there are good access points.

One is a road that leads to communications facilities on the hill above Golfito. The turn-off is to the right as you're heading into town near the first plaza (somewhat overgrown, so it's easy to miss). The road is steep, but is made of cement, so you won't have difficulty driving it even in rainy weather. It winds up the hill through thick forest, but there are a few areas to park off the roadway and bird up or down. If you don't have a car, a taxi ride to the top of the hill costs a few dollars. This area is one of the few in Costa Rica where **White-shouldered Tanagers** are very common. I also saw fair numbers of **Black-headed Antshrikes** and **Scarlet-thighed Dacnis**, fewer numbers of **Philadelphia Vireos, Red-eyed Vireos, Sulphur-bellied Flycatchers** and **Bright-rumped Attilas**, as well as other more common species along the road. In any case, go to near the top of the hill for a nice view of Golfito, Golfo Dulce and the Península de Osa in the distance.

Near the northwestern end of the inner gulf are several other interesting trails into the refuge. Watch for **Ruddy-breasted Seedeaters** in this area and also **White-throated Crakes** along the road near water. I saw a family of the latter species taking a bath in a small stream early one evening. The young appeared quite downy and lacked the distinct barred underbelly of the adult. There are also quite a few water birds on the extensive tide flats near the northeast of town and some mangroves—a good place to look for **Yellow-billed Cotingas**.

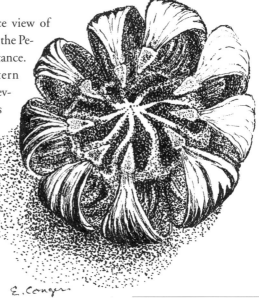

Strangler fig trees are common throughout Costa Rica. Small bits of edible tissue in opened seed pods attract a variety of birds.

There is a road that winds north through the refuge, passes an area known as Gamba and joins the Interamerican Highway at Villa Brieño. Although this road is supposed to be passable by car, there was one very rough crossing at a small stream just south of Gamba that I wouldn't do again. Maybe it will be fixed by the time you get there.

The area where a bridge crosses a small tributary in the headwaters of Quebrada Gamba was especially productive. Some melastome trees along the roadway attracted **Green Honeycreepers, Bay-headed Tanagers** and **Golden-hooded Tanagers**, while both **Scarlet-rumped** and **Yellow-billed Caciques** were also present. I made other good sightings just across the first bridge. A **Rufous-tailed Jacamar** was very co-operative, sitting for several minutes on an exposed twig, while a **Mourning Warbler** was harder to see as it foraged in a thicket and sometimes on the ground along the roadway. Flycatchers were also present, including some fairly uncommon species such as **Golden-crowned Spadebills, Mistletoe Tyrannulets** and **Yellow-olive Flycatchers**.

Wading in the Heliconia-lined stream was productive for viewing hummingbirds. I spotted a nest hung on the underside of a Heliconia leaf and

LIST OF BIRDS SIGHTED IN GOLFITO AREA

(a=abundant; c=common; u=uncommon; s=scarce; r=rare)

Species	Jan-Mar	Apr-Jun	Jul-Sep
Magnificent Frigatebird	c		
Cattle Egret	c		
Little Blue Heron	a		
White Ibis	a		
Roseate Spoonbill	u		
Turkey Vulture	c		
Black Vulture	c		
White-throated Crake	u		
Northern Jacana	u		
Spotted Sandpiper	u		
Short-billed Pigeon	c		
Ruddy Ground-dove	a		
Blue Ground-dove	u		
White-tipped Dove	c		
Orange-chinned Parakeet	c		
Squirrel Cuckoo	u		
Smooth-billed Ani	c		
Bronzy Hermit	u		
Long-tailed Hermit	c		
White-necked Jacobin	u		
Purple-crowned Fairy	u		
Black-throated Trogon	u		
Ringed Kingfisher	u		
Green Kingfisher	u		
Blue-crowned Motmot	u		
Rufous-tailed Jacamar	s		
Fiery-billed Aracari	c		
Chestnut-mandibled Toucan	a		
Golden-naped Woodpecker	c		
Pale-billed Woodpecker	u		
Black-hooded Antshrike	c		
Masked Tityra	u		
Black-crowned Tityra	u		
Rufous Piha	s		
Blue-crowned Manakin	u		
Tropical Kingbird	c		
Piratic Flycatcher	u		
Bright-rumped Attila	s		
Sulphur-bellied Flycatcher	u		
Gray-capped Flycatcher	a		
Social Flycatcher	c		

Species	Jan-Mar	Apr-Jun	Jul-Sep
Great Kiskadee	c		
Eastern Wood-pewee	c		
Golden-crowned Spadebill	u		
Yellow-olive Flycatcher	s		
Mistletoe Tyrannulet	s		
Barn Swallow	c		
Southern Rough -winged Swallow	c		
Northern Rough -winged Swallow	c		
Riverside Wren	c		
House Wren	c		
Clay-colored Robin	c		
Swainson's Thrush	c		
Tropical Gnatcatcher	u		
Red-eyed Vireo	s		
Bananaquit	c		
Mangrove Warbler	u		
Chestnut-sided Warbler	u		
Mourning Warbler	r		
Scarlet-rumped Cacique	u		
Yellow-billed Cacique	u		
Bronzed Cowbird	a		
Northern (Baltimore) Oriole	u		
Red-breasted Blackbird	c		
Golden-hooded Tanager	c		
Bay-headed Tanager	u		
Green Honeycreeper	u		
Scarlet-thighed Dacnis	u		
Blue-gray Tanager	c		
Palm Tanager	c		
Scarlet-rumped Tanager	c		
Black-cheeked Ant-tanager	u		
White-shouldered Tanager	c		
White-collared Seedeater	c		
Variable Seedeater	c		
Ruddy-breasted Seedeater	r		
Thick-billed Seed-finch	c		
Blue-black Grassquit	u		
Orange-billed Sparrow	u		
Black-striped Sparrow	c		

shortly thereafter a **Bronzy Hermit** settled down to incubate the eggs inside. **Long-tailed Hermits** and **Purple-crowned Fairies** were also present, but I'll never forget a stunning **White-necked Jacobin** that hovered 2 meters (6 feet) away at eye-level for 10–15 seconds. It slowly revolved and struck several poses, as if making sure that I saw all the taxonomically important details that marked it. That all hummers should be so co-operative! But the find of the day was a **Black-cheeked Ant-tanager** in thick undergrowth along the stream. This species is endemic to Costa Rica, being found only around Golfo Dulce and on the adjacent Peninsula de Osa.

Inner Golfo Dulce near Golfito.

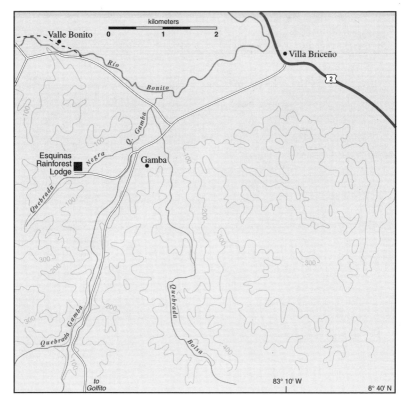

ESQUINAS RAINFOREST LODGE

This newly opened "luxury" lodge was constructed with funds from the nonprofit organization Rainforest of the Austrians. It now is owned by the Austro-Costa Rican nonprofit Association Progamba. Rainforest of the Austrians also paid more than $600,000 for over 3,000 hectares (7,500 acres) of forest, which it in turn donated to the Costa Rican National Park Service. This land is now the Esquinas Section of Piedras Blancas National Park, which is officially also part of Corcovado National Park. And so, owing to the Austrian effort, this valuable resource has been saved. Local people are now involved in eco-tourism in the region instead of farming by traditional methods, which have largely destroyed most forested land in Costa Rica. Although staying at the lodge is expensive if you are by yourself ($95 single occupancy), rates go down significantly for double ($65 per person) or triple ($45 per person) occupancy—not bad if you're with a group, especially considering this includes guides, meals and taxes. The advertisement also indicates that special rates may be negotiated for children, groups, students and Costa Ricans. Contact the manager, Favier Salgar (775-0845, 775-0131 or 284-3074).

LIST OF BIRDS SIGHTED IN ESQUINAS RAINFOREST LODGE AREA

(a=abundant; c=common; u=uncommon; s=scarce; r=rare)

Species	Jan-Mar Apr Jun Jul Sep	Species	Jan-Mar Apr-Jun Jul-Sep
Turkey Vulture	c	Barn Swallow	c
Black Vulture	c	Northern Rough -winged Swallow	c
Ruddy Ground-dove	a	Riverside Wren	u
Blue Ground-dove	u	House Wren	c
White-tipped Dove	c	Clay-colored Robin	u
White-crowned Parrot	u	Swainson's Thrush	c
Squirrel Cuckoo	u	Bananaquit	c
Smooth-billed Ani	c	Yellow Warbler	u
Spectacled Owl	u	Chestnut-sided Warbler	u
Long-tailed Hermit	u	Bronzed Cowbird	a
Ringed Kingfisher	u	Northern (Baltimore) Oriole	u
Blue-crowned Motmot	u	Red-breasted Blackbird	c
Fiery-billed Aracari	c	Golden-hooded Tanager	u
Chestnut-mandibled Toucan	c	Green Honeycreeper	u
Red-crowned Woodpecker	u	Blue-gray Tanager	u
Masked Tityra	c	Palm Tanager	u
Tropical Kingbird	c	Black-cheeked Ant-tanager	s
Gray-capped Flycatcher	a	White-collared Seedeater	c
Social Flycatcher	u	Variable Seedeater	c
Great Kiskadee	c	Blue-black Grassquit	u
Eastern Wood-pewee	c	Orange-billed Sparrow	c
		Black-striped Sparrow	c

I birded the area one morning with Augustino, the resort's local guide (see sidebar, page 60). He put me in contact with another **Black-cheeked Ant-tanager** near the lodge, and some more common birds of the region— **Orange-billed Sparrows, Chestnut-mandibled Toucans, Riverside Wrens** and even a pair of **Spectacled Owls**. There is an extensive trail system into the park behind the lodge and more is under construction. We saw the owls in the forest, but most of the other birds were on the lodge grounds in adjacent second growth.

While you are passing through this area, watch for **Red-breasted Blackbirds** in the fields or on fences. They are an invader from Panama and are, so far, only found in extreme southwest Costa Rica. I saw a number of them in mid-April. At that time, it was also great to watch several male **Bronzed Cowbirds** displaying to females, who unconcernedly continued feeding in the fields. The males leap into the air and hover for several seconds above a female, wings beating furiously. They then descend slowly to alight directly in front of the female and immediately crouch and puff out all their feathers. I hadn't associated cowbirds with beauty and dramatics before I saw this display, but

the aerial acrobatics and the stance of the male before the female with his newly minted breeding plumage shining in the sunlight are very impressive.

Also watch for **Fork-tailed Flycatchers** in open country in this region; they are another specialty of southwestern Costa Rica.

THE SOUTHEASTERN LOWLANDS

Beautiful Sunbitterns are becoming increasingly rare in Costa Rica. They can still be seen occasionally along secluded foothill streams.

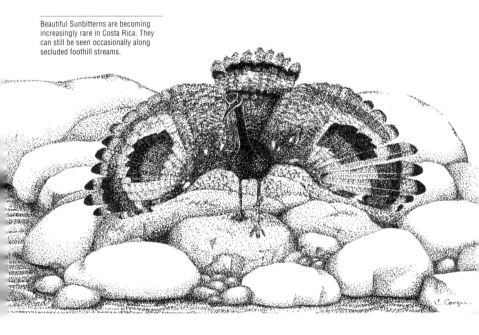

The southeastern lowlands of Costa Rica consist of a relatively narrow strip of land, which extends southeast from Siquirres and Limón to the Panama border, between the higher foothills of Cordillera de Talamanca and the Caribbean Sea. In this region, spurs of the Talamancas extend eastward for considerable distances, in some cases coming close to the Caribbean. This is in great contrast to the broad expanses of lowlands found in northeastern Costa Rica. The uniform sandy coast of this region is interrupted by low rocky outcrops only near Limón and the small towns of Cahuita and Puerto Viejo de Talamanca in extreme southeastern Costa Rica. (The latter town is not to be confused with Puerto Viejo de Sarapiquí in northeastern Costa Rica). Major rivers draining the Talamancas are the Río Pacuare, Río Chirripo, Río Estrella and Río Sixaola, which forms part of the Costa Rica–Panama border. The latter two river systems drain low valleys, Valle de la Estrella and Valle de Talamanca, which extend for considerable distances towards the mountains.

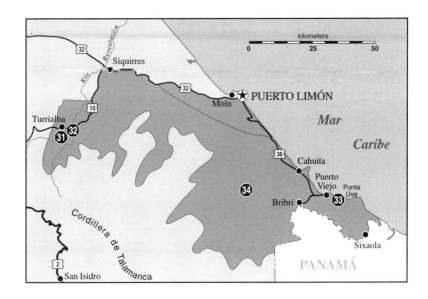

Birding Locations in the
Southeastern Lowlands of Costa Rica

31 Turrialba
32 CATIE
33 Puerto Viejo de Talamanca and Punta Uva
34 Hitoy Cerere Biological Reserve

Most lowlands in this region have long been cleared of forest for banana plantations, especially along the highway to Limón and in lower reaches of Valle de la Estrella. Cocoa was once a key crop in the area, but a fungal disease has greatly reduced its importance. Other land uses include palm oil plantations, rice fields and cattle pastures. However, second-growth forest is widespread in Valle de Talamanca and some primary forest still remains, primarily south and west in low foothills near Puerto Viejo. Two small parks, Cahuita National Park, 1,067 hectares (2,635 acres), and Gandoca–Manzanillo Wildlife Refuge, 5,013 hectares (12,380 acres), were recently created to protect some coastal forests, although it is mostly second growth. A much more significant area is Hitoy–Cerere Biological Reserve, 9,154 hectares (22,610 acres), in the south central Valle de la Estrella, which protects extensive areas of primary, very wet lowland and mountain jungle.

This region of Costa Rica also contains significant foothill areas, which are primarily accessible via the highway from San José through Turrialba to the town of Siquirres. Here at higher elevation, major crops are coffee and sugar cane and much of the land is cleared.

Unlike most other areas of Costa Rica, September and October are rather dry along the coast of this region, and a wetter dry season usually occurs in February and March. However, rainfall becomes much more prevalent throughout the year as elevation increases, and there is virtually no dry season in lower foothills of the mountains.

TRAVEL

The only major highway penetrating southeastern Costa Rica extends southeast from Limón to the Panama border, although there are some secondary roads that branch off to Puerto Viejo and from the highway between Cartago and Limón. If you are driving, be prepared for potholes south of Limón and rough gravel roads south of Cahuita. San José/Turrialba buses (Trantusa 556-0073) leave hourly from C13, A6 & 8. The trip takes about 1.5 hours. Transportes Mepe (221-0524) runs three buses a day from San José to Cahuita and Sixaola from A11, C Central & 1. Or if you are already in Limón, buses to Cahuita, Puerto Viejo and Sixaola leave from Radio Casino—C4, A4—at least four times daily.

TROPICAL BIRD SPECIALTIES OF THE SOUTHEASTERN LOWLANDS

Within Costa Rica, only three species of birds are restricted to the southeastern lowlands (see Appendix I, Group 8). Of these, the **Black-chested Jay** and the **Sulphur-rumped Tanager** are quite uncommon and difficult to find. The other species, the **Spotted-crowned Antvireo**, is relatively common only near Sixaola.

Within Costa Rica, five species are restricted to southern lowland areas (Appendix I, Group 13). Of these, the **Whistling Wren** is fairly common, and the **Blue-crowned Manakin** and the **Red-rumped Woodpecker** are again common only near the Panama border. Refer to the previous chapter for a listing of 31 species that are common specialties of the eastern lowlands.

SE LOWLANDS

Flycatcher nest.

TURRIALBA

There are several good birding areas near Turrialba, a moderate-sized town directly east of San José and Cartago. The town itself is perched on the slopes of Volcán Turrialba, which last erupted in the 1860s. It looks down on the Río Reventazón valley and serves as a center for this agricultural area, growing mainly sugar cane, coffee and a wide variety of vegetables. Although still quite busy, especially on market days, Turrialba and the towns along Highway 10 are quieter now than when all San José to Puerto Limón traffic used the route. (Most east-west traffic now takes the shorter route on the newer and better Highway 32, which goes through Parque Nacional Braulio Carrillo.) Turrialba is at an altitude of about 650 meters (2,150 feet), so it's a good area to see a mixture of lowland and foothill bird species.

There are two bus terminals in Turrialba—the upper (A4, C2) is for buses to and from Siquirres, Cartago and San José; the lower terminal (near A2, C2) serves the small communities surrounding Turrialba.

If you want to stay in Turrialba, try the cheap and passably clean Interamericano Hotel (556-0142). It's close to the bus stations and the town center, yet set off in a relatively quiet area across the old railroad tracks. The hotel has a spacious lounging area downstairs and lots of tables still in place from a defunct restaurant. It's a good place to use as a base while birding surrounding areas and to catch up on your birding notes. Look for large flocks of **Crimson-fronted Parakeets** that use the palm trees beside the hotel in the mornings and evenings. **Black Phoebes** and **Torrent Tyrannulets** are also fairly common; the former in town along the river, the latter along streams in the countryside.

LIST OF BIRDS SIGHTED IN THE TURRIALBA AREA
(a=abundant; c=common; u=uncommon; s=scarce; r=rare)

Species	Jan-Mar	Apr-Jun	Jul-Sep
Cattle Egret	a		
Turkey Vulture	a		
Black Vulture	a		
Roadside Hawk	u		
Ruddy Ground-dove	c		
White-crowned Parrot	c		
Rufous-tailed Hummingbird	u		
Hoffmann's Woodpecker	c		
Slaty Spinetail	s		
Black Phoebe	u		
Tropical Kingbird	a		
Social Flycatcher	a		
Torrent Tyrannulet	u		

Species	Jan-Mar	Apr-Jun	Jul-Sep
Yellow-bellied Elaenia	u		
Northern Rough-winged Swallow	c		
Brown Jay	c		
Bananaquit	u		
Montezuma Oropendola	a		
Great-tailed Grackle	a		
Blue-gray Tanager	c		
Palm Tanager	c		
Scarlet-rumped Tanager	c		
Yellow-faced Grassquit	c		
Variable Seedeater	c		
Black-striped Sparrow	u		
Rufous-collared Sparrow	c		

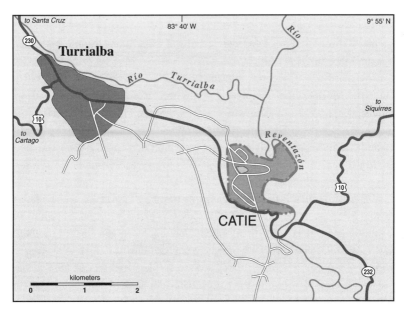

CATIE

Centro Agronómico Tropical de Investigación y Enseñanza (CATIE) is 4 kilometers (2.5 miles) east of Turrialba on the main highway toward Siquirres. It is a world-famous research center for tropical agriculture. It is of interest to birders because it consists of more than 1,000 hectares (2,470 acres) of land on a steep bluff overlooking the Reventazón River. Much of the land is landscaped lawns and flower beds, but there are many large trees and thickets. In

LIST OF BIRDS SIGHTED IN THE CATIE AREA

(a=abundant; c=common; u=uncommon; s=scarce; r=rare)

Species	Jan-Mar	Apr-Jun	Jul-Sep	Species	Jan-Mar	Apr-Jun	Jul-Sep
Yellow-crowned Night-heron	u			Great Kiskadee	c		
Cattle Egret	a			Common Tody-flycatcher	u		
Green-backed Heron	a			Banded-backed Wren	u		
Little Blue Heron	c			House Wren	c		
Turkey Vulture	c			Clay-colored Robin	c		
Black Vulture	c			Chestnut-sided Warbler	c		
Purple Gallinule	a			Montezuma Oropendola	u		
Northern Jacana	a			Great-tailed Grackle	c		
Short-billed Pigeon	c			Yellow-crowned Euphonia	u		
Orange-chinned Parakeet	c			Yellow-throated Euphonia	u		
Crowned Woodnymph	u			Golden-hooded Tanager	u		
Keel-billed Toucan	u			Summer Tanager	u		
Tropical Kingbird	a			Black-headed Saltator	u		

addition there is a small pond on the grounds where you are assured of seeing **Purple Gallinules, Green-backed Herons, Little Blue Herons, Northern Jacanas** and other water birds.

One morning I saw some colorful tropical species, including **Keel-billed Toucans, Montezuma Oropendolas, Golden-hooded Tanagers, Yellow-crowned Euphonias** and **Yellow-throated Euphonias.** The brilliant green throat and chest of the otherwise violet **Crowned Woodnymph** was especially beautiful in the morning sun as the hummer perched on twigs overhanging the steep bluff of the river. A few **Banded-backed Wrens** were also present in thickets along the rim of the bluff.

CATIE shouldn't be considered a prime birding destination, but if you are passing by the area anyway and have an hour or two, it's a very pleasant place to stop in at, especially in the morning. Walking along the edge of the bluff was most productive for me. From there you can bird the thickets, as well as scan the large trees in adjacent open areas for warblers, tanagers and euphonias. A steep trail that descends to the river might offer good birding. The guard at the entrance to CATIE is accustomed to visitors and tourists. Just ask if you can enter to look at the birds.

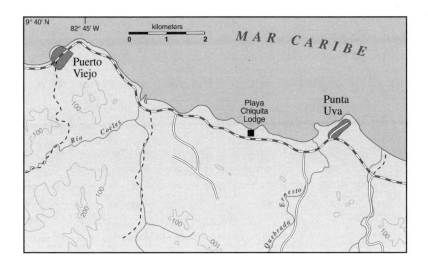

PUERTO VIEJO DE
TALAMANCA AND PUNTA UVA

The area around Puerto Viejo de Talamanca is one of the most under-rated birding destinations in Costa Rica, because of the ease with which you can see a great variety of species. Unlike many regions in Costa Rica, large cattle pastures are a rarity in this area, as are large monoculture farms. Much of the land is covered with large second-growth forest and seeing significant stands of primary forest on adjacent hillsides is the norm rather than the exception. Colorful parrots, toucans, trogons and tanagers abound in the area while a variety of antbirds and woodcreepers are present to challenge your skills.

Tourism has boomed in Costa Rica. Tourists drawn to the beautiful beaches, surfing and coral reef snorkeling in the Talamanca region have rapidly transformed the small towns of Cahuita and Puerto Viejo from quiet fishing villages to busy (but still quite small) tourist centers. There is a great variety of accommodations available ranging from cheap one-room cubicles to luxury resorts. Check your guide book for hosts of alternatives.

A moderately priced and nicely laid out establishment is Playa Chiquita Lodge (233-6613) about 6 kilometers (3.75 miles) east of Puerto Viejo near Punta Uva. Any of the buses will drop you off if you ask, or take a taxi from Puerto Viejo. Beaches, estuaries, mangrove swamps (in the Gandoso River), crop and farmlands and large patches of secondary and primary forest are all nearby. In addition, Playa Chiquita Lodge is about 50 meters (165 feet) or so from the ocean.

Small fruits from the many species of melastome trees are favorite bird foods.

If you stay at the lodge, watch for **Bay Wrens** in the thickets along the path to the beach. Their powerful songs will alert you to their presence but they are sometimes quite difficult to spot. **Northern Waterthrushes** also feed along the wet margins of the path, and a variety of shorebirds and seabirds can be seen on the beach, depending on the season. In March, there was some movement along the coast and **Spotted Sandpipers** and **Ruddy Turnstones** were showing signs of molting into their breeding plumage.

Playa Chiquita Lodge also has a garden with a variety of flowers, shrubs and trees, and the manager was in the process of installing some feeders when I was last there. **Long-tailed Hermits** were especially abundant, feeding on heliconias, and **Olive-backed Euphonias** were common higher up in the trees. Small flocks of migrant **Prothonotary Warblers** occasionally passed through the garden and **White-crowned Parrots, Montezuma Oropendolas, Squirrel Cuckoos, Collared Aracaris, Wedge-billed Treecreepers** and several species of flycatcher were common. I was also treated to the appearance of **Black-cheeked Woodpeckers, Lineated Woodpeckers** and one beautiful and more uncommon **Cinnamon Woodpecker**. All were seen while sitting on the deck or standing in the garden.

There is good birding along the main road and the many side roads and paths in the vicinity. Large flocks of **Turkey Vultures,** intermixed with occasional **Broad-winged Hawks** and **Swainson's Hawks,** were using mid-morning updrafts to gain altitude when I was there. They migrate through the region in mid-March and open areas along the main road were good places to observe the migration. Many thousands of birds can be seen daily during peak migration periods. **White-crowned Parrots** and the occasional **Brown-headed Parrot** are also easily seen along the road along with the more common open country flycatchers and seedeaters.

One kilometer (.6 miles) down the road from Chiquita Lodge, a road branches to the right and is passable with a light car for about 1 kilometer (.6 miles). There is a sign at the junction which reads Caminata Guida al Bosque.

Great birding can be had by walking the road and paths in the area. Look especially in melastome trees along the road. Their ripe fruit is a favorite for many species, especially tanagers and honeycreepers. I observed 11 species in one morning, including the relatively uncommon **Rufous-winged Tanager, Tawny-crested Tanager, Green Honeycreeper** and **Shining Honeycreeper**, all brilliantly colored species with contrasting shades of green, blue, chestnut, yellow and black. Be especially aware of the lighting in this area; keep it behind you if at all possible to get the full effect. I also spotted a **Rufous Piha** along a

Restful scene from near a beach.

LIST OF BIRDS SIGHTED IN PUERTO VIEJO DE TALAMANCA AND PUNTA UVA

(a=abundant; c=common; u=uncommon; s=scarce; r=rare)

Species	Jan-Mar	Apr-Jun	Jul-Sep
Brown Pelican	u		
Yellow-crowned Night-heron	u		
Cattle Egret	c		
Little Blue Heron	c		
Tricolored Heron	s		
Snowy Egret	c		
Turkey Vulture	a		
Black Vulture	a		
Semiplumbeous Hawk	s		
Common Black-hawk	u		
Broad-winged Hawk	u		
Purple Gallinule	u		
Semipalmated Plover	c		
Wilson's Plover	u		
Whimbrel	c		
Willet	c		
Spotted Sandpiper	c		
Ruddy Turnstone	u		
Sanderling	u		
Western Sandpiper	u		
Least Sandpiper	u		
Short-billed Pigeon	c		
Gray-chested Dove	u		
Brown-hooded Parrot	u		
White-crowned Parrot	u		
Squirrel Cuckoo	c		
Groove-billed Ani	c		
Black-and-white Owl	s		
Swift	?		
Long-tailed Hermit	c		
Rufous-tailed Hummingbird	a		
Slaty-tailed Trogon	u		
Violaceous Trogon	u		
Amazon Kingfisher	c		
Broad-billed Motmot	u		
Pied Puffbird	r		
Collared Aracari	a		
Keel-billed Toucan	a		
Chestnut-mandibled Toucan	c		
Black-cheeked Woodpecker	c		
Cinnamon Woodpecker	s		
Lineated Woodpecker	u		
Wedge-billed Woodcreeper	c?		

Species	Jan-Mar	Apr-Jun	Jul-Sep
Streaked-headed Woodcreeper	c		
Masked Tityra	u		
Black-crowned Tityra	u		
Rufous Piha	s		
Snowy Cotinga	u		
White-collared Manakin	c		
Long-tailed Tyrant	u		
Tropical Kingbird	c		
Bright-rumped Attila	r		
Gray-capped Flycatcher	s		
Social Flycatcher	u		
Great Kiskadee	a		
Great-crested Flycatcher	s		
Dusky-capped Flycatcher	s		
Tropical Pewee	u		
Barn Swallow	u		
Northern Rough -winged Swallow	c		
Mangrove Swallow	c		
Bay Wren	c		
House Wren	c		
Clay-colored Robin	c		
Prothonotary Warbler	u		
Chestnut-sided Warbler	a		
Northern Waterthrush	u		
Buff-rumped Warbler	r		
Montezuma Oropendola	a		
Northern (Baltimore) Oriole	u		
Olive-backed Euphonia	a		
Golden-hooded Tanager	c		
Rufous-winged Tanager	u		
Green Honeycreeper	u		
Shining Honeycreeper	u		
Blue-gray Tanager	u		
Palm Tanager	u		
Scarlet-rumped Tanager	c		
Summer Tanager	u		
White-lined Tanager	u		
Tawny-crested Tanager	u		
White-collared Seedeater	c		
Variable Seedeater	c		
Thick-billed Seed-finch	u		
Blue-black Grassquit	u		
Black-striped Sparrow	c		

forest edge, and a few **Masked Tityras**, **Black-crowned Tityras** and **Snowy Cotingas** higher up in the trees, mostly roosting on bare branches. A special treat was a **Pied Puffbird** placidly sitting next to a **Black-crowned Cotinga**.

I went birding one day with Martin Hernandez Meza, the local guide who put the sign on the road. He is considered the best all-round local guide in the area. His house sits on a small hillside about 500 meters (1,600 feet) from the main road, on the left side. Martin charges about $12 for a half-day or $18 for a full day. Although he is not an expert birder, he is very knowledgeable of all the more common species. His family's farm includes some large tracts of primary forest and very interesting trails. With Martin's help, I saw a **Semiplumbeous Hawk** and a beautiful **Black-and-white Owl**. The latter was perched high beneath the canopy of a great tree, but afforded a terrific view with the spotting scope. According to Martin, both species are fairly common in the area, along with **White Hawks**, which we didn't see that day. Other very interesting sightings included **Broad-billed Motmots**, **White-collared Manakins**, a **Bright-rumped Attila**, **Violaceous Trogons**, **Slaty-headed Trogons** and a **Buff-rumped Warbler** gathering nesting material beside a small stream. Other fairly common birds in the area are **Great Curassow**, **Crested Guan**, **Spectacled Owl**, **Fasciated Antshrike**, **Great Antshrike** and **Black-chested Jay**. In Costa Rica, the latter species is restricted to the southeast Caribbean lowlands and foothills.

Martin has a specially constructed screened frame *cabina* in a secluded section of the forest. He uses it for guests who want to stay overnight and learn something about the sights and sounds of life in the jungle after sunset. Sounds interesting. Maybe next time!

HITOY-CERERE

How would you like to have a private tropical rainforest of more than 9,000 hectares (22,230 acres) to bird and stroll around in? That's very likely what you will get if you go to Reserva Biologica Hitoy-Cerere in the near future. That is, before word spreads that access to the reserve has been improved and that it is a veritable tropical wonderland. It's largely untouched rainforest with many huge trees laden with mosses, epiphytes and lianas and beautiful clear rivers and streams winding through rugged foothills of the Talamancas.

As of March 1996, a regular car can get to within 500 meters (1,600 feet) of the administration and accommodations buildings of the reserve. There are friendly farm families at the end of the passable road where you can park your car. Signs to the park from the turnoff at Penshurt on Highway 36 were adequate, although passage through the banana farms in the flatlands of Valle de Estrella is still a bit confusing. If you are not sure of where you are, ask at any

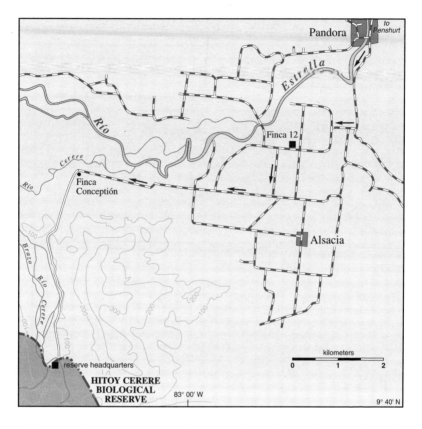

of the many banana-processing plants or *pulperias* (general stores) along the way. If you don't have a car, getting to the reserve is more difficult, but it can still be done. Buses run from Limón to Valle de Estrella several times a day and the end of the line is Finca 12. From there, taxis can be arranged to take you to the reserve and pick you up again. On the way through Valle de Estrella I saw some **Purple Gallinules**, egrets and herons feeding along marshy streams, along with many other open country birds.

There are no hotels near the reserve, but it is usually possible to sleep in bunk bed-style rooms and to eat with park staff at their headquarters for a nominal cost. Calling in advance is recommended (try the central office in San José, 257-0922, at C25, A8 & 10, or the office in Limón, 758-3796), although I had no difficulty when I just showed up. Lodging with a farm family might also be arranged. If you have difficulties, talk to Sherman Barr. He owns the second to last farm (house on the right) before the end of the road. You can also camp at the reserve headquarters but be prepared for rain. The area gets more than 3.5 meters (11.5 feet) of rain a year. There is really no dry season, but the least amount of rain falls in February and March and September and October.

LIST OF BIRDS SIGHTED IN HITOY-CERERE AREA
(a=abundant; c=common; u=uncommon; s=scarce; r=rare)

Species	Jan-Mar	Apr-Jun	Jul-Sep	Species	Jan-Mar	Apr-Jun	Jul-Sep
Cattle Egret	a			Wedge-billed Woodcreeper	c		
Great Blue Heron	u			Plain Antvireo	u		
Turkey Vulture	c			White-flanked Antwren	u		
Black Vulture	c			Dotted-winged Antwren	u		
Swainson's Hawk	u			Chestnut-backed Antbird	c		
Great Curassow	s			White-collared Manakin	c		
Purple Gallinule	u			Long-tailed Tyrant	u		
Northern Jacana	u			Tropical Kingbird	c		
Short-billed Pigeon	c			Gray-capped Flycatcher	u		
Ruddy Ground-dove	c			Social Flycatcher	c		
Crimson-fronted Parakeet	c			Great Kiskadee	c		
White-crowned Parrot	c			Gray-breasted Martin	c		
Blue-headed Parrot	s			Southern Rough -winged Swallow	c		
Squirrel Cuckoo	c			Clay-colored Robin	u		
Groove-billed Ani	c			Philadelphia Vireo	u		
Striped Cuckoo	u			Golden-winged Warbler	r		
Long-tailed Hermit	u			Chestnut-sided Warbler	c		
Blue-chested Hummingbird	c			Montezuma Oropendola	a		
Rufous-tailed Hummingbird	u			Golden-hooded Tanager	c		
Slaty-tailed Trogon	u			Palm Tanager	c		
Violaceous Trogon	u			Scarlet-rumped Tanager	u		
Amazon Kingfisher	u			Summer Tanager	u		
White-whiskered Puffbird	s			Variable Seedeater	u		
Keel-billed Toucan	a			Black-striped Sparrow	c		
Black-cheeked Woodpecker	c						

There aren't many trails in the reserve and you should be prepared with rubber boots, because there are some soggy patches in most seasons. The trail system begins behind and to the left of the kitchen and winds up a small ridge. Thick second growth first greets you, in which **Bay Wrens**, **Black-throated Wrens** and **Song Wrens** are to be watched for. **White-collared Manakins** were especially abundant when I was there. Their small wing pops, which sound like fire crackers, could be heard constantly, and they were a real joy to watch as they displayed briefly on low exposed twigs.

There is a short trail called Sendero Tepesquintle which branches to the right, curls up a gentle ridge, then descends steeply to the Río Cerere. From there you can walk up the riverbed (old tennis shoes are good for this) for a number of kilometers if the river is low. Bird densities were fairly low and the heavy jungle made spotting birds difficult, but I did see **Keel-billed Toucans**, **Chestnut-backed Antbirds**, **Slaty-tailed Trogons** and, quite high in a vine tangle, a lovely pair of **Dot-winged Antwrens**. In addition, I got to study a **White-whiskered Puffbird** to my heart's content as it perched on a low branch above the trail. I had yet more luck with the antbirds on the return trip along this trail, spotting **Plain Antvireos** and **White-flanked Antwrens**, along with **Squirrel Cuckoos, Long-tailed Hermits** and **Violaceous Trogons**, a beautifully colored species I never tire of looking at.

If you continue on the main trail, another branch to the right called Sendero Espavél will take you up a fairly steep ridge and down the other side to Río Moin in about 9 kilometers (5.6 miles). About 1 kilometer (.6 miles) from the main junction is the giant espavél tree after which the trail was named. The tree's circumference is about 13 meters (43 feet), a sight worth the walk for its own sake.

Birding is also good at the reserve entrance near the park building. One hot afternoon on the deck of the bunkhouse I spotted several birds that became active after a brief shower. **Blue-chested Hummingbirds** were especially common feeding on flowers near the buildings. **Black-cheeked Woodpeckers, Philadelphia Vireos** and a few **Golden-winged Warblers** were busy feeding in more distant trees, along with **Chestnut-sided Warblers** in beautifully patterned, newly molted breeding plumage.

Walking back along the road in morning or evening will reward you with a host of more open country species. **Montezuma Oropendolas** are everywhere. Also common are **Crimson-fronted Parakeets, White-crowned Parrots, Keel-billed Toucans, Long-tailed Tyrants** and a number of tanagers and flycatchers. **Striped Cuckoos** and **Blue-headed Parrots** are also present, along with the more uncommon **Chestnut-headed Oropendola**. They don't nest nearby, as the **Montezuma Oropendola** does, but they'd fly by regularly, especially towards evening. Look for a smaller, more sleek oropendola and it's likely the **Chestnut-headed Oropendola**.

Some very good birding could also be had on farms near Hitoy-Cerere. Substantial tracts of jungle remain on most hilltops and in gullies and good mixtures of birds should be present within the region. Spending several days (or weeks) in this area would be a real treat. It's on the threshold of truly great expanses of untouched rainforest that extend west to the very tops of the Talamancas and beyond. No matter how much time you have, it would not be enough to more than scratch the surface of the vast birding potential of the region.

CENTRAL VALLEY–
VALLE CENTRAL

The fluid song of the Montezuma Oropendola echoes and flows through the forest.

The Valle Central or Meseta Central, the area adjacent to San José, is a moderately high plateau, which lies between Cordillera Central to the north and Cordillera Talamanca to the south. Because much of the land is 1,000 meters (3,300 feet) or higher in elevation and the area is influenced to some extent by the Guanacaste climate from the northwest, Valle Central is relatively cool and dry. Light jackets or sweaters are not unusual apparel for early morning or evening bird walks.

Most land of Meseta Central drains to the west into Río Tárcoles. The capital city of Costa Rica, San José, lies near the center of this region and Heredia, Alajuela and numerous other smaller communities surround San José. The low pass forming the continental divide is called Ochomogo. East of the pass lies a smaller valley that contains Cartago as the principal community and drains into the Caribbean via Río Reventazón.

More than half the population of Costa Rica lives in the Valle Central and the area was heavily populated by Indians hundreds of years ago when the Spanish first arrived. Its good climate and fertile soil has long attracted farmers and settlers and the region is largely deforested. Today, coffee, sugarcane, pasture, nurseries and a host of other croplands, together with cities, towns and suburbs, occupy most of the Valle Central. Small stands of second-growth forest dot hillsides and sometimes blanket very steep ravine slopes, which are too steep and unstable to farm.

We reached Lankester Gardens in the morning after catching the first bus out of Orosi and birded in the very early morning in some nearby wetlands. I was well satisfied, because I had seen numerous **Sedge Wrens** and **White-throated Flycatchers**, both species highly restricted in distribution within Costa Rica. We were more than ready for a snack and a cup of coffee. To our disappointment, the gates were firmly shut, and a worker on the other side of the bars informed us they didn't open for another hour. We sat disconsolately on the edge of a flower bed, and, as usual, were soon joined by a curious Tico—a truck driver who was also waiting for the gardens to open to deliver some supplies. After he had studied my telescope and looked at some **White-eared Ground-sparrows**, I asked him if he knew whether there was a restaurant or cafe inside the gardens. "No, nothing," he said. He must have noted our dismay, since he went to his truck and returned a few moments later with two warm chicken *empanadas* which he gave to us. We thanked him profusely as we savored what was probably his mid-morning snack and carried on a conversation in broken Spanish.

TRAVEL

Most travelers coming to Costa Rica will arrive by air, landing in the Central Valley at the Juan Santamaría International Airport near San José. If you have to stay in the Central Valley, I recommend you avoid San José and stay in one of the surrounding smaller towns, which are much more pleasant and slower-paced, unless you specifically want to see a fast-paced, congested Central American metropolis.

San Antonio de Belen is a short taxi-ride south of the airport. The community has only one hotel, but it is a dandy! The new Apartotel Oro (239-0403 or 0993) provides beautiful, fully furnished, modern two-bedroom apartments for about $50 per night, or $500 per month. It's a good deal if you want a private, secure base of operations in the Central Valley while in Costa Rica.

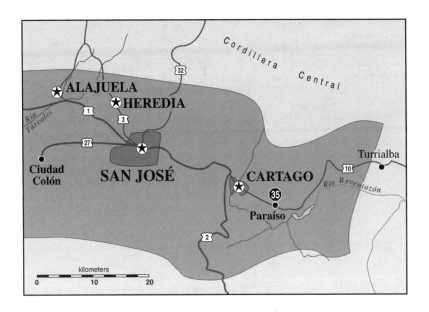

Birding Locations in the
Valle Central of Costa Rica

35 Paraiso and Lankester Gardens

Everything is provided, including television, telephone and a full complement of kitchen appliances, pots, pans and dishes. Alajuela and Heredia are other pleasant moderately sized towns near the airport. Consult your guide book for possible accommodations to fit every pocketbook.

TROPICAL BIRD SPECIALTIES OF VALLE CENTRAL

White-throated Flycatchers and **Prevost's Ground-sparrows** are largely restricted to the Valle Central within Costa Rica (Appendix I, Group 14). These two species are the region's only unique tropical specialties. Although not a tropical specialty, one other species, the **Sedge Wren**, is worth note, since within Costa Rica it is largely restricted to the Valle Central, mainly near Cartago.

Because of the congestion, pollution and habitat destruction that has occurred in the Valle Central, it's not a great place to spend time if you are interested in birds and the environment. In fact, since there are very few species of birds in the Valle Central that cannot be seen in other areas in much more pleasant surroundings, I recommend leaving the area as soon as possible.

E. Couyer

After all, fabulous places such as Vara Blanca and Póas Volcano are only about an hour's drive from the airport, and the Tárcoles/Carara area is little more than two hours away. The one area that I do recommend birding in the Valle Central is described below.

PARAISO–LANKESTER GARDENS

The area immediately south of Cartago and Paraiso, especially the wetland regions, is one of the few places in Costa Rica where there is a good chance of seeing **Prevost's Ground-sparrows**, **Sedge Wrens** and **White-throated Flycatchers**, all in the same general vicinity. In addition, from October to early May, marshes in this area harbor substantial numbers of **Common Yellowthroats**, a species quite difficult to find in other regions of Costa Rica. If you base your birding efforts around the world-famous Lankester Gardens, which grow more than 800 species of orchids and many other plants—and thus contain some good bird habitat—your day can be that much more enjoyable.

LIST OF BIRDS SIGHTED IN THE PARAISO/LANKESTER GARDENS AREA

(a=abundant; c=common; u=uncommon; s=scarce; r=rare)

Species	Jan-Mar	Apr-Jun	Jul-Sep	Species	Jan-Mar	Apr-Jun	Jul-Sep
Turkey Vulture		u		Clay-colored Robin	a		
Black Vulture		u		Orange-billed Nightingale-thrush	a		
Red-billed Pigeon		u		Gray-crowned Yellowthroat	a		
Rufous-tailed Hummingbird		u		Great-tailed Grackle	u		
Hoffmann's Woodpecker		s		Eastern Meadowlark	u		
Tropical Kingbird		u		Blue-gray Tanager	u		
Great Kiskadee		u		Buff-throated Saltator	u		
Dusky-capped Flycatcher		u		Grayish Saltator	u		
White-throated Flycatcher		c		White-collared Seedeater	u		
Yellow-bellied Elaenia		u		Blue-black Grassquit	u		
Blue-and-white Swallow		c		Yellow-throated Brush-finch	u		
Brown Jay		c		White-eared Ground-sparrow	u		
Sedge Wren		c		Rufous-collared Sparrow	c		
Rufous-and-white Wren		s					
House Wren		u					

When I birded this area, I used the small town of Orosi as a base, since I also wanted to do some birding in the nearby Tapantí National Park. Numerous buses filled with workers leave from Orosi very early in the morning and go to Paraiso and Cartago. There are also at least hourly Cartago–Paraiso buses. Tell the driver you want to get off at the stop near Lankester Gardens, about 1 kilometer (.6 miles) west of Paraiso; they all know where it is. If you're driving, take the road south opposite the Fibrelite factory and bus stop. The gardens are only about .5 kilometers (.3 miles) away, an easy walk.

There is a small wetland area immediately south of the highway at the turn-off to Lankester Gardens. In early May 1996, a new road cut through the middle of this vacant land and construction of a large tank (oil-storage?) near one corner of the field was in progress, so I don't know how much longer this wetland will exist. A pity. Early one misty morning, numerous **Sedge Wrens** were flying about and several perched for considerable periods of time on tufts of swamp grass. **White-throated Flycatchers** were also plentiful. Look for them perching on higher shrubs in the marsh and in thickets around the edges. Their name aptly describes their most striking distinguishing characteristic. Although **Gray-crowned Yellowthroats** seemed to be everywhere, I never did see any **Common Yellowthroats**. Perhaps I was a bit late in the year, and they had already migrated north.

When we were through birding the marsh, a short walk down the road to Lankester Gardens yielded **Eastern Meadowlarks** and a **Dusky-capped Flycatcher**. Although guide books say the gardens open at 8 a.m., their hours

(at least in May, after the peak tourist season) are from 9 a.m. to 3:30 p.m.—
not great for birding—but we did manage to see several species. **Orange-billed
Nightingale-thrushes** were especially abundant, along with **Yellow-throated
Brush-finches** and a few **White-eared Ground-sparrows, Rufous-and-white
Wrens** and several other more common species. Of course, there were also
quite a few orchids around!

There are a few other wetlands and small lakes in the region, so if you get
there and a huge oil-storage yard is developed along the highway where I birded,
don't despair. A marsh and small lake are located just south of the gardens.
Stop in at the house near the marsh and ask to bird the land. I believe the
owner's name is Carmen Castro, and she is used to such requests from birders.

MOUNTAINS

The Emerald Toucanet is a common species in mountainous regions.

The major mountains of Costa Rica lie in a loose chain, which extends in a northwest–southeast direction across the country, with elevations increasing southward. All of the major peaks of Cordillera de Guanacaste, Cordillera de Tilarán and Cordillera Central are dormant or active volcanoes. The major range in the south is upper regions of Cordillera de Talamanca and it is not of recent volcanic origin. Our definition of mountainous regions includes elevations between about 1,000 meters and 1,700 meters (about 3,300 to 5,600 feet). These elevations encompass virtually all of the upper regions of Cordillera de Guanacaste and Cordillera de Tilarán in northern Costa Rica and most of the Cordillera Central, but only mid-slope regions of the Talamancas, where elevations are greatest. Only in the Cordillera de Tilarán and Cordillera Central does the land flatten somewhat to form rolling highland plateaus and low ridges. Other regions, especially in the Talamancas, are very precipitous.

Rainfall in this region is generally high, especially on the east slope, where wet air from the Caribbean cools as it encounters the mountains. It is significantly drier on the Pacific side of the mountains, especially from January to

If you are driving to Monteverde in the early morning, you might just as well stop along the road and do some lowland birding on your way, because you won't arrive until mid-day anyway. A nicely treed trail to stop at is 3.1 kilometers (2 miles) after you have turned off the highway near the Río Lagarto bridge. It's a right turn off the road and it's possible to drive a car down the lane and park out of sight of the main road. (Don't try it if it's wet!) I spent a few hours there one January morning and saw a beautiful **Blue-crowned Motmot** and a pair of **Black-headed Trogons. Rufous-naped Wrens** were singing merrily, seemingly near every fence post, and **Scissor-tailed Flycatchers** were common. My best bird of the morning was a large **Barred Woodcreeper**, which obligingly perched on a tree trunk for several minutes. **Inca Doves, White-tipped Doves, Hoffmann's Woodpeckers, Masked Tityras, Brown Jays** and **Striped-headed Sparrows** were also present.

March or April. The west side of Cordillera de Guanacaste is especially dry. During clear weather, a jacket or sweater for a morning bird walk is normal apparel. Wet cloudy weather, sometimes accompanied by high winds, especially on ridge tops, also makes for cool conditions when extra clothing may be needed.

Although cattle ranches and farms predominate in the area, upper ridges are often treed and the many steeply incised valleys hold beautiful gallery forests. In addition, many protected areas lie within this region. From north to south, the most significant are Guanacaste National Park, 700 square kilometers (280 square miles), and Rincon de la Vieja, 14,084 hectares (26,775 acres), both of which protect high slopes of volcanoes in their northeastern reaches. The private reserves of Monteverde Cloud Forest Preserve, 11,100 hectares (27,417 acres), and the Children's Rainforest Preserve, 7,285 hectares (18,000 acres), Póas National Park, 5,599 hectares (13,829 acres), Braulio Carrillo

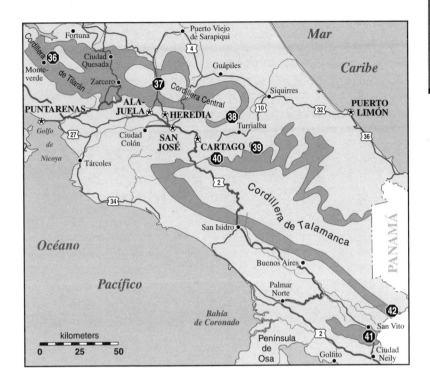

Birding Locations in the Mountainous Regions of Costa Rica

- **36** Monteverde–Santa Elena Region
- **37** Vara Blanca
- **38** Santa Cruz
- **39** Rancha Naturalista
- **40** Orosi and Tapantí Nature Preserve
- **41** San Vito and Wilson Botanical Gardens
- **42** Alturas and Zona Protectora Las Tablas

National Park, 44,099 hectares (108,924 acres), Irazú Volcano National Park, 2,309 hectares (5,703 acres), Tapantí Wildlife refuge, 4,715 hectares (11,647 acres), Chirripó National Park, 50,150 hectares (123,871 acres) and La Amistad National Park, 193,927 hectares (479,000 acres), are also significant. The latter two parks protect much of the higher slopes of the Talamancas and form one of the last great mountain wilderness areas in Central America.

TRAVEL

There are no major centers of population at these altitudes and access is from centers previously described or from small towns in the region. However, a major point of access and travel is the Interamerican Highway as it crosses over the Talamancas between Cartago and San Isidro. The highway between San José and Guápiles also crosses this zone as it goes over a pass in the Cordillera Central. Similarly, the highway that passes through Naranjo and Zacero to Ciudad Quesada attains considerable altitude as it goes over ridges in the western part of Cordillera Central.

TROPICAL BIRD SPECIALTIES OF THE MOUNTAINS

Birding in the mountains of Costa Rica can be as grueling or as relaxed and luxurious as you like. Pick and choose accommodations from camping alongside wet jungle trails to sipping cocktails on a balcony as you watch arrivals at feeders!

Twenty-nine of the 82 species (see Appendix I, Group 15) that are restricted to mountainous regions within Costa Rica are considered common tropical specialties. These range from parrots, hummingbirds, trogons and flycatchers to thrushes and tanagers and include:

Black Guan	Three-wattled Bellbird
Ruddy Pigeon	Yellowish Flycatcher
Sulphur-winged Parakeet	Tufted Flycatcher
Barred Parakeet	White-throated Spadebill
Chestnut-collared Swift	Mountain Elaenia
Green Hermit	Gray-breasted Wood-wren
Violet Sabrewing	White-throated Robin
Green-crowned Brilliant	Pale-vented Robin
Striped-tailed Hummingbird	Mountain Robin
Purple-throated Mountain-gem	Slaty-backed Nightingale-thrush
Resplendent Quetzal	Slate-throated Redstart
Collared Trogon	Golden-browed Chlorophonia
Emerald Toucanet	Spangled-cheeked Tanager
Spotted-crowned Woodcreeper	Yellow-throated Brush-finch
Plain Antvireo	

MONTEVERDE-SANTA ELENA REGION

The Monteverde region is world renowned because of the Monteverde Cloud Forest Biological reserve. It began with a Quaker settlement in the early 1950s, which protected a significant portion of their land from development. Over the years, the core has been added to so the reserve now consists of about

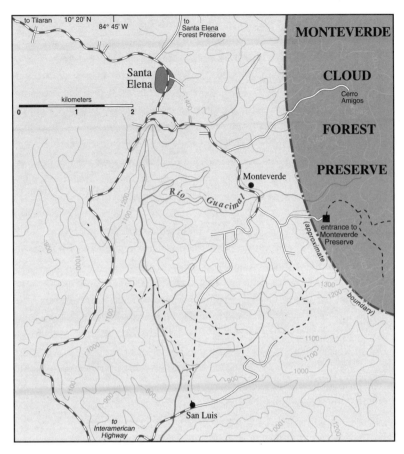

11,000 hectares (27,170 acres) and is administered by the Tropical Science Center of Costa Rica. Using Monteverde as an example, the Children's Rainforest Preserve was created; it abuts Monteverde with another 7,000 hectares (17,290 acres) of protected land on the Caribbean slope. The nearby Santa Elena Reserve (also called Centro Ecologico Bosque Nuboso de Monteverde) protects another 360 hectares (890 acres). Several other private acreages and trail systems are also present in the area, giving many alternatives to the sometimes crowded main Monteverde reserve.

All travel to the region is on roads notorious for their poor condition. Roads are rough, rocky and sometimes steep. If you're driving, take it slow and easy—bird-watch along the way and you'll be all right. After all, several buses make the trip every day. Two roads will get you to the Monteverde region from the Interamerican Highway. The first, as you're traveling north from San José, is at Rancho Grande Bar, just over 16 kilometers (10 miles) from the highway turn-off to Puntarenas. The next road is about 15 kilometers (nine miles) further north just before the Río Lagarto bridge. Both roads are marked with signs, but they are easily missed. Both roads were in equally poor condition when I traveled them, but I have heard rumors of some recent improvements.

Buses from San José to Monteverde are operated by Tilarán (222-3854) and leave from C14, A9 & 11, usually once a day, but possibly more frequently during the busy season. An alternative route is to bus to Puntarenas in the morning (leaves San José from C12, A9) and catch the afternoon Puntarenas bus to Santa Elena from the beach between C2 & 4. If you start early enough you get a few hours in Puntarenas and you can perhaps spot a seabird or two.

The town of Monteverde consists mostly of tourist accommodations, a few cafes and a bakery, strung out along the last 3-4 kilometers (two miles) of the road before the entrance to the Monteverde reserve. A turn to the left before Monteverde will lead you in a few hundred meters to the town of Santa Elena, a more typical Tico community with the normal complement of businesses, plus some lower cost inns and hotels. In Santa Elena, I've stayed at the Pensión Tucán (645-5017) and at Pensión Santa Elena (645-5051). Both are very economical but neither room had a private bathroom. The Tucán was noisy but friendly and clean, with very good food. If you prefer something a little more modern and private, try the moderately priced Cabanas El Bosque (645-5129) in Monteverde at about $30 for a double room with private bath. They also allow camping for $4 a night. Look for **Eastern Meadowlarks** hopping about on the lawn and **Blue-and-white Swallows** nesting in the eaves. Consult your guide book for many more choices.

Tourists abound in this area, but it is still a far cry from the crowded conditions in some popular North American parks and European resorts. December through March is the busiest period and also the driest. When I was there one February, high winds were fairly common, making rather dusty, unpleasant conditions along roads. I prefer other times of the year, when the vegetation is greener and there are fewer people about.

Despite the influx of tourists, people are still friendly in the region, especially in Santa Elena. You will find that some restaurants (*sodas*) are patronized almost exclusively by tourists. Go there if you want to meet tourists, buy what passes for a burger and fries and pay fairly high prices. Across the street or next door may be a small *soda* where the locals go—not a tourist in sight! Food will generally be good to excellent, cheap and served by friendly staff.

Getting around the Monteverde area is by taxi or by foot if you don't have a car. It's fairly easy to hitchhike, but your chances are cut down because it seems that most locals get around on motor bikes. Taxis are not all that expensive, but fares can add up over a stay of several days. Five dollars was the standard charge in 1995 for a ride from Santa Elena to the Monteverde Cloud Forest entrance. Morning birding walks along roads to reserves and hitchhiking back in the afternoon is feasible in many cases. There *is* one bus that takes workers to the Monteverde Cloud Forest early in the morning and returns in mid-afternoon. Ask the locals for details. The bus is supposedly only for workers but it will stop for tourists if space is available.

There are many trails and roads in the area you can walk to see many mountain bird species. A favorite of mine starts on the northern outskirts of Santa Elena. To take this walk, turn left and follow a small road along the near side of the soccer field on the outskirts of town. After a few hundred meters, take another left at a T-junction. Of course, you will see birds all along the route, but an especially active area in June and August was near the small rise just past the T-junction. Here, I spotted **Band-tailed Pigeons, Crimson-fronted Parakeets, Emerald Toucanets**, a beautiful **Blue-crowned Motmot** and a host of flycatchers. The best sightings were **Yellow-bellied Elaenias** and a **Sulphur-bellied Flycatcher**.

Continue down the road to the local cemetery, opposite, which is a well-used path (the gate was open when I was there) that bears local foot traffic. The path branches and fades into open fields in less than a kilometer (.6 miles), but walking and sitting along it proved rewarding for me. I spotted **Hoffmann's Woodpeckers, Emerald Toucanets, Dusky-capped Flycatchers, Rufous-and-white Wrens, Brown Jays** and a **Rufous-capped Warbler**. In addition, I could depend on seeing an **Orange-billed Nightingale-thrush** every morning in the same spot on the path. They are very predictable. If you see one, you can return to the same spot the next day and have a very good chance of getting another look at it.

Morning walks along the road to Monteverde Cloud Forest are also productive. Saltators and seedeaters are common in lower reaches as are **White-eared Ground-sparrows, Red-legged Honeycreepers** and the equally colorful **Golden-browed Chlorophonias, Yellow-crowned Euphonias** and **Yellow-throated Euphonias**. Euphonias and honeycreepers seemed especially abundant near Stella's Bakery. There was also a sloth sleeping in a tree nearby! My best sightings along the road were a **Rufous-browed Peppershrike** and a difficult to identify **Lesser Greenlet**—look for the white eye-ring and gray head.

Monteverde is also great for hummingbirds and there's no better place to go for a bonanza of sightings than the Hummingbird Gallery located near the Monteverde Reserve entrance, where hummingbird feeders are maintained year-round. When I was there in June there were virtually hundreds of hummers feeding or perched patiently on bushes surrounding the feeders. In all, seven species were present!

LIST OF BIRDS SIGHTED IN MONTEVERDE AREA

(a=abundant; c=common; u=uncommon; s=scarce; r=rare)

Species	Jan-Mar	Apr-Jun	Jul-Sep	Species	Jan-Mar	Apr-Jun	Jul-Sep
Cattle Egret		c	c	Blue and white Swallow	a	a	
Turkey Vulture		c	c	Brown Jay	u	u	u
American Swallow -tailed Kite		u	u	Plain Wren		c	c
Band-tailed Pigeon		c	a	Rufous-and- white Wren		c	c
Red-billed Pigeon		c	c	House Wren		u	c
Ruddy Dove		u		Gray-breasted Wood-wren		u	
Crimson-fronted Parakeet		c		Clay-colored Robin		u	
White-fronted Parrot			u	Mountain Robin	c	c	c
Green Hermit		a		Black-faced Solitaire		r	
Violet Sabrewing		c		Slaty-backed Nightingale-thrush		r	
Green Violet-ear		c		Orange-billed Nightingale-thrush		u	u
Steely-vented Hummingbird			u	Rufous-browed Peppershrike		r	
Rufous-tailed Hummingbird			c	Yellow-green Vireo	u	u	
Striped-tailed Hummingbird		u		Lesser Greenlet		r	
Coppery-headed Emerald		c		Bananaquit		u	
Purple-throated Mountain-gem		a		Three-striped Warbler		u	
Green-crowned Brilliant		u		Slate-throated Redstart	u	u	
Resplendent Quetzal		u		Collared Redstart	u		
Orange-bellied Trogon	u	u		Rufous-capped Warbler		r	
Blue-crowned Motmot		u		Eastern Meadowlark		u	
Emerald Toucanet		u	c	Golden-browed Chlorophonia		c	c
Hoffmann's Woodpecker		c	c	Yellow-crowned Euphonia		u	
Golden-olive Woodpecker			r	Yellow-throated Euphonia		c	c
Spotted Barbtail		r		Red-legged Honeycreeper		c	c
Slaty Antwren		r		Blue-gray Tanager		u	a
Masked Tityra		c	c	Common Bush -tanager	u	u	
Three-wattled Bellbird		u		Buff-throated Saltator		u	
Long-tailed Manakin			r	Grayish Saltator		u	
Tropical Kingbird	a	a	a	Yellow-faced Grassquit			a
Boat-billed Flycatcher		u		Variable Seedeater		u	
Sulphur-bellied Flycatcher		u	u	Slaty Flowerpiercer		r	
Social Flycatcher		a	a	White-eared Ground sparrow			u
Great Kiskadee		u	a	Rufous-collared Sparrow	a	a	a
Dusky-capped Flycatcher		c	u				
Tufted Flycatcher		r					
Yellow-bellied Elaenia		c	c				
Mountain Elaenia		c	c				

Striking **Violet Sabrewings** were fairly common, as were **Green Hermits**, with their elongated white-fringed tails. **Green Violet-ears** were slightly more difficult to identify until sunlight revealed their violet ear patch. **Purple-throated Mountain-gems** were also common and easily identified by their purple gorget and white stripe behind the eye. Also look for hummingbirds in flowering bushes anywhere along roadsides and paths. **Steely-vented Hummingbirds** and the ever-present **Rufous-tailed Hummingbirds** are quite common near Santa Elena.

The famous **Resplendent Quetzal** is also quite common in the Monteverde region. I saw an immature male along the road to Monteverde and mature birds near the entrance to the Santa Elena Reserve. The staff of the reserve told me they are frequently found in this location early in the morning. Quetzals move about during the year. Ask local people and guides where they can be sighted when you arrive.

Many trails are on private land near Monteverde. The Baje del Tigre trail is on a 30 hectare (74 acre) preserve administered by the Monteverde Conservation League. Sendero Tranquillo is on a 200 hectare (494 acre) reserve where only 12 people are allowed at one time, and there are trails in the 17 hectare (42 acre) Finca Ecológico. For a free hike walk the road up to the towers on Cerro Amigo. The view from the top is great and you're sure to see some birds. All in all, you could spend several weeks in the Monteverde area and still not exhaust the region. Michael Fogden, owner of the Hummingbird Gallery, has put together a bird list of the region (including lowland areas) which has more than 452 entries. He has been compiling it since 1979.

MONTEVERDE CLOUD FOREST RESERVE

The first time I visited Monteverde Cloud Forest Reserve, I took one of the guided tours and was lucky enough to draw Alexander Villegas (645-5343) as a guide. He is a local Tico with an amazing knowledge of local birds. With his help, I got some great mountain birds in a few hours along the Waterfall Trail. These included a **Gray-breasted Wood-wren**, **Common Bush-tanagers**, a striking **Black-faced Solitaire**, a **Slaty-backed Nightingale-thrush**, **Three-striped Warblers**, a **Spotted Barbtail**, a **Slaty Antwren** and a **Slaty Flowerpiercer**.

I hired Alexander as a guide for an afternoon and he again proved his worth. In a few hours, he managed to put me in view of **Slate-throated Redstarts**, **Tufted Flycatchers**, an **Orange-bellied Trogon**, a **Long-tailed Manakin**, a **Three-wattled Bellbird** and many, many more. The bellbird is famous for the far-reaching cry of the male, audible for .5 kilometers (.3 miles) or more! Alexander also showed me differences between the **Red-billed Pigeon** and the **Ruddy Pigeon**, two species that are extremely difficult to differentiate in the field, although their voices are quite different. (These species are so similar that only the **Red-billed Pigeon** is illustrated in *The Birds of Costa Rica*.)

Other common mountain species and some more difficult to find birds that are relatively easy to find at moderate elevations in the reserve are **Highland Tinamou, Double-toothed Kite, Black-chested Hawk, Barred Forest-falcon, Black Guan, Black-breasted Wood-quail, Brown-headed Parrot, Bare-shanked Screech-owl, Mottled Owl, Magenta-throated Woodstar, Smoky-brown Woodpecker, Spotted Woodcreeper, Red-faced Spinetail, Lineated Foliage-gleaner, Streaked-breasted Treehunter, Plain Antvireo, Silvery-fronted Tapulco** (difficult to sight), **Bright-rumped Attila, Golden-bellied Flycatcher, White-throated Spadebill, Eye-ringed Flatbill, Olive-striped Flycatcher, Azure-hooded Jay, Ochraceous Wren** and **Black-thighed Grosbeak.**

SANTA ELENA RESERVE

The Santa Elena Reserve, 5 kilometers (3 miles) northwest of town, is much less crowded than Monteverde and, according to local guides, is as good as or even better for birding than the Monteverde Reserve. The only time I tried to bird the area, the wind was howling over the crest of the divide, driving heavy fog and light rain with it. I really didn't see much of anything; even nearby trees were difficult to distinguish, let alone birds! I'd like to try the area again when the weather is better. However, a tourist from Germany did see a mountain lion on one of the trails earlier in the day; all the guides were envious. Some had been working in the area for more than 20 years and had never seen one.

VARA BLANCA

Vara Blanca is a small collection of houses and business establishments at an altitude of about 1,700 meters (5,600 feet) located very near the crest of the continental divide in the Cordillera Central. The headwaters of the Río Sarapiquí flow north through spectacularly incised canyons that fall away to the Caribbean lowlands. Nearby, to the west, Póas Volcano looms up another 900 meters (2,950 feet), and to the east is Volcán Barva, nearly as high. To the south, the floor of the central valley lies about 1,000 meters (3,300 feet) below. The scenery in this region is spectacular, and great birding for mountain and highland species is nearby in epiphyte-laden forests, groves of oak trees and mixed farmland. And it's less than an hour's drive from the international airport. So why stay in San José?

The easiest way to get to Vara Blanca is to drive through Alajuela and take Highway 127, which turns into Highway 9 as it winds its way through coffee plantations and then pasture land for the high altitude dairy farms on the slopes of Cordillera Central. Look for **Gray Jays, Acorn Woodpeckers** and

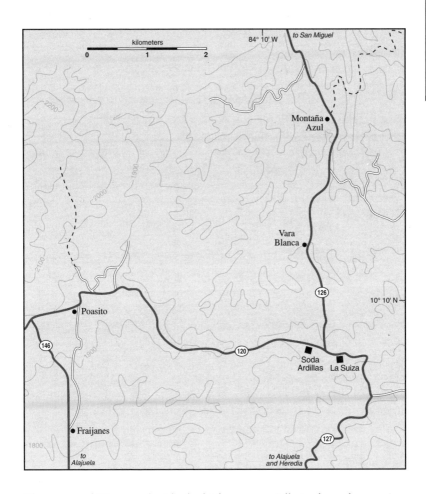

Blue-crowned Motmots beside the highway, especially in the early morning. In 25 short kilometers (15.5 miles) you will gain 1,000 meters (3,300 feet) of elevation and be in a climate where nights are refreshingly cool. Getting to this area by bus is a bit inconvenient, but it can be done. Some of the San José–Puerto Viejo de Sarapiquí buses (A11; C Central & 1) take this route while others go via Braulio Carrillo. Schedules change so you will have to inquire about routings. There are, however, more frequent local buses from Alajuela (C8; A Central & 1) or Heredia (C Central, A1&3), with some buses continuing down the Caribbean side of the mountain to San Miguel.

Although many guide books say accommodation is limited or non-existent in the area, there are a few places to stay near the highway junction at the crest of the ridge. La Suiza advertises *cabinas*, horseback riding and birding. The dirt road turn-off is just before the junction. Restaurante Vara Blanca (at the

A common melastome berry at mid-elevations of Costa Rica.

junction) also advertises *cabinas* as does at least one farm on the right of the highway to Póas. The moderately high priced Póas Volcano Lodge (255-3486, and not really that close to the volcano despite its name) is also a few kilometers from the junction on the highway to Póas. A moderately low priced private chalet-type *cabina* is located on a strawberry farm about 100 meters (328 feet) from the junction towards Póas. It's easily missed but it's right next to the small Soda Ardillas. It is definitely a bargain. The over-priced Juanbo Restaurante and Cabinas is 2.2 kilometers (1.4 miles) down the road towards Puerto Viejo. Since there is no real town in the area, all of the above establishments are in country settings with attached acreages.

The weather in this area can make birding problematic. The most usual pattern is for cloud-laden air to flow over the divide from the Caribbean; fog and clouds dissipate upon mixing with the warm, drier air of the Central Valley. A good strategy is to stay in the Vara Blanca area and keep your options open depending on daily weather conditions. The highland areas of Póas Volcano are nearby but are most often enshrouded in cloud, so bird that area on a priority basis any time it is clear. If it's cloudy and foggy at Vara Blanca, try birding at Virgen del Socorro, which is at a considerably lower elevation and only about 15 kilometers (9 miles) to the north. This area is often relatively clear and dry while higher elevations are foggy or rainy.

Birding around Vara Blanca will yield a mixture of mountain and highland species. **Red-tailed Hawks** reside in these moderate elevations and can occasionally be seen soaring over pasture land and mixed forest. **Band-tailed Pigeons** and **White-crowned Parrots** are also commonly seen. When I was birding behind the chalet on the strawberry farm, warblers—**Yellow Warblers, Wilson's Warblers, Black-throated Green Warblers, Slate-collared Redstarts** and **Black-and-white Warblers**—were quite common in oak stands and thickets, while **Three-striped Warblers, Townsend's Warblers** and **Collared Redstarts** were present but only occasionally seen.

There is great birding along a right-of-way near Montaña Azul, about 2 kilometers (1.2 miles) north of Vara Blanca. It's not passable for vehicles, but it's used by horsemen and hikers for access to more remote farms on the eastern slope of Volcan Barva. Epiphyte-laden trees line the path in some areas, where I saw three different groups of **Resplendent Quetzals**, including beauti-

LIST OF BIRDS SIGHTED IN VARA BLANCA AREA
(a=abundant; c=common; u=uncommon; s=scarce; r=rare)

Species	Jan-Mar Apr-Jun Jul-Sep	Species	Jan-Mar Apr-Jun Jul-Sep
Cattle Egret	c	Yellow Warbler	c
Turkey Vulture	c	Townsend's Warbler	r
Black Vulture	c	Black-throated Green Warbler	a
Red-tailed Hawk	s	Wilson's Warbler	c
Band-tailed Pigeon	a	Slate-throated Redstart	a
Red-billed Pigeon	c	Collared Redstart	s
White-tipped Dove	u	Great-tailed Grackle	c
Chiriquí Quail-dove	r	Eastern Meadowlark	u
White-crowned Parrot	c	Golden-browed Chlorophonia	u
Resplendent Quetzal	c	Silver-throated Tanager	c
Tropical Kingbird	c	Spangled-cheeked Tanager	u
Western Wood-pewee	c	Flame-colored Tanager	u
Blue-and-white Swallow	a	Common Bush-tanager	a
House Wren	c	Yellow-faced Grassquit	u
Mountain Robin	a	Yellow-throated Brush-finch	u
Wood Thrush	u	Rufous-collared Sparrow	a
Black-and-white Warbler	u		
Three-striped Warbler	s		

ful males with fully developed long tail coverts. **Common Bush-tanagers** and **Slate-collared Redstarts** were plentiful in thickets. In March, there were several fruit-laden melastome trees near the path, which attracted a variety of colorful tanagers. I watched one tree for about half an hour and was rewarded by sighting several **Spangled-cheeked Tanagers, Silver-throated Tanagers** and a few **Golden-browed Chlorophonias**. A **Flame-colored Tanager** put in a brief appearance as I was heading back to the highway in late afternoon. My special bird of the day was a **Chiriquí Quail-dove**, which I also spotted as I was back-tracking. It was walking along the trail in front of me for several minutes, so I had ample opportunity to study its bold facial markings. This species is only found in mountainous regions of Costa Rica and western Panama, and is not frequently seen, so it was a very satisfactory way to end an already good day of birding.

SANTA CRUZ

Santa Cruz is a small town about 15 kilometers (9 miles) northwest of Turrialba at an elevation of about 1,500 meters (4,900 feet), about halfway up to the top of the 3,329 meters (9,987 feet) high Volcán Turrialba. There is a road, suitable only for four-wheel drive vehicles or hiking, that winds up the mountain for another few kilometers. It starts near the Santa Cruz sign on the western edge of town. If it's a clear day, it's worth going to Santa Cruz if only for the view of the Reventazón valley which lies at your feet and the distant Caribbean Sea. Buses run infrequently from Turrialba and a taxi costs about

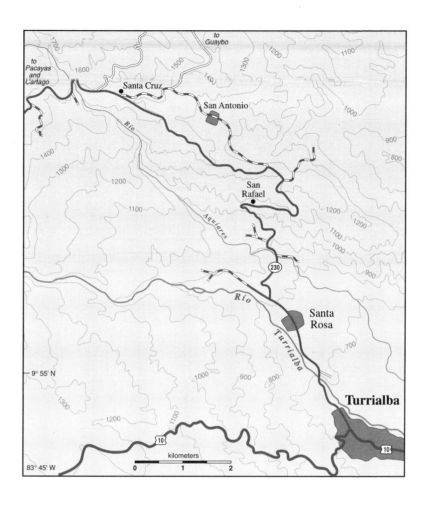

$8. If you have a car, access is easy. The road is paved and is a good alternative way to go to Cartago.

Although it was past the good birding in the morning, I managed to see an **Eastern Wood-pewee**, a **Black-crowned Tityra** and a few other more common species. Friendly farmers invited me in for coffee twice as I was walking up the steep trail. They said that **Resplendent Quetzals** are fairly common in the area, in addition to **Golden-browed Chlorophonias**, **Spangled-cheeked Tanagers**, **Flame-Colored Tanagers** and, at slightly higher elevation, **Yellow-bellied Siskins**.

LIST OF BIRDS SIGHTED IN THE SANTA CRUZ AREA
(a=abundant; c=common; u=uncommon; s=scarce; r=rare)

Species	Jan-Mar	Apr-Jun	Jul-Sep	Species	Jan-Mar	Apr-Jun	Jul-Sep
Cattle Egret	c			Eastern Wood-pewee	s		
Turkey Vulture	c			Blue-and-white Swallow	u		
Black Vulture	c			Brown Jay	a		
Black-crowned Tityra	u			Rufous-collared Sparrow	u		
Social Flycatcher	u						

Although much of the land is in pasture, some patches of second-growth forest are present, which should be good, especially in early morning. The area might contain specialties such as the **Ashy-throated Bush-tanager**, largely restricted to mid-elevations of the east slope of Cordillera Central.

RANCHO NATURALISTA

Rancho Naturalista (San José 267-7138; Lodge 284-5894; U.S. 1-800-597-3305) caters to birders and, together with their operation at Tarcol Lodge, can be considered one of the foremost privately operated destinations for serious birders in Costa Rica. The very capable and expert birder Jay Vandergaast serves as guide. All-inclusive packages (three days minimum) include transport to and from San José, all food and natural juice drinks, American-style accommodation, laundry service and daily intensive birding walks with a resident guide. Although costs are not cheap, around $100 a day for one week or $114 per day (double occupancy), they are comparable to other well-known nature destinations in Costa Rica, such as La Selva. The latter tends to be quite impersonal owing to the large number of people passing through the area. In contrast, Rancho Naturalista has a maximum capacity of 18 people and at least one professional guide at their beck and call more or less constantly. I was told that they like to have one guide for every five people, but groups are likely to be somewhat larger in the busy season (December to April and June–July).

If you drive to Rancho Naturalista, take the main highway east out of Turrialba for about 7 kilometers (4.3 miles) and turn right at the signpost for La Suiza and Tuis. Pavement turns to gravel between the two small towns. Most of Tuis is off the main road. Don't go into town, but continue on and bear right at the first major fork in the road, about 1 kilometer (.6 miles) past Tuis. (The left-hand road goes over the ridge to a small town called Cien Manzanas.) About 1 kilometer (.6 miles) further up the road you will see a small Rancho Naturalista sign on the left. The road to the lodge is steep but in very good condition. If you go by bus, take the one to Tayutic (named Platanillo on most maps), the next town up the road, and ask the driver to let you off at the sign. The bus costs about 40 cents from Turrialba. Taxi is another option.

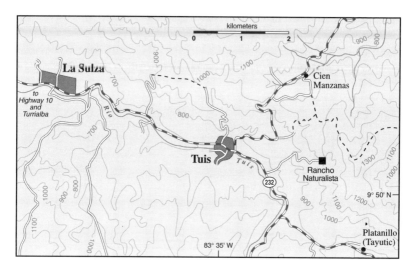

Rancho Naturalista consists of a 50 hectare (124 acre) farm, part of which is still in coffee and other crops. Well-developed second-growth forest covers its upper reaches. Since it is at about 1,000 meters (3,300 feet) in altitude, a mixture of mountain and lowland bird species is found in the area. Their bird list currently has more than 400 species, although this includes sightings in surrounding valleys and river bottoms as well.

Everything considered, if you're really serious about seeing numerous species of birds, including some that are difficult to find, you should give Rancho Naturalista a try. Among the difficult species they *regularly* see are **Purplish-backed Quail-dove, Black-crested Coquette, Green Thorntail, Snowcap, Tawny-throated Leaftosser, Dull-mantled Antbird, Black-headed Antthrush, White-crowned Manakin, Gray-headed Manakin, Tawny-chested Flycatcher, Rufous-browed Tyrannulet, Black-headed Nightingale-thrush, Chestnut-headed Oropendola, Speckled Tanager** and **Ashy-throated Bush-tanager**.

One February day I walked up the road to Rancho Naturalista and saw 34 species in a very short time. Most were common birds, but I was pleased with **Green Thorntails, Slaty Spinetails** and **White-lined Tanagers**. If you stay for a few days and bird with their resident guide, your list will certainly be in the hundreds, if not more!

LIST OF BIRDS SIGHTED IN RANCHO NATURALISTA AREA
(a=abundant; c=common; u=uncommon; s=scarce; r=rare)

Species	Jan-Mar	Apr-Jun	Jul-Sep
Cattle Egret	u		
Turkey Vulture	c		
Black Vulture	c		
Gray-headed Chachalaca	u		
Ruddy Ground-dove	c		
White-tipped Dove	c		
Crimson-fronted Parakeet	c		
White-fronted Parrot	c		
Green Thorntail	c		
Rufous-tailed Hummingbird	c		
Hoffmann's Woodpecker	c		
Slaty Spinetail	u		
Tropical Kingbird	c		
Social Flycatcher	c		
Great Kiskadee	c		
Yellow-bellied Elaenia	u		
Southern Rough-winged Swallow	c		

Species	Jan-Mar	Apr-Jun	Jul-Sep
Northern Rough-winged Swallow	c		
Brown Jay	c		
Clay-colored Robin	c		
Bananaquit	u		
Montezuma Oropendola	a		
Great-tailed Grackle	a		
Golden-hooded Tanager	u		
Blue-gray Tanager	c		
Palm Tanager	c		
Scarlet-rumped Tanager	u		
Hepatic Tanager	u		
White-lined Tanager	u		
Black-headed Saltator	u		
Yellow-faced Grassquit	c		
Variable Seedeater	c		
Black-striped Sparrow	u		
Rufous-collared Sparrow	c		

OROSI AND TAPANTÍ NATIONAL PARK

Orosi is a small town nestled in a deep river valley in the upper part of the Río Reventazón drainage, just above a small lake formed by the Cachi hydro-electric dam. Because the valley is quite scenic, it gets a moderate number of tourists and tour buses. If this is one of the areas you visit first in Costa Rica, you will be impressed. If you have been to Póas Volcano, Cerro de La Muerte, have taken the highway from San Vito to Cuidad Neily, or to other areas in Costa Rica, you probably won't be overly enthusiastic, especially when you see some of the highly eroded hillsides where attempts are made to grow coffee on 45° slants!

But when you leave the coffee farms behind and step into Tapantí National Park 12 kilometers (7.4 miles) away from Orosi, it's like stepping into another world. The park contains excellent birding in low mountain rainforest at elevations beginning at about 1,300 meters (4,300 feet). The park also contains lots of higher elevation forest, which is quite inaccessible because all the maintained trails and roads that are open to the public are at fairly moderate elevations.

A bus to Orosi leaves from Cartago every 1.5 hours from a stop just southeast of the ruined church. (This church is a landmark in Cartago—you can't miss it.) The trip takes about an hour and costs less than $1. I stayed at Montaña Linda (533-3345), one of the few hotels in the town proper, where $5 will get you a bed and kitchen privileges. Don't expect anything fancy, but it's a very

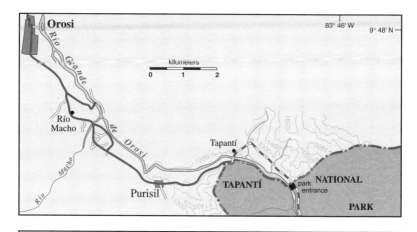

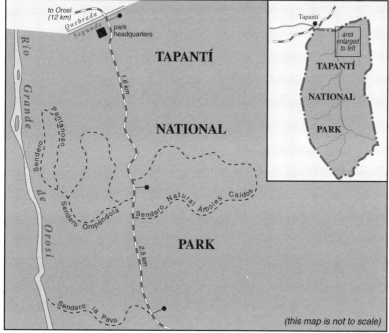

(this map is not to scale)

friendly atmosphere. Birding near Orosi isn't too exciting, but staying in town will give you access to taxis and buses if you don't have a car.

If you want to bird Tapantí for a few days, you might want to try Kiri Lodge (533-3040). I was told its prices are moderate. It's off the main road about 1 kilometer (.6 miles) before the park entrance. A Tico family also has an economical *cabina* for rent even closer to the park (up the hill from a colorful rain shelter on the left). There was no sign when I was there. If you are interested and can't find it, ask a taxi driver or, better yet, talk to the Director of Tapantí, Sergio Leon. He is very interested in seeing local people benefit from the park. Another alternative is to stay with park personnel if they have room.

Unlike many other Costa Rican parks and reserves, Tapantí has a fairly well-developed system of trails and a road extends for about 13 kilometers (8 miles) through the park up the Río Grande de Orosi valley. Birding was fairly steady in Tapantí when I was there, although showers and mist persisted. However, I birded Sendero Pavo, an area of primary forest, in midday and saw zilch. Senderos Oropéndola and Pantaroso, on the other hand, were very productive. Along the latter trail were **Yellow-throated Brush-finches** and the difficult-to-find **Chestnut-capped Brush-finch** and **Black-headed Nightingale-thrush**. Look for all these birds along trails or in thickets close to the ground. **Slate-throated Redstarts** and **Red-eyed Vireos** were also common in overhead trees along with many species of tanagers. An especially good sighting of the day was a **Black-faced Solitaire**, which perched briefly in a tree across the river.

Birding along the main road is great for a large assortment of colorful tanagers. Specialties of the Tapantí area are **Blue-and-gold Tanagers, Spangled-cheeked Tanagers, White-winged Tanagers** and **Blue-hooded Euphonias**, all of which are more easily found here than in many other areas of Costa Rica. According to Stiles and Skutch (1989), **Blue-and-gold Tanagers** were not recorded in the foothills of the Talamancas, but they do occur in the Tapantí region in considerable numbers. Numerous **Silver-throated Tanagers, Bay-headed Tanagers** and **Crimson-collared Tanagers** are also present. Walk slowly along the road from the park entrance early in the morning and you will be busy keeping track of all these colorful birds, as well as an assortment of others.

Flycatchers are abundant, although you will probably see only one or two individuals of a certain species in a few days of birding. When I was there in early May, a **Yellowish Flycatcher** had a nest beside the road about 300 meters (1,000 feet) from the park office. It was in a curtain of moss and slender vines, which draped the road embankment, but it was so well camouflaged that it would have been impossible to see if I hadn't seen the bird flutter and settle into it, with only a tiny white spot, her eye-ring, visible to the naked eye. Another fairly difficult species to observe in Costa Rica, the **Olive-sided Flycatcher**, was gleaning insects from small bushes along a steep road embankment that was cleared of large vegetation. Other interesting species in Tapantí include **Bright-rumped Attilas, Mistletoe Tyrannulets, Tufted Flycatchers** and **Black Phoebes**. Look for the latter species along the river.

Hummingbirds are common in Tapantí, although somewhat difficult to observe. I was glad to see a **White-tailed Mountain-gem** along with the more common **Purple-crowned Fairies** and **Green Hermits**.

LIST OF BIRDS SIGHTED IN OROSI AND TAPANTÍ NATIONAL PARK AREA

(a=abundant; c=common; u=uncommon; s=scarce; r=rare)

Species	Jan-Mar	Apr-Jun	Jul-Sep	Species	Jan-Mar	Apr-Jun	Jul-Sep
Green-backed Heron		u		Blue-and-white Swallow		c	
Turkey Vulture		u		House Wren		c	
Black Vulture		u		Clay-colored Robin		c	
Spotted Sandpiper		u		Mountain Robin		u	
Rock Dove		u		Black-faced Solitaire		r	
Band-tailed Pigeon		u		Swainson's Thrush		u	
Red-billed Pigeon		u		Black-headed			
White-tipped Dove		u		Nightingale-thrush		s	
Common Pauraque		c		Yellow-throated Vireo		u	
Green Hermit		c		Red-eyed Vireo		c	
Rufous-tailed				Bananaquit		a	
Hummingbird		u		Slate-throated Redstart		c	
White-bellied				Chestnut			
Mountain-gem		s		-headed Oropendola		c	
Purple-crowned Fairy		u		Montezuma Oropendola		c	
Collared Trogon		u		Great-tailed Grackle		c	
Blue-crowned Motmot		u		Blue-hooded Euphonia		r	
Russet Antshrike		s		Silver-throated Tanager		a	
Black Phoebe		s		Bay-headed Tanager		u	
Tropical Kingbird		c		Spangled-cheeked			
Bright-rumped Attila		u		Tanager		c	
Sulphur-bellied Flycatcher		u		Blue-and-gold Tanager		c	
Social Flycatcher		c		Blue-gray Tanager		u	
Rufous Mourner		s		Scarlet-rumped Tanager		u	
Dusky-capped Flycatcher		u		Crimson-collared Tanager		u	
Olive-sided Flycatcher		u		White-winged Tanager		u	
Western Wood-pewee		u		Common Bush-tanager		a	
Eastern Wood-pewee		u		Buff-throated Saltator		u	
Yellowish Flycatcher		s		Black-faced Grosbeak		u	
Tufted Flycatcher		s		Yellow-faced Grassquit		u	
Yellow-bellied Elaenia		u		Yellow-throated			
Mistletoe Tyrannulet		u		Brush-finch		u	
Olive-striped Flycatcher		s		Chestnut-capped			
Northern				Brush-finch		s	
Rough-winged Swallow		c		Rufous-collared			
				Sparrow		u	

Chestnut-headed Oropendolas are also common along roads and forest edges in Tapantí. This species is considerably less abundant and more difficult to find in Costa Rica than the larger **Montezuma Oropendola**. It was a treat to see large flocks of them in trees along the roadway.

Hand-out literature on Tapantí states that about 260 types of birds are found in the area. This total includes high-altitude species but, even so, birding in lower altitudes of Tapantí for several days will yield continued surprises even if you go to the area near the end of your stay in Costa Rica.

SAN VITO AND THE WILSON BOTANICAL GARDENS

San Vito is a moderate-sized town in southwestern Costa Rica, close to the Panama border. Unlike most other Tico towns, it's situated near a crest of the ridge in hilly terrain, where it's impossible to have a neat grid system of streets with a nice flat central plaza. Consequently, streets go off in all directions, and there are some wild intersections, where six or seven streets all seem to come together. Some are one-way, others are not. Fortunately for the tourists even taxis seem to go more slowly in San Vito than in other Costa Rican towns.

This area is at an altitude of about 1,000 meters (3,300 feet) at the head of the Valle de Coto Brus, which lies between the Talamanca Range and the lower, but still imposing, Fila Costeña to the southwest. The latter range of mountains isolates this perched valley from the Pacific lowlands. Because of its isolation and unusually dry climate (compared with the surrounding region), Valle de Coto Brus harbors a number of bird specialties. **Ruddy Foliage-gleaners, Lance-tailed Manakins, Thick-billed Euphonias** and **Black-headed Brush-finches** are more easily found in this area than in other portions of southwestern Costa Rica. One, the **Masked Yellowthroat**, is sometimes considered a separate species called the **Chiriquí Yellowthroat**, since the population that occurs in this region is separated by the length of Panama from other populations.

The San Vito area can easily be accessed from San José by Tracopa bus lines (221-4214). There is one direct bus daily but at least four others that make more stops along the way. If you are driving, take the Interamerican Highway south, through San Isidro de General, and turn left about 85 kilometers (53 miles) down the road. There is a sign for La Amistad Park at the junction. A fairly recent bridge over the Térraba River at this point replaces an old ferry.

There is a variety of places to stay in San Vito. Cabinas Las Mirlas (773-3054) is inexpensive and only about 50 meters (165 feet) from the Tracopa bus terminal. Separate *cabinas* look onto a small park–ravine that is near the center of the town but seems isolated. (If you stay there, check beneath the mattresses for nest of ants.) Slightly more expensive is Hotel el Ceibo (773-3025) with hot water for showers. This hotel also backs onto the park.

A relatively expensive alternative is to stay at the OTS station (773-3278) at the Wilson Botanical Gardens, 6 kilometers (3.7 miles) south of San Vito. One advantage of this is you can bird the gardens early and late, rather than only between 8 a.m. and 4 p.m., when the gates officially open. Your $8 daily entrance fee to the gardens is also included in the cost of accommodations and meals. There is also one place called Las Cascadas Cabinas just .5 kilometers (.3 miles) north of the gardens.

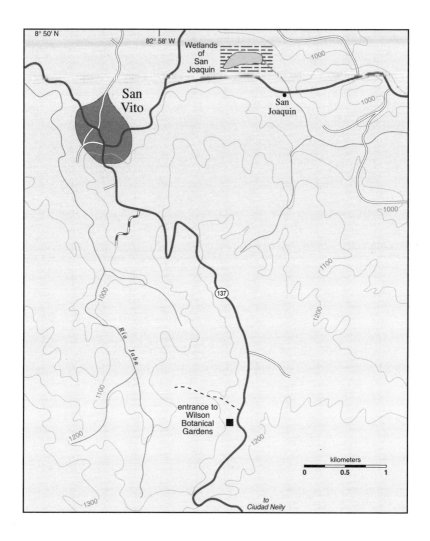

The San Vito countryside is largely devoted to coffee production, and the more common tanagers, pigeons, hummingbirds, thrushes and warblers abound. In the small park in San Vito, I saw **Bay-headed Tanagers**, **Eastern Wood-pewees**, **Buff-throated Saltators** and other more common species. One big surprise was a **Gray-necked Woodrail** bathing in the stream in the bottom of the ravine. Another special treat was seeing two newly hatched **Clay-colored Robins** in a nest in a steep grassy road embankment.

There is a marshy area called the Wetlands of San Joaquín about 2 kilometers (1.2 miles) northeast of San Vito where interesting species can be seen. To get there, take the road towards Lourdes. Go past a landing strip on the left side of the road (check the small pond on the right for water birds) and continue on for a few hundred meters. Watch for a small pond on the left that is visible from the road and a dirt road just past the pond. If you're driving, park here. The marsh is a conservation area paid for with donations from Canadians, I believe, and is administered by the Association for the Protection of Natural Resources of Coto Brus. When I was there, a wooden explanatory sign split in several sections was lying in the grass. The sign may or may not be replaced.

A very nice roofed observation tower is located on the northeast edge of the marsh. The marsh is a great place to see both **Common Gallinules** and **Purple Gallinules, Least Grebes, Bran-colored Flycatchers, Ruddy-breasted Seedeaters, Common Yellowthroats** and that specialty of the San Vito area, the **Masked Yellowthroat**. Look for it in marshy vegetation and adjacent areas. This marsh is also a very good place to see **White-throated Crakes**, abundant but difficult to spot. From the observation tower, watch for them in the marsh and along its edges at dawn or dusk when they are inclined to come out of the dense marsh vegetation to feed.

Little undisturbed forest remains in the area, so the small bit protected by the Wilson Botanical Gardens and Las Cruces Biological Station 6 kilometers (3.7 miles) south of San Vito serves as a sanctuary for a myriad of mid-elevation tropical animals, including many birds. This land, administered by OTS, consists of 10 hectares (25 acres) of world-famous botanical gardens and a further 145 hectares (358 acres) of forest, mostly secondary growth in fairly advanced stages of development. It's a great place to bird, but most of the trail system within the forested portion of the reserve is off limits unless visitors are accompanied by a guide. A further 6 kilometers (3.7 miles) or so of very rough trail is off limits to everyone except researchers. Despite a sign saying otherwise, anyone can walk the River Trail unaccompanied to the Río Jaba if you ask at the administration building or, better yet, talk to the station director, Luis Diego Gómez. He is very cordial and is accustomed to special requests from birders.

Even if access to the forest were completely prohibited, birding within the 10 hectare (25 acre) gardens is still a great experience and you are likely to see new species. **Tawny-winged Woodcreepers, Streaked Saltators** and **White-throated Robins** were nice to see in early April one year. Waves of **Swainson's Thrushes** and **Eastern Wood-pewees** seemed to be passing through, since they appeared to be everywhere I looked. The gardens are also a very good place to see tanagers and related species. **Scarlet-thighed Dacnis** are especially common in the gardens and in the San Vito area in general. I saw several **Bay-headed Tanagers, Golden-hooded Tanagers, Yellow-crowned Euphonias** and a few **Silver-throated Tanagers**. Coloration of the latter species was a little dingier than the individuals I've seen on the Caribbean slope. A few **Speckled Tanagers** were also present, a species most easily seen at mid-elevations in southwestern Costa Rica

There are fewer birds in the forest than in the gardens and species composition is quite different. On the trail down to the river, I saw **Riverside Wrens, Orange-billed Nightingale-thrushes, Rufous-capped Warblers, Ruddy Quail-doves, White-ruffed Manakins, Blue-crowned Motmots, Baird's Trogons** and several other more common species.

There is a bird list, compiled over the last 20 or so years, of more than 350 species for the Las Cruces Biological Station. You don't have much of a chance to see rare or uncommon species listed in a few days birding, but some of the more common specialties to look for include **Barred Forest-falcon, Marbled Wood-quail, Spotted Wood-quail, Barred Parakeet, White-winged Sicklebill, Violet Sabrewing, Barred Woodcreeper, Spotted Barbtail, Black-faced Antthrush, Great Antshrike, Bicolored Antbird, Yellow-bellied Flycatcher, Ruddy-tailed Flycatcher, White-throated Spadebill, Ochre-bellied Flycatchers, Blue-hooded Euphonia, Red-crowned Ant-tanager** and a host of warblers and vireos. Some common good ones to look for are **Rufous-browed Peppershrike, Green Shrike-vireo, Tawny-crowned Greenlet, Lesser Greenlet, Golden-winged Warbler, Blackburnian Warbler, Ovenbird, Kentucky Warbler, Canada Warbler, Golden-crowned Warbler** and **Buff-rumped Warbler.**

LIST OF BIRDS SIGHTED IN SAN VITO AREA

(a=abundant; c=common; c=uncommon; s=scarce; r=rare)

Species	Jan-Mar	Apr-Jun	Jul-Sep
Cattle Egret		a	
Green-backed Heron		c	
Turkey Vulture		c	
Black Vulture		c	
American Swallow -tailed Kite		c	
Yellow-headed Caracara		c	
Gray-necked Wood-rail		u	
Common Gallinule		c	
Northern Jacana		c	
Short-billed Pigeon		c	
Ruddy Ground-dove		c	
Gray-chested Dove		u	
Ruddy Quail-dove		c	
Crimson-fronted Parakeet		c	
White-crowned Parrot		u	
Red-lored Parrot		u	
Squirrel Cuckoo		u	
Smooth-billed Ani		c	
White-collared Swift		c	
Long-tailed Hermit		u	
Green Hermit		c	
Scaly-breasted Hummingbird		c	
Rufous-tailed Hummingbird		u	
Green-crowned Brilliant		u	
Purple-crowned Fairy		c	
Baird's Trogon		u	
Blue-crowned Motmot		u	
Emerald Toucanet		u	
Fiery-billed Aracari		u	
Tawny-winged Woodcreeper		u	
Streaked-headed Woodcreeper		c	
Masked Tityra		c	
White-ruffed Manakin		c	

Species	Jan-Mar	Apr-Jun	Jul-Sep
Tropical Kingbird		c	
Boat-billed Flycatcher		u	
Sulphur-bellied Flycatcher		u	
Streaked Flycatcher		u	
Social Flycatcher		c	
Great Kiskadee		c	
Eastern Wood-pewee		a	
Yellow-bellied Elaenia		c	
Riverside Wren		u	
House Wren		c	
White-throated Robin		c	
Clay-colored Robin		c	
Swainson's Thrush		a	
Orange-billed Nightingale-thrush		u	
Yellow Warbler		u	
Chestnut-sided Warbler		u	
Rufous-capped Warbler		s	
Bronzed Cowbird		u	
Great-tailed Grackle		c	
Northern (Baltimore) Oriole		u	
Yellow-crowned Euphonia		u	
Speckled Tanager		u	
Silver-throated Tanager		u	
Golden-hooded Tanager		c	
Bay-headed Tanager		u	
Scarlet-thighed Dacnis		a	
Blue-gray Tanager		a	
Palm Tanager		c	
Buff-throated Saltator		u	
Streaked Saltator		u	
Yellow-faced Grassquit		c	
Variable Seedeater		c	
Blue-black Grassquit		c	
Black-striped Sparrow		u	
Rufous-collared Sparrow		c	

ALTURAS AND ZONA
PROTECTORA LAS TABLAS

The greatest mountain wilderness area remaining in Central America is Parque International de Amistad, which protects about 200,000 hectares (494,000 acres) of mostly mountainous jungle in Costa Rica, and a further 200,000 adjoining hectares in Panama. Various other reserves and protected areas surround most of the park and nearly double the amount of land set aside for special treatment. Access to this region is notoriously difficult, typically consisting of tracks suitable for four-wheel drive vehicles and then an uphill hike of several kilometers to, perhaps, a park headquarters where you can pitch a tent. If you have energy or time left after that, you can begin to explore the park.

There is one little known and fascinating area accessible with any car and a modicum of driving skill in a little over an hour's drive from San Vito. There is also a once-a-day bus that goes to a small mountain village called Alturas (on maps) or Coton (by locals) that also puts you on the edge of this wilderness area. The protected region is called Zona Protectora Las Tablas. The southern boundary lies in the mid-level foothills of the Talamancas, while most of its northeastern boundary forms the border with Panama and its northwestern edge abuts La Amistad.

Alturas, or Coton, is actually a company town wholly contained on a huge 10,000 hectare (24,700 acre) combination ranch, farm and logging operation owned by a single Costa Rican family. The northern boundary of this holding in turn abuts the southern edge of Las Tablas. To make dreams come true, there is a small research station at an altitude of about 1,800 meters (5,900 feet) a few kilometers north of Coton, within a few meters of the boundary of Las Tablas. Birders are welcome to stay at the station if there is room and if advance notice is given. This gives birders all of the 10,000 hectares of mixed farmlands, pastures, coffee fields and primary and secondary forest of the farm empire to bird, in addition to the vast tracts of primary forest contained in Zona Protectora Las Tablas.

If you want to stay at the research station, contact Luis Gomez (773-3278). The station was a joint effort between Stanford University and OTS, but Stanford recently discontinued its support. Señor Gomez is in charge of Las Tablas Research Station as well as Las Cruces Biological Station at the Wilson Botanical Gardens near San Vito. Current rates are $30/day/person including meals, or $20 without meals. Accommodation is in dormitory-style bunk beds and electricity is provided for a few hours every evening. According to Edgar Quiros, the on-site manager who is also engaged in botanical research, the

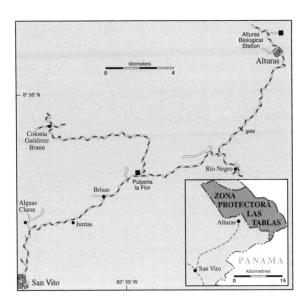

busiest research months are January and February. Otherwise you are likely to have the place to yourself.

We are so inured to the stress of noise pollution in everyday life that it is a surprising relief to go to an area where silence reigns. It's also surprisingly difficult to find such an area. The peace and quiet at Alturas make it a favorite place of mine. The jaguar padding by in the adjacent forest is soundless, as is the raptor swooping down on its prey. You probably won't see them but you know they are there.

Access to this areas is relatively easy by car. There is a gate at the southern boundary of the farm that is manned constantly. Tell the person you are going to the research station to look at birds and you shouldn't have any problem getting in. Alternatively, take the bus from San Vito and walk the last few kilometers, or you can probably arrange to meet Edgar in San Vito when he comes in for supplies (at least once a week) and ride back with him.

If you have little time or are in a hurry to get lots of birds on your list, you probably shouldn't go to Las Tablas. Bird densities are relatively low, especially in the forest, and the lower elevations of the area share many birds with the San Vito area. Go to the area because of its quiet remoteness. There are, however, a number of uncommon raptors in this region. **Black-chested Hawks, Solitary Eagles** and **Black Hawk-eagles** are considered common in this area, while **Bicolored Hawks, Black-and-white Hawk-eagles** and **Ornate Hawk-eagles** have also been sighted in the vicinity.

Alturas Research Station on the edge of Zona Protectora Las Tablas.

In early April, there was no one else at the station except Edgar. Mornings were typically clear, but clouds built over the Talamancas in the early afternoons and brief showers were common. A nice series of trails in the nearby forest has been laid out by researchers and you will be given a map when you arrive. Walks in the forest yielded a number of good species, but birds were never abundant. I did see **Ruddy Quail-doves** along the trails, and **Collared Trogons** and **Baird's Trogons**. **Chestnut-mandibled Toucans** were difficult to sight but could be heard calling from high in the canopy. **Tawny-winged Woodcreepers** and **Wedge-billed Woodcreepers** were common, and I did see one **Ruddy Treerunner**, a more uncommon species in the area, as it searched for food, often upside-down, on the underside of small branches.

Plain **Antvireos**, **Black-hooded Antshrikes** and **Dusky Antbirds** were fairly common. Flycatchers were also in the forest and this is a good area to look for some of the more uncommon species. **Bright-rumped Attilas, Yellowish Flycatchers, Tufted Flycatchers, Sulphur-rumped Flycatchers, Bran-colored Flycatchers, White-throated Spadebills, Eye-ringed Flatbills, Scale-crested Pygmy-tyrants, Lesser Elaenias** and migrant **Eastern Kingbirds** and **Least Flycatchers** are all considered common here, while many other species are sighted more infrequently. I also saw **White-ruffed Manakins** but didn't manage to see any **Blue-crowned Manakins** or **Thrush-like Manakins**, reported to be common in the area.

There were not many hummingbirds in the forest or in the more open pasture land, but heliconias grow profusely all along the forest/pasture boundary and their flowers attracted a number of species. **Green Hermits** and **Green-crowned Brilliants** were common, but fewer numbers of **Purple-crowned**

Fairies, Violet Sabrewings and Striped-tailed Hummingbirds also occurred. The best way to see them is to sit down in an area where they are active and then, hopefully, you will be near some of their favorite perching twigs, where you will get a chance to really see their colors. Remember to put yourself in the best viewing light possible.

Birds were constantly on the move in the open areas near the research station, where a nearby cecropia tree with numerous mature fruit spikes attracted them. **Scarlet-thighed Dacnis, Palm Tanagers, Scarlet-rumped Tanagers, Scarlet Tanagers, Golden-hooded Tanagers** and **Bay-headed Tanagers** made visits to the tree to eat the fruit along with numerous **Swainson's Thrushes** and a few **Clay-colored Robins**. Even **Lineated Woodpeckers, Acorn Woodpeckers, Fiery-billed Aracaris, Eastern Wood-pewees** and **Social Flycatchers** occasionally partook of the fruit. Flocks of **Sulphur-winged Parakeets** flew by the station daily and a **Broad-winged Hawk** commonly perched in a dead tree near the station. In the same tree one morning, I had a chance to admire for several minutes a beautiful **Cedar Waxwing**, a species that seems to only sporadically winter in fairly small numbers as far south as Costa Rica and Panama.

Cecropia trees provide food and shelter for many species of birds throughout Costa Rica.

LIST OF BIRDS IN ALTURAS/LAS TABLAS AREA

(a=abundant; c=common; u=uncommon; s=scarce; r=rare)

Species	Jan-Mar	Apr-Jun	Jul-Sep
Cattle Egret		u	
Turkey Vulture		u	
Black Vulture		u	
Broad-winged Hawk		u	
Band-tailed Pigeon		c	
Ruddy Pigeon		c	
Ruddy Ground-dove		a	
White-tipped Dove		c	
Ruddy Quail-dove		u	
Sulfur-winged Parakeet		a	
White-crowned Parrot		c	
Smooth-billed Ani		c	
Chestnut-collared Swift		u	
Vaux's Swift		u	
Green Hermit		c	
Violet Sabrewing		u	
Striped-tailed Hummingbird		u	
Green-crowned Brilliant		c	
Purple-crowned Fairy		u	
Baird's Trogon		u	
Collared Trogon		u	
Turquoise-browed Motmot		u	
Emerald Toucanet		u	
Fiery-billed Aracari		c	
Chestnut-mandibled Toucan		a	
Acorn Woodpecker		c	
Red-crowned Woodpecker		c	
Lineated Woodpecker		u	
Tawny-winged Woodcreeper		c	
Wedge-billed Woodcreeper		c	
Ruddy Treerunner		s	
Black-hooded Antshrike		c	
Plain Antvireo		u	
Dusky Antbird		u	
Masked Tityra		u	
White-ruffed Manakin		u	
Boat-billed Flycatcher		u	
Sulphur-bellied Flycatcher		u	

Species	Jan-Mar	Apr-Jun	Jul-Sep
Gray-capped Flycatcher		c	
Social Flycatcher		s	
Dusky-capped Flycatcher		u	
Eastern Wood-pewee		a	
Tropical Pewee		u	
Tufted Flycatcher		c	
White-throated Spadebill		c	
Scale-crested Pygmy-tyrant		u	
Yellow-bellied Elaenia		u	
Southern Rough-winged Swallow		c	
Northern Rough-winged Swallow		c	
House Wren		c	
White-throated Robin		u	
Clay-colored Robin		u	
Mountain Robin		u	
Swainson's Thrush		a	
Cedar Waxwing		r	
Black-and-white Warbler		u	
Golden-winged Warbler		u	
Tennessee Warbler		u	
Yellow Warbler		c	
Black-throated Green Warbler		u	
Great-tailed Grackle		u	
Northern (Baltimore) Oriole		u	
Speckled Tanager		u	
Golden-hooded Tanager		c	
Bay-headed Tanager		u	
Scarlet-thighed Dacnis		a	
Palm Tanager		c	
Scarlet-rumped Tanager		c	
Scarlet Tanager		c	
Buff-throated Saltator		u	
Streaked Saltator		u	
Rose-breasted Grosbeak		s	
Yellow-faced Grassquit		c	
White-collared Seedeater		c	
Rufous-collared Sparrow		c	

HIGHLANDS

The crater of Póas Volcano, one of the primary tourist attractions in Costa Rica.

The highlands of Costa Rica include land above 1,600–2,000 meters (5,200–6,600 feet). They are largely restricted to the tops of volcanoes (Volcans Póas, Barva, Irazú and Turrialba) of Cordillera Central and the highest reaches of the Cordillera de Talamanca. A small amount of land in Monteverde Cloud Forest Preserve and a few of the peaks of Cordillera de Guanacaste are above 1,700 meters (5,600 feet). However, these areas are of secondary importance and are largely inaccessible compared with the more mountainous regions to the south.

Cool or even cold weather combined with steep, rocky terrain means that few crops can be grown in these regions. Still, many slopes have been logged and turned into cattle pasture, and small-scale farming persists. Fortunately large regions in the highlands are protected in the previously mentioned parks and refuges, most notably Chirripó National Park and La Amistad National Park. Forests of oak are common from about the 1,500 meters (4,900 feet) level up to about 2,500 meters (8,200 feet). Timberline is usually at 3,000 meters (9,800 feet). *Páramo* is found above 3,000 meters (9,800 feet) or lower

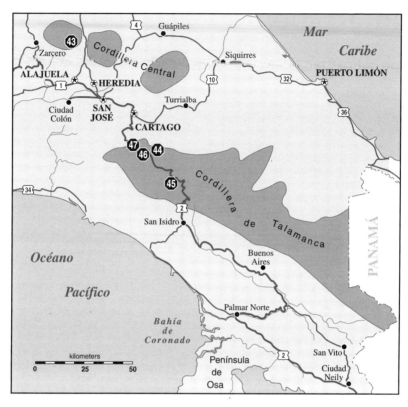

Birding Locations in the
Highland Regions of Costa Rica

43 Volcán Poás   **46** Albergue de Montaña Tapantí
44 Monte Sky   and Finca el Jaular
45 Cerro de la Muerte   **47** El Empalme

in previously burned areas, such as the summit of Cerro de la Muerte. *Páramo* consists of stunted, windblown shrubs, bamboo and tree ferns, similar to vegetation found at high altitudes in the South American Andes.

Clouds and fog are relatively common year-round at these high altitudes. However, rainfall at the summits of mountains is often substantially less than on the lower slopes, especially those facing the Caribbean. Relatively dry weather prevails from November to May, with February being the sunniest month. Mornings tend to be clear, whereas fog and rain often develop in the afternoons. Mornings can be downright cold; underwear, sweaters, jackets and even gloves are welcome, especially when clutching the cold legs of a tripod.

COMMON TROPICAL BIRD
SPECIALTIES OF THE HIGHLANDS

Highland birding in Costa Rica is especially rewarding because of the large number of specialties that can be easily seen, owing to the more open nature of some of the terrain. Of the 40 species (See Appendix I, Group 16) that are restricted to highland regions, 20 are common tropical specialties which you have a very good chance of seeing with a few days birding in the highlands. These include:

Green Violet-ear	Black-billed Nightingale-thrush
Fiery-throated Hummingbird	Long-tailed Silky-flycatcher
Gray-tailed Mountain-gem	Black-and-yellow Silky-flycatcher
Magnificent Hummingbird	Flame-throated Warbler
Volcano Hummingbird	Collared Redstart
Buffy Tuftedcheek	Sooty-capped Brush-tanager
Black-capped Flycatcher	Slaty Flowerpiercer
Timberline Wren	Large-footed Finch
Sooty Robin	Yellow-thighed Finch
Ruddy-capped Nightingale-thrush	Volcano Junco

TOP OF THE WORLD

My fingers ached with cold as I slowly trudged up the bare hillside, changing hands often to keep the tripod and spotting scope on one shoulder or the other. The early dawn light was just beginning to illuminate the Caribbean lowlands more than 3,350 meters (11,000 feet) below me. Looking down on banks of clouds from an airplane is sometimes nice, but it's really something else to have your feet planted on firm ground near the summit of a mountain and to see clouds rising, forming and moving far below. Closer, the crystal clear air gave

sharp outlines to nearby peaks and clear sky above, promised warmth from the sun just beginning to overcome a low cloud bank to the east.

I stood in shadows watching the birth of the new day, tripod leaning somewhat precariously on my chest, both hands in my jacket pockets, feeling awed, insignificant, but thankful to be there, waiting for the warmth of a patch of sunlight that was creeping down the hillside towards me. Mornings are the best times in the highlands and some mornings are simply grand.

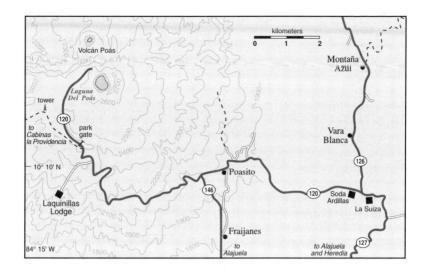

PÓAS VOLCANO

Póas Volcano lies within the 5,599 hectare (13,830 acre) Póas National Park, which protects the remaining cloud forest near the summit of the volcano. The volcano is still active and the park is closed from time to time owing to gas emissions. The last real eruption, a minor one of ash, was in 1989. Birding aside, a trip to Póas is worthwhile just for a view inside the crater (if it's a clear day). A short trail takes you to the rim of the crater, which is about 1.3 kilometers (.8 miles) in diameter and 300 meters (1,000 feet) deep with an extremely acid lake at the bottom. Guillermo Alvarado, in his book *Costa Rica Land of Volcanoes*, wrote the lake has a pH of "practically zero, which makes it the world's most acid natural lake."

Birding at Póas, at an altitude of more than 2,700 meters (8,900 feet), can be a bit difficult because of fog and rain (least from December to April). Go to the area whenever it's clear. Average temperatures range from 9–14°C (48–50°F) with a maximum of 21°C (70°F) and a minimum of –6°C (21°F). Bring warm clothes! Care must also be taken to avoid high altitude sunburn. When the sun does shine, the air remains strangely cold, while surfaces become quite warm. Because this park is popular and is very close to the major population centers in the Central Valley, it gets severely crowded on sunny weekends, especially Sundays. Birding its limited trail system then becomes virtually impossible. If you have a car, be at the park entrance at 8 a.m. when it opens and try to do so on a weekday. The crowds don't show up until about 9:30 or 10 a.m., so you can have an hour or so of quiet along the main trails, even on weekends.

Access to Póas is normally via Alajuela. The best and most scenic road is Highway 125 and 9 to the junction near Vara Blanca, then Highway 120 through the small town of Poasito and on to the volcano. Look for **Bare-shanked Screech-owls** along the way, especially in the evening. To get to the area by bus, call

Blackberry bushes grow profusely at high elevations.

the TUASA office in San José (233-7477) at C12, A2 & 4 or Alajuela (441-1431) at Parque Central. Both companies have buses that go to the park, at least on Sundays and perhaps holidays. Other local buses may run towards Póas from Alajuela, but I don't know any details. A taxi from Alajuela costs about $20—not out of the question, especially for a group.

Accommodation near Póas is quite limited and prices reflect the scarcity. (In Costa Rica costs seem to increase with altitude, especially when tourist attractions are involved!) La Providencia Cabinas y Restaurante (231-7884) is on a farm of more than 500 hectares (1,235 acres) which abuts the park and has about 200 hectares (500 acres) of high altitude cloud forest. Thirty-eight dollars rents a small cabin (no electricity) on a hillside about .5 kilometers (.3 miles) away from the restaurant and farm buildings—quite isolated with a great view of the Central Valley. Food at the restaurant is very expensive by Costa Rican standards. The road to La Providencia is a left turn just before the park gate.

An alternative place to stay is Laguinillas Lodge, which is another left turn about one kilometer (.6 miles) before the park gate. The road (passable for a regular car, but it might be difficult getting back up the hill if it's wet) descends steeply to a very pleasant lodge and restaurant, where food is prepared in the traditional wood-burning raised hearth and stove. Rooms are $30 for a single. The owner of this farm/lodge complex is quite knowledgeable about the more common birds in the area.

I saw a number of **Resplendent Quetzals**, **Flame Tanagers**, flycatchers and warblers when I stopped there briefly in early April. Good birding can be had from the restaurant or *cabinas*. On another excursion to the lodge in mid-April, I saw a **Black Guan** early in the morning, a **Buffy Tuftedcheek** and what was probably an **Ochraceous Wren** along the trails in the forest. Bird densities were quite low in the forest, and it might take a bit of exploring to find the best spots, but the habitat is there.

If you want to stay near the top of Póas, Laguinillas Lodge is recommended. But at lower elevations near Vara Blanca, more options are available depending on the weather. Patronage of either of the above restaurants will inevitably result in some good sightings and the friendly family that operates Laguinillas Lodge seems amenable to "drop-in" birders.

LIST OF BIRDS SIGHTED IN VOLCÁN PÓAS AREA

(a=abundant; c=common; u=uncommon; s=scarce; r=rare)

Species	Jan-Mar	Apr-Jun	Jul-Sep	Species	Jan-Mar	Apr-Jun	Jul-Sep
Turkey Vulture		u		Sooty Robin	a		
Swainson's Hawk		u		Black-billed Nightingale-thrush	a		
Black Guan		u					
Band-tailed Pigeon		a		Long-tailed Silky-flycatcher	c		
Ruddy Pigeon		c					
Magnificent Hummingbird		c		Black-and-yellow Silky-flycatcher	u		
Volcano Hummingbird		c		Black-throated Green Warbler	c		
Buffy Tuftedcheek		u		Wilson's Warbler	c		
Olive-sided Flycatcher		u		Flame-colored Tanager	u		
Western Wood-pewee		c		Sooty-capped Bush-tanager	a		
Mountain Elaenia		c					
Blue-and-white Swallow		a		Slaty Flowerpiercer	u		
Ochraceous Wren		u?		Large-footed Finch	u		
Timberline Wren		c		Yellow-thighed Finch	u		
Mountain Robin		u		Rufous-collared Sparrow	c		

There is also good birding on the roads to both the above establishments—something to keep in mind, since the gates to the park don't open until 8 a.m. The road to La Providencia passes the crest of a hill with some communication towers and then descends steeply to the lodge. I birded the road between the main highway and the tower in mid-April. **Volcano Hummingbirds** and **Magnificent Hummingbirds** were quite common near flowering gorse-like shrubs that lined the road near the summit. **Black-billed Nightingale-thrushes** were very common along the road, along with a few **Large-footed Finches** and **Yellow-thighed Finches**. I often heard **Timberline Wrens** and I finally got lucky and saw one as it briefly perched on a low twig overhanging the road, before it disappeared into the thicket.

Bird near the gate of the park as you wait for park personnel to arrive in the morning. Near the beginning of the divider, I saw a pair of very tame **Black-and-yellow Silky-flycatchers**. The male was beautifully colored and sat posing for several minutes before being joined by a female. She was very drably colored in comparison, showing a fairly bright yellow only on her flanks, which were concealed much of the time. I also got a chance to have a close look at a **Slaty Flowerpiercer** as it worked some flowers in a thicket beside the road. It strongly reminded me of the path of my mother's crochet hook as it descended to one flower, looped over, often upside-down, to repeat the process over and over.

Within the park there are some interesting areas along the road for a kilometer or so before you reach the parking lot. These roadside areas are usually peaceful even when the trails are crowded. I saw **Sooty Robins**, **Black-billed Nightingale-thrushes**, **Wilson's Warblers**, **Black-throated Green Warblers**, **Western**

Wood-pewees and **Long-tailed Silky-flycatchers** in this area. Also watch for other high altitude species such as **Ochraceous Wren, Ruddy Pigeon, Spotted Wood-quail, Buffy-crowned Wood-partridge, Zeledonia, Red-tailed Hawk** and **Black-capped Flycatcher.**

From the parking lot there is a short main trail that leads to the rim of the volcano, with a spur that leads to a secondary crater. Thick stunted cloud forest predominates here, especially along the latter trail, which can make birding very difficult. **Black-and-yellow Silky-flycatchers, Long-tailed Silky-flycatchers, Slaty Flowerpiercers, Sooty-capped Bush-tanagers, Sooty Robins, Large-footed Finches** and **Yellow-thighed Finches** are found in this area. High altitude hummers are also quite common near the top of the crater. I saw **Volcano Hummingbirds** and **Magnificent Hummingbirds**, but also watch for **Fiery-throated Hummingbirds** and **Green Violet-ears.**

CERRO DE LA MUERTE

Access to this area is easy via the Interamerican Highway, which winds over a major ridge of the Talamanca mountains between Cartago and San Isidro. The highest summit near the highway is called Cerro de La Muerte (also Cerro Buenavista on some maps) and is 3,491 meters (10,473 feet) in elevation. The Mountain of Death gained its grizzly name in the early 1900s when travelers walked back and forth between San José and San Isidro. Deaths were not uncommon when the unwary and unprepared lost their way on the fog-shrouded ridges and died of hypothermia. Although temperatures may be quite balmy in clear weather, they can plummet by tens of degrees when fog and rain suddenly reduce visibility to a few meters. In addition, clear nights bring frosty mornings.

If you are driving a car, the Mountain of Death can be birded while staying in the Central Valley or San Isidro, although a day trip to the area tends to mean you are driving instead of birding during the best hours of the day.

There are no sizable towns at this high elevation but there a few small villages and small lodges in the region, some of which specialize in birding. The closest accommodation near the summit of Cerro de La Muerte is the Hotel Georgina (at kilometer 99—mile 61.4— of the highway), which is why I chose it as a base for birding. Hotel Georgina serves as a bus stop and it's a little strange to have the restaurant filled one moment and entirely vacant the next. Food is good typical Tico fare, but if you want fresh fruit and vegetables bring your own. However, you can usually get excellent locally grown apples and sometimes grapes. Rooms are basic, clean and economical; $7 or $8 for one with private bath, less without. The staff are friendly and courteous. Draw-

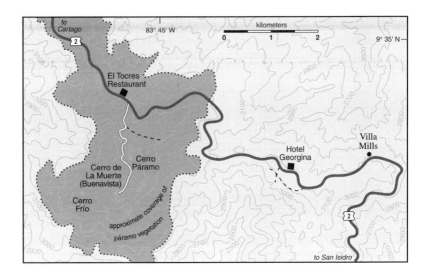

backs to the location are highway noise and lack of a covered patio for sitting around or birding in rainy weather.

On the first day of a June birding trip at Cerro de La Muerte, we were glad to see a mostly clear dawn, since the day before it had rained heavily most of the afternoon and into the night. Looking out the back window of the Hotel Georgina we could see some towering cumulus clouds over the distant cloud-covered Caribbean Sea. Some nearer clouds obscured the foothills of the Talamancas but most of the nearby high peaks were clear and a large patch of blue sky was overhead. **Sooty Robins** were abundant near the hotel. While a few showed the dark glossy plumage and bright orange bills and legs of adult-hood, most were in muted grayish-brown juvenile plumage. Although very common in this area, this species is found only in mountainous areas of Costa Rica and northern Panama.

About 100 meters (328 feet) down the highway towards San Isidro is a path leading down the slope on the left side of the highway. The way had been re-cently cleared but the heavy rain from the day before had drenched the vegeta-tion and grass and the deep litter of the cloud forest floor was sodden. Few birds were in evidence at dawn but we did spot a family of **Black-billed Nightingale-thrushes.** They were quite tame and hopped about on the ground while search-ing for food, flying only a few feet when approached too closely. Later, when the sun was shining in the tops of the trees, I spotted three or four **Flame-throated Warblers** flitting nervously from branch to branch in a tree high overhead. Most were females or juveniles, apart from one male with his more vividly colored orange throat, made more beautiful by the bright sunshine.

A walk northward along the power line from the hotel can be productive. Bird activity was greatest between 7 a.m. and 10:30 a.m. **Long-tailed Silky Flycatchers** were common. Although few landed until later in the morning, the white "windows" in their long tails were good characteristics for positive identification as they flew overhead across the

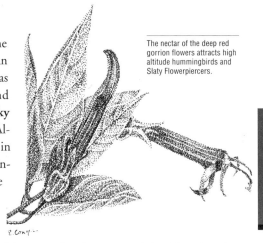

The nectar of the deep red gorrion flowers attracts high altitude hummingbirds and Slaty Flowerpiercers.

open power line right-of-way. Most were females, more subdued in coloration but showing the crested head nonetheless.

Several **Sooty-capped Bush-tanagers** were in the area, flitting from bush to bush. These tanagers are a favorite highland bird of mine. They tend to forage in flocks and seem friendly because they often approach quite closely as they go about their business. Their plump bodies seem underpowered by their short wings, and their bursts of flight from bush to bush, wings beating furiously, seem to exhaust them as they land unceremoniously at their next destination. One **Yellow-thighed Finch** was also briefly spotted. Their bright yellow thighs are usually concealed, making identification difficult, but they are easily seen if the bird is above you and can also be viewed when a bird is launching for flight. I also spotted a **Blue Seedeater**, another somewhat rare resident of the highlands.

In some areas, the steeper bank on the western side of the power line is heavily overgrown with shrubs, grasses and small trees. In one particularly sunny spot, a great profusion of red flowers (called *gorrion* by the local people) was growing, forming a heavy copse of intertwined leaves, branches and long red flowers. *Gorrion* nectar is a favorite food for hummingbirds. Both **Magnificent Hummingbirds** and **Fiery-throated Hummingbirds** made repeated visits to the flower bed. The sun fully exposed the yellow-bordered red sun-like spot on the throat of the latter species for brief instants—tiny explosions of color! I was also finally able to view a **Slaty Flowerpiercer** in this area. It was in the same flowering *gorrion* bush but kept well hidden and seldom ventured into plain view. This tiny finch feeds on nectar and is often attacked and driven from its food by the more aggressive hummingbirds, only finding refuge by diving deep into the foliage.

One afternoon, we birded between bouts of fog and rain, using the hotel as a base of operation. **Hairy Woodpeckers** perched on fence posts near the back of the hotel. I also spotted the clown of the avian world, the **Acorn Wood-**

pecker, its large white eye encircled by black and set under its brilliant red head giving it a comical wondrous look. Several **Large-footed Finches** were also in the yard. Their sleek charcoal-gray heads are accentuated with black stripes while their bodies are glossy olive. They were foraging for food by jumping vigorously upon the ground or grass and raking their feet strongly backwards, propelling their bodies backward simultaneously. Quick forward lunges then captured any revealed food. I watched a female for several minutes as she attempted to teach two newly fledged young this method of food collection. Although they did give a few desultory scratches, they seemed most content to watch and have mother give them encouragement by feeding them the juiciest morsels.

To find a little used path, cross the highway and head northwest towards the buildings a hundred or so meters away. Bear left along the fence line and you will find an old road that winds to the southwest. One evening, fog drifted over bamboo thickets and enveloped bromeliad-covered trees, also draped with vines, mosses and lichens—quite ethereal! Closer looks revealed the greens, reds, blues and oranges of a variety of small berries and flowers beside the trail. Few birds were moving; I saw a few **Long-tailed Silky-flycatchers** and had brief glimpses of a **Black-and-yellow Silky-flycatcher** and a juvenile **Black-capped Flycatcher**. The latter didn't have the very dark cap of the adult, but did have the characteristic eye-ring, wing bars and tawny chest. A **Magnificent Hummingbird** also obligingly landed on a nearby branch.

It is much drier on top of the Talamancas from January to March, although even then it's not unusual for wet mist or light rain to come sweeping over the ridges as air races westwards, especially in the afternoons. But mornings and early afternoons are usually bright and sunny. Indeed, be careful of sunburn. Remember that you are at over 3,000 meters (9,800 feet) elevation and you can really get fried quickly.

On a few days in February, winter resident warblers from North America were fairly common. It's a good place to see **Black-throated Green Warblers** and **Wilson's Warblers** and the rarer **Townsend's Warbler**. All these species prefer to spend their winters in high mountain habitats, and all three reach their southernmost limit of distribution in Costa Rica and western Panama. I also saw an adult **Black-capped Flycatcher**, a species found only in the high Talamancas, and a beautiful male **Resplendent Quetzal**. The manager of the Hotel Georgina said they are very common in the area from March to May, but a few occur there year-round.

On the path across the highway from Hotel Georgina in mid-April, I saw more than 30 **Swainson's Hawks** pass overhead one morning on their way north. **Flame-throated Warblers** were especially co-operative and perched fairly

LIST OF BIRDS SIGHTED IN CERRO DE LA MUERTE AREA
(a=abundant; c=common; u=uncommon; s=scarce; r=rare)

Species	Jan-Mar	Apr-Jun	Jul-Sep
Turkey Vulture		c	
Black Vulture	c		
Swainson's Hawk		c	
Band-tailed Pigeon		c	
Fiery-throated Hummingbird			u
Magnificent Hummingbird			u
Volcano Hummingbird	s		u
Resplendent Quetzal	s		
Acorn Woodpecker	c	u	
Hairy Woodpecker		c	
Buffy Tuftedcheek			u
Olive-sided Flycatcher			r
Black-capped Flycatcher	s	u	
Mountain Elaenia			u
Blue-and-white Swallow	c	c	
Mountain Robin		c	
Sooty Robin	c	a	
Black-billed Nightingale-thrush		c	
Cedar Waxwing		r	
Long-tailed Silky-flycatcher		a	
Black-and-yellow Silky-flycatcher			u
Flame-throated Warbler	c	u	
Townsend's Warbler	r		
Black-throated Green Warbler	c	s	
Wilson's Warbler	c	u	
Sooty-capped Bush-tanager	c	a	
Blue Seedeater			r
Large-footed Finch		c	
Yellow-thighed Finch		r	
Volcano Junco		c	
Rufous-collared Sparrow	c	c	

quietly for several seconds in low bushes along the road. They are normally high in the trees and difficult to get a good close view of. Two close sightings of **Buffy Tuftedcheeks**, a high altitude ovenbird, were especially nice. More unexpected were sightings of an **Olive-sided Flycatcher** and a **Cedar Waxwing**, both in full view on high exposed branches for long periods of time. The former species winters in South America and is a common migrant at lower altitudes, but is seldom seen so high.

Cedar Waxwings sporadically winter as far south as Costa Rica and Panama but they are considered relatively rare. The winter of 1995-96 may have seen an influx of **Cedar Waxwings**, since I had spotted another one two weeks earlier in the foothills of the Talamancas above San Vito. I also heard several **Timberline Wrens** as they sang from heavy thickets, but never glimpsed one. Some other birders saw a small group of **Silver-throated Jays** in the same area, a species that is fairly common in this region, although I've never run across it.

When you are on Cerro de La Muerte, be sure to bird the *páramo* near the summit of the mountain. This vegetation type is dominated by miniature bamboo, which grows in thick clumps and occurs in almost pure stands in some areas. Normally several species of shrubs are mixed in with the bamboo to form very dense thickets. The easiest way to bird the *páramo* is to drive up the road to the radio-television relay towers that clutter the peaks of Cerro de La Muerte. The road is a right turn as you're heading towards San Isidro. It's a few hundred

HIGHLANDS

meters past Las Torres Restaurant, which is very close to the highest point of the highway near kilometer 89 (mile 51.2). This road will take you to an elevation of about 3,400 meters (11,200 feet). You will be aware of this if you do any walking, especially if it's uphill. If you are not used to the high altitude, take it easy!

Birding the dense thickets of the *páramo* can be difficult, but there are several hillsides and rocky outcrops along the road where visibility is better. Early one morning, the birds didn't really start moving until after 7 a.m., when the sun had taken at least part of the chill from the air. A few **Volcano Hummingbirds** and **Sooty Robins** were highly visible as they perched on wires and other vantage points. **Sooty-capped Bush-tanagers** were easily seen as they rummaged through thickets, but **Large-footed Finches** and **Black-billed Nightingale-thrushes** were more difficult to locate as they foraged on or close to the ground in thickets. A few **Black-capped Flycatchers** perched near the tops of bushes in typical flycatcher fashion.

But the specialty of this area is the **Volcano Junco**, a species endemic to the highest mountains of Costa Rica and western Panama. Although **Volcano Juncos** can be found lower down the mountain in cleared areas, they are more abundant in open areas and along the road to the communication towers. These chunky birds are very tame and will approach to within a few meters. The black mask around their eyes gives them a very distinctive appearance.

ALBERGUE DE MONTAÑA TAPANTÍ

Albergue de Montaña Tapantí is beside the road at kilometer 62 (mile 38.4) of the Interamerican Highway at an altitude of about 2,500 meters (8,200 feet). It's a nicely laid out lodge with all the amenities, except heat. The rooms are quite chilly at night and on cloudy days, so bring warm clothes. However, there is a very nice fireplace in the common area next to the restaurant, which serves good meals as reasonable prices. Rates are moderately expensive, about $40, which include a light breakfast. Lower rates may be negotiated, especially during slow periods. The lodge is located on 5 hectares (12 acres) of sparsely treed land, and nearby roads lead down to the Río Macho.

I arrived at Montaña Tapantí late one morning and saw some birds that afternoon, despite banks of clouds that rolled intermittently over the area. I saw **Band-tailed Barbthroats** feeding on flowers beside the kitchen, a species that must be reaching the upper limit of its distribution in this area. A small flock of **Slaty Finches** were feeding on grass seeds on the open slope below the lodge. This high altitude seedeater is quite uncommon, and I was very pleased to see it so easily. **Flame-colored Tanagers** and **Flame-throated Warblers** flitted about in the tree-tops, while numerous **Ruddy-capped Nightingale-thrushes**

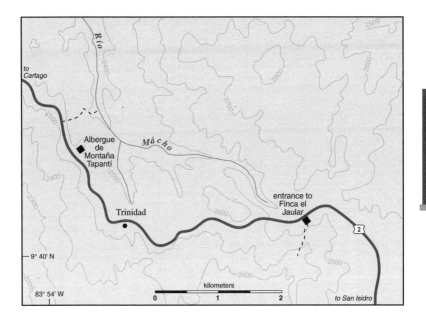

hopped about in the yards and on roadways. The latter species was especially common in this area, and seems to prefer lower elevations than the **Black-capped Nightingale-thrush**, which is common at even higher elevations. **Long-tailed Silky-flycatchers** were also very abundant. The lodge has a resident **Bare-shanked Screech-owl** which nests in a tree beside the guest lodgings. A fledgling was found on the ground when I was there.

On another morning, I walked down a road that winds through mixed farmland and second growth with a few monster trees scattered about, and then crosses the headwaters of the Río Macho. It's to the right just north of Albergue Tapantí. Birding was steady all morning, with many of the species I had seen previously. Ho-hum, more **Resplendent Quetzals, Buffy Tuftedcheeks**, etc. Species I hadn't seen in the previous few days included some very tame **Yellow-thighed Finches**, a **Spotted-crowned Woodcreeper** and a **Yellow-winged Vireo**. The latter species is endemic to the high mountains of Costa Rica and western Panama and is sometimes quite difficult to find. I also had the pleasure of watching a pair of quite tame **Black-capped Flycatchers** as I crossed and re-crossed their territory during the morning's walk.

Finca el Jaular

Another good place to bird near Albergue de Montaña Tapantí is Finca el Jaular, at kilometer 66.6 (mile 41.3). At this point, a good road leads down the Pacific side of the mountain slope from the right side of the highway. This is

LIST OF BIRDS SIGHTED IN ALBERGUE DE MONTAÑA TAPANTÍ AREA

(a=abundant; c=common; u=uncommon; s=scarce; r=rare)

Species	Jan-Mar	Apr-Jun	Jul-Sep
Dark shanked Screech-owl		c	
Band-tailed Pigeon		a	
Ruddy Pigeon		s	
Band-tailed Barbthroat		s	
Magnificent Hummingbird		c	
Resplendent Quetzal		u	
Hairy Woodpecker		u	
Spotted-crowned Woodcreeper		s	
Buffy Tuftedcheek		u	
Tropical Kingbird		r	
Western Wood-pewee		c	
Black-capped Flycatcher		u	
Blue-and-white Swallow		c	
Gray-breasted Wood-wren		u	
Clay-Colored Robin		s	
Mountain Robin		a	
Ruddy-capped Nightingale-thrush		a	

Species	Jan-Mar	Apr-Jun	Jul-Sep
Black-billed Nightingale-thrush		a	
Long-tailed Silky-flycatcher		c	
Black-and-yellow Silky-flycatcher		u	
Yellow-winged Vireo		r	
Nashville Warbler		u	
Collared Redstart		c	
Black-cheeked Warbler		r	
Golden-browed Chlorophonia		u	
Blue-hooded Euphonia		s	
Flame-colored Tanager		u	
Sooty-capped Bush-tanager		s	
Blue Seedeater		r	
Slaty Finch		r	
Large-footed Finch		c	
Yellow-thighed Finch		c	
Rufous-collared Sparrow		a	

private land and the gate is usually locked, but a procedure has been set up for birders to access the area. If you stay at Montaña Tapantí, you can get a key there at no extra charge. Alternatively, you can get a key for a few dollars from the *pulpería* at Trinidad at kilometer 63 (mile 39). Try to get the key the day before, so you can bird the area early in the morning.

The road from the highway winds through some absolutely beautiful climax montane forest, filled with some of the biggest epiphyte-laden trees I've ever seen at this high elevation. Birding in the very early morning was rather slow, with only a few **Band-tailed Pigeons**, flycatchers and **Sooty-capped Bush-tanagers** flying about, with the occasional **Black-billed Nightingale-thrush** foraging on the road. At about 8 a.m., the sun managed to shine through a few holes in the low overcast

Epiphytes flourish in humid forests throughout Costa Rica. Aquatic invertebrates living in small pools of water trapped between their leaves provide food for birds, and the pools serve as bathtubs for small birds.

sky and bird activity increased substantially. Several wrens sang in the underbrush, but I only managed to spot one, a **Gray-breasted Wood-wren**.

I also got lucky when a **Black-cheeked Warbler** foraged among some low bushes close to the road for a minute or so. This species is only found in the high mountains of Costa Rica and western Panama and is fairly difficult to find. I also saw two groups of **Buffy Tuftedcheeks** rummaging about moss- and epiphyte-covered tree trunks. **Collared Redstarts** were fairly common, as were **Golden-browed Chlorophonias**. The yellow of the former species and the bright green of the latter shone through the occasional patch of fog that was moving through the area by mid-morning. **Magnificent Hummingbirds** occasionally perched briefly on nearby twigs, and **Large-footed Finches** foraged on the ground.

At one point we saw a pair of **Hairy Woodpeckers** being harassed by a squirrel. **Long-tailed Silky-flycatchers** were common, and I also saw several

AN OWL IN THE HAND

Under normal circumstances, baby **Bare-shanked Screech-owls** would probably be all right when they fall out of the nest. They will usually climb up the nearest tree and wait there to be fed. But this one chick had fallen onto the tiled pathway of the Albergue Montaña Tapantí, and the manager's dog was more than curious about it. So Bernie, the manager, had picked it up (gathering not a few bites and scratches on the way) and put it into a box in his office. When I dropped in to visit Bernie, he took me to see "his baby." It had climbed out of the box and was sitting in a corner with a large moth in its mouth. Remembering his last encounter, Bernie reached down

his gloved hand to pick the chick up—what a display of ferocity ensued! The fledgling puffed itself up to cantaloupe size, spread its wings, which were almost fully feathered, and hissed menacingly, making pecking motions at the advancing hand. I think it may have been safe from the dog after all! I was glad for the opportunity to see it close at hand, but rather anxious for its survival. Bernie had called a reserve further down the Interamerican Highway, and they were on their way to collect the owlet, so that it could be fed, reared and released back to the wild.

Resplendent Quetzals are the most sought after species for birders in Costa Rica.

Black-and-yellow Silky-flycatchers. The latter species are quite tame and sluggish and can easily be observed for minutes on end. One grassy clearing beside the road was especially productive. A **Resplendent Quetzal** whizzed by and I spotted some **Blue-hooded Euphonias** in a nearby tree, along with several **Blue Seedeaters** foraging in the grass. Both the latter species are fairly rare and difficult to find and to see both almost simultaneously was quite a treat.

EL EMPALME

El Empalme is a small settlement composed mostly of roadside stands that sell locally produced strawberries, honey, cheese, flowers and apples to passersby at kilometer 51 (mile 31.6) of the Interamerican Highway. It's at an altitude of about 2,000 meters (6,600 feet), considerably lower than the Hotel Georgina on Cerro de La Muerte, and also lower than the nearby Albergue Tapantí. Until recently, there were no accommodations near El Empalme, but Alberto Solano has recently built a *cabina* on his farm which is about one kilometer (.6 miles) west of El Empalme on a good dirt road. It's called Cabañas La Montaña (382-4148) and standard rates are $25 a day. The *cabina* has cooking facilities and a fireplace, which is very welcome on chilly evenings, and can sleep four with ease. The atmosphere is very warm and friendly, with Alberto's wife Aurelia's welcoming, "*Mi casa es su casa!*"—"my house is your house—anything you need, knock on my door, my house is right over there."

LIST OF BIRDS SIGHTED IN EL EMPALME AREA
(a=abundant; c=common; u=uncommon; s=scarce; r=rare; vr=very rare)

Species	Jan-Mar	Apr-Jun	Jul-Sep
American Swallow-tailed Kite		u	
Cooper's Hawk		vr	
Band-tailed Pigeon		c	
Squirrel Cuckoo		s	
Green-crowned Brilliant		s	
Magnificent Hummingbird		c	
Volcano Hummingbird		c	
Resplendent Quetzal		c	
Hairy Woodpecker		u	
Ruddy Treerunner		c	
Western Wood-pewee		a	
Yellowish Flycatcher		s	
Black-capped Flycatcher		a	
Tufted Flycatcher		s	
Olive-striped Flycatcher		s	
Blue-and-white Swallow		c	

Species	Jan-Mar	Apr-Jun	Jul-Sep
Ochraceous Wren	r		
Clay-colored Robin	s		
Mountain Robin	a		
Ruddy-capped Nightingale-thrush	u		
Black-billed Nightingale-thrush	a		
Long-tailed Silky-flycatcher	c		
Black-and-yellow Silky-flycatcher	a		
Yellow-winged Vireo	s		
Flame-throated Warbler	c		
Spangled-cheeked Tanager		s	
Sooty-capped Bush-tanager	a		
Slaty Flowerpiercer	c		
Large-footed Finch	c		
Yellow-thighed Finch	c		
Yellow-throated Brush-Finch		s	
Rufous-collared Sparrow	c		

The 46 hectare (114 acre) piece of land where the *cabina* is located is near a ridge with a great view of Cartago in the valley below. A newly constructed trail leads through the mixed forest, some of it selectively logged. Alberto's brother guided me on my first walk through the area and he proudly pointed out all the fruit trees preferred by **Resplendent Quetzals**. The high point of my day was spotting an **Ochraceous Wren,** a species I had been seeking for quite some time, foraging on a moss-covered tree trunk. The species looks like a small **House Wren** with a light wash of ochre coloration; however, the habits and habitats of the two species are very different. We also saw a stunning **Resplendent Quetzal** in "full dress," which flew above our heads and perched in full view a short distance away.

The next day in the same area, I saw several **Ruddy Treerunners**, another mountain specialty that is locally common (in other words, difficult to find unless you know where to look), **Yellow-winged Vireos, Flame-throated Warblers** and a **Spangled-cheeked Tanager.** I found **Black-and-yellow Silky-flycatchers, Yellow-thighed Finches, Black-billed Nightingale-thrushes, Western Wood-pewees, Black-capped Flycatchers, Resplendent Quetzals** and **Magnificent Hummingbirds** to be especially abundant in the area. **Volcano Hummingbirds** were also fairly common and I saw one **Green-crowned Brilliant.**

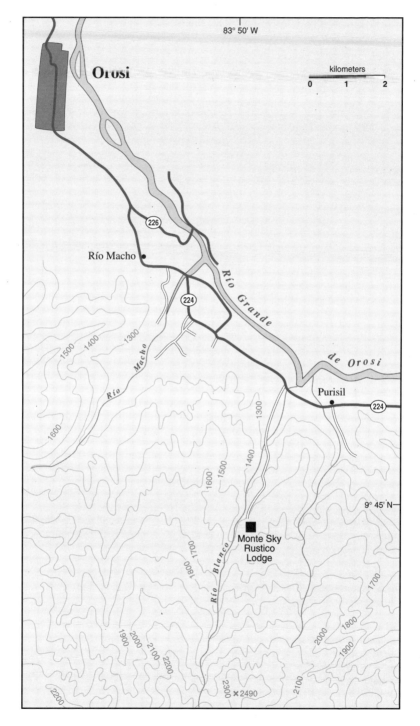

The last morning I was in the area, I was very lucky to see a **Cooper's Hawk**, quite rare in Costa Rica, perched high above the surrounding trees on an old dead snag.

All in all, the avifauna of this area is mostly composed of highland and mountain species, with a few of the lower elevation species, such as the **Yellow-throated Brush-finch** and even **Squirrel Cuckoos**, also present. People in this area seem to be especially aware of **Resplendent Quetzals** and the different times of year when various fruits ripen and are eaten by the birds. If you are desperate to see a **Resplendent Quetzal**, this is a good place to visit, since they occur here in abundance year-round.

MONTE SKY

Monte Sky (220-2237) is a new eco-development on the northeastern slopes of the Talamancas above the small town of Orosi. It consists of a small, very rustic guest house and more than 550 hectares (13,600 acres) of land with a fairly well-developed trail system. The house was built in the 1920s and it's a stiff climb from the parking lot. Altitudes vary from a low of about 1,700 meters (5,600 feet) to more than 2,490 meters (8,100 feet) in the Three Peaks area. About 80 percent of the land is primary forest, the remainder secondary growth with some small clearings around the house.

This area is not for the faint-hearted. There is little armchair birding here, except from the house, which has a tremendous view of the Central Valley and the volcanoes of the Central Cordillera. The trouble is that this is real cloud forest and the area is often enveloped in thick fog. But the people are very friendly and Paulo Orias, the guide, is very eager to learn more about birds. The prices are extremely reasonable: $15 for an overnight stay with three meals, and $4 for a day visit, which includes at least a guided orientation and a snack!

If you bird this area, take warm clothes, especially for an overnight stay. I would be tempted to stay in Orosi and take a four-wheel drive taxi to Monte Sky if it's clear. If not, bird Tapantí National Park or adjacent areas like Lankester Gardens near Paraiso.

COCOS ISLAND

Cocos Island (5°30'N; 37°18'W) is in the Pacific Ocean more than 500 kilometers (310 miles) southwest of Costa Rica. It is the country's only oceanic holding. Aside from its unique flora and fauna, the island lays claim to being the world's largest uninhabited island (about 2,400 hectares, or 5,900 acres). Since the entire island was declared a national park, it may retain this status for years to come.

Although the main ecological attraction of this area is an amazing array of marine life popular with snorkelers and scuba divers, there are good reasons why birders visit this remote area. More than 70 species of birds (see Appendix I, Group 19) occur on the island, and three are endemic: **Cocos Cuckoo, Cocos Flycatcher** and **Cocos Finch**. Aside from the endemics, seabirds are another reason to venture to Cocos Island. Although many of the seabirds are common in other countries, this is about the most reliable area in Costa Rica where you have a good chance of seeing **Great Frigatebirds, Red-footed Boobies, Brown Noddies, Black Noddies** and **White Terns**. In addition, if you arrive by boat, you could see some pelagic species on the way, such as **Wedge-rumped Storm-petrels, Black Storm-petrels** and perhaps even a **Red-billed Tropicbird**.

Now for the bad news. There is no regularly scheduled transportation to Cocos Island, so it is a very expensive place to visit. Over the years, charter companies have come and gone, reflecting the infrequency of travel to the area. Diving near Cocos Island is popular, with Agressa Fleet (U.S. 1-800-348-2628 or 504-385-2528) and Tropical Sceneries (224-2555) both offering 10–12 day all-inclusive excursions to the area for between $2,000 and $3,000. Cocos Island Airways (232-4373) also offers trips from San José. If you're seriously contemplating a trip to Cocos Island, it might be an idea to contact a good tour wholesaler like Horizontes (222-2022) in San José for latest information on tours and transportation to the region.

COSTA RICAN BIRD SPECIALTIES

The popularity of Costa Rica as a birding destination is substantially increased because many bird species originated in the region. Only four species of birds, **Mangrove Hummingbird, Coppery-headed Emerald, Gray-tailed Mountain-gem** and **Black-cheeked Ant-tanager** are wholly restricted to mainland Costa Rica. However, almost one-tenth (77 species) of the country's avifauna can be found only in or near Costa Rica. Although many of these birds are found in extreme western Panama or, in unusual cases, in eastern Nicaragua, they are much more widespread in Costa Rica. Thus, if bird watchers wish to see these species, the majority are most easily seen in Costa Rica.

Below is a table showing Costa Rican bird specialities, their distribution, how difficult it is to locate them, and where to find them. If you are just starting to bird watch, you will certainly enjoy seeing even just a few of these birds. If you are a serious birder, the list will help you to maximize the number of endemics you see while you are in Costa Rica. For example, from the table you can see that most of the birds with very restricted distributions are found in mid to high elevations in the mountains, especially the Talamancas, which extend into western Panama. Modest numbers are also found in east slope areas and Southwestern Lowlands (Chapter 3), but there are none in the Northwestern Lowlands (Chapter 2).

Species	Distribution	Degree of Difficulty	Where to Find It
Curassows, Guans			
Black Guan	Above 1,000 m (3,300 ft) in mountains of CR & W Panama	M	In protected areas–Póas Volcano; Monteverde; parks of the Talamancas; Cerro de la Muerte; Alturas
Quail			
Black-breasted Wood-quail	Mid-elevations of northern mountains; E slope of Talamancas to W Panama	D	Best looked for in protected areas –Monteverde region, Guanacaste Park
Pigeons, Doves			
Buff-fronted Quail-dove	Mountain areas of CR & W Panama, above 1,000 m (3,300 ft)	FD	Santa Elena Reserve; Monteverde; Vara Blanca; El Empalme; Finca el Jaular
Chiriquí Quail-dove	Mid-elevations of mountains of CR & W Panama	M	Monteverde; Vara Blanca; Tapantí; Alturas

CR= Costa Rica; E=easy; M=moderate; MD=moderately difficult;
ME=moderately easy; FD=fairly difficult; D=difficult; VD=very difficult

Species	Distribution	Degree of Difficulty	Where to Find It

Parrots

Species	Distribution	Degree of Difficulty	Where to Find It
Crimson-fronted Parakeet	Mainly lowlands of E slope from E Nicaragua to W Panama	E	Puerto Viejo de Sarapiquí, Fortuna; Puerto Viejo de Talamanca
Sulfur-winged Parakeet	Mid- & high elevations of the Talamancas to W Panama	M	Rancho Naturalista; Alturas
Red-fronted Parrotlet	Low to mid-elevations from Cordillera Central south along Talamancas to W Panama	M	La Selva; Quebrada Gonzales; Hitoy-Cerere

Cuckoos

Species	Distribution	Degree of Difficulty	Where to Find It
Cocos Cuckoo	Cocos Island	D	Cocos Island

Owls

Species	Distribution	Degree of Difficulty	Where to Find It
Bare-shanked Screech-owl	Above 1,000 m (3,300 ft) in CR to W Panama (sometimes to NW Colombia)	D	Póas; Albergue de Montaña Tapantí; Cerro de La Muerte; Alturas

Hummingbirds

Species	Distribution	Degree of Difficulty	Where to Find It
White-crested Coquette	300–1,200 m (1,000–3,900 ft); SW CR to W Panama	D	Los Cusingos; Las Ventanas de Osa; Golfito
Fiery-throated Hummingbird	Mountains of CR & W Panama; above 1,400 m (4,600 ft)	M	Santa Elena Reserve; Póas; Cerro de La Muerte;
Beryl-crowned Hummingbird	SW CR to W Panama; sea level to 1,200 m (3,900 ft)	D	Tárcoles area; Las Ventanas de Osa; San Vito; Golfito
Mangrove Hummingbird	Mangroves of W coast of CR only	D	Curú; Colorado; Terrabá estuary; Golfito
Snowy-bellied Hummingbird	Mid-elevations of SW CR to E Panama	D	General and Coto Brus valleys; Los Cusingos; San Vito; Buenos Aires
Black-bellied Hummingbird	Mid-elevations of E slope CR from Cordillera Central to W Panama	D	Rancho Naturalista; Hitoy-Cerere; Braulio Carrillo
Coppery-headed Emerald	E slope mid-elevations of Cordilleras Guanacaste, Tilarán & Central; W slope at higher elevations	E	Monteverde; Arenal Observatory
White-bellied Mountain-gem	E slope low to mid-elevations of Cordillera Tilarán south to W Panama	MD	Arenal Observatory, Rancho Naturalista, Hitoy-Cerere
Gray-tailed Mountain-gem	Above 1,800 m (5,900 ft) in Talamancas	D	El Empalme; Albergue de Montaña Tapantí; Cerro de La Muerte
Magenta-throated Woodstar	Mid-elevations of W slope CR to W Panama	MD	Monteverde; Los Cusingos
Scintillant Hummingbird	W slope CR to W Panama, above 1,000 m (3,300 ft)	D	Monteverde, Alturas
Volcano Hummingbird	Above 1,800 m (5,900 ft) from Cordillera Talamanca south to W Panama	MD	Póas; Cerro de La Muerte; El Empalme

Trogons

Species	Distribution	Degree of Difficulty	Where to Find It
Lattice-tailed Trogon	Low to mid-elevations; E slope CR to W Panama	MD	Fortuna; Arenal Observatory; Jardin Las Cusingas; Hitoy-Cerere
Baird's Trogon	SW CR to W Panama	E	Tárcoles–Carara area; Las Ventanas de Osa; Golfito; Los Cusingos; San Vito
Orange-bellied Trogon	Mid-elevations of CR & W Panama	MD	Monteverde; Santa Elena Reserve; Arenal Observatory; Braulio Carrillo

Species	Distribution	Degree of Difficulty	Where to Find It

Woodpeckers and Allies

Species	Distribution	Degree of Difficulty	Where to Find It
Prong-billed Barbet	Mid-elevations of CR to W Panama	MD	Monteverde; Virgen del Socorro; Rancho Naturalista
Fiery-billed Aracari	SW CR to W Panama	E	Los Cusingos; Tárcoles area; Las Ventanas de Osa; Golfito
Golden-naped Woodpecker	SW CR to W Panama	E	Los Cusingos; Tárcoles area; Las Ventanas de Osa; Golfito

Ovenbirds

Species	Distribution	Degree of Difficulty	Where to Find It
Ruddy Treerunner	Above 1,200 m (3,900 ft) in CR to W Panama	D	Santa Elena Reserve; Vara Blanca; El Empalme; Finca el Jaular; Alturas
Streaked-breasted Treehunter	Above 700 m (2,300 ft) in CR to W Panama	D	Monteverde; Vara Blanca; El Empalme; Tapantí

Antbirds

Species	Distribution	Degree of Difficulty	Where to Find It
Black-hooded Antshrike	SW CR to W Panama	E	Carara area; Las Ventanas de Osa; Golfito
Black-crowned Antpitta	E slope CR to Panama & NW Colombia	D	Quebrada Gonzales; Virgen del Socorro; Hitoy-Cerere

Tapaculos

Species	Distribution	Degree of Difficulty	Where to Find It
Silvery-fronted Tapaculo	Above 1,000 m (3,300 ft) in CR & Panama	VD	Mountains; widespread but difficult to see

Cotingas

Species	Distribution	Degree of Difficulty	Where to Find It
Turquoise Cotinga	SW CR to W Panama; to 2,000 m (6,600 ft)	VD	Palmar Norte; Carara area; Golfito
Yellow-bellied Cotinga	SW CR to W Panama	VD	Mangrove areas of Tárcoles, Terrabá estuary; Golfito
Bare-necked Umbrellabird	Foothills E slope; CR & W Panama	D	Arenal Observatory; Quebrada Gonzales; Jardin Las Cusingas; La Selva

Manakins

Species	Distribution	Degree of Difficulty	Where to Find It
Orange-collared Manakin	SW CR to W Panama	ME	Carara; Las Ventanas de Osa; Los Cusingos

Flycatchers

Species	Distribution	Degree of Difficulty	Where to Find It
Golden-bellied Flycatcher	Mid-elevations E slope CR to W Panama	D	Monteverde; Braulio Carrillo; Santa Cruz above Turrialba; Rancho Naturalista
Dark Pewee	Mid- to high elevations from Cordillera Tilarán to W Panama	D	Santa Elena Reserve; El Empalme; Monte Sky; Cerro de La Muerte
Ochraceous Pewee	High elevations of Cordillera Central to W Panama	D	Póas; Monte Sky; El Empalme; Finca el Jaular
Black-capped Flycatcher	High elevations of Cordillera Central to W Panama	E	Póas; El Empalme; Cerro de La Muerte
Tawny-chested Flycatcher	Lowlands & foothills of mainly	D	Quebrada Gonzales; La Selva;

CR= Costa Rica; E=easy; M=moderate; MD=moderately difficult;
ME=moderately easy; FD=fairly difficult; D=difficult; VD=very difficult

BIRD SPECIALTIES

Species	Distribution	Degree of Difficulty	Where to Find It
Flycatcher	NE CR to E Nicaragua		Rancho Naturalista; Arenal Observatory
Cocos Flycatcher	Cocos Island	M	Cocos Island
Zeledon's Tyrannulet	Mid-elevations E slope CR to W Panama	D	Arenal Observatory; Quebrada Gonzales; Jardin Las Cusingas

Jays

Species	Distribution	Degree of Difficulty	Where to Find It
Silvery -throated Jay	High elevations of Cordillera Central to W Panama	D	Cerro de La Muerte; Hotel Georgina; Póas

Wrens

Species	Distribution	Degree of Difficulty	Where to Find It
Striped -breasted Wren	Lowlands of E slope Nicaragua to C Panama	ME	Oro Verde; Los Chiles; Puerto Viejo de Talamanca; La Selva
Riverside Wren	Lowlands of SW CR to W Panama	E	Carara; Las Ventanas de Osa; Golfito; Palmar Norte
Black -throated Wren	Lowlands of E slope, SE Nicaragua to NW Panama	MD	Los Chiles, Oro Verde, La Selva; Puerto Viejo de Talamanca
Black-bellied Wren	SW CR to NW Colombia	MD	Carara; Las Ventanas de Osa; Golfito
Ochraceous Wren	Mid- to high elevations of Cordillera Tilarán south to E Panama	MD	Póas; El Empalme; Finca el Jaular; Alturas
Timberline Wren	High elevations of Cordillera Central to W Panama	MD	Póas; Cerro de La Muerte
Whistling Wren	Lowlands & foothills of S CR to E Panama	D	Puerto Viejo de Talamanca; Hitoy-Cerere; Las Ventanas de Osa; Golfito

Thrushes, Robins

Species	Distribution	Degree of Difficulty	Where to Find It
Sooty Robin	High elevations of Cordillera Central south to W Panama	E	Póas; Cerro de La Muerte
Black-faced Solitaire	Mid- to high elevations of CR to W Panama	MD	Monteverde; Tapantí; El Empalme; Finca el Jaular; Alturas
Black-billed Nightingale-thrush	High elevations of Cordillera Central south to W Panama	E	Póas; Cerro de La Muerte; El Empalme

Silky-flycatchers

Species	Distribution	Degree of Difficulty	Where to Find It
Long-tailed Silky-flycatcher	High elevations of Cordillera Central south to W Panama	E	Póas; Cerro de La Muerte; El Empalme
Black-and-yellow Silky-flycatcher	Mid- to high elevations in mountains of CR & W Panama	E	Santa Elena Reserve; Póas; Cerro de La Muerte; El Empalme

Vireos

Species	Distribution	Degree of Difficulty	Where to Find It
Yellow-winged Vireo	High elevations of Cordillera Central south to W Panama	D	El Empalme; Finca el Jaular; Cerro de La Muerte

Species	Distribution	Degree of Difficulty	Where to Find It

Warblers

Flame-throated Warbler	High elevations of Cordillera Central south to W Panama	E	Cerro de La Muerte; El Empalme
Zeledonia	Mid- to high elevations of mountains of CR & W Panama	VD	Monteverde; Póas; Vara Blanca; El Empalme; Cerro de La Muerte; difficult to observe

Tanagers

Golden-browed Chlorophonia	Mid- to high elevations of CR & W Panama	E	Monteverde; Vara Blanca; Póas; El Empalme; Albergue de Montaña Tapantí
Tawny-capped Euphonia	Foothills of E slope of CR to NW Colombia	ME	Quebrada Gonzales; Hitoy-Cerere
Spotted-crowned Euphonia	Low and mid-elevations of SW CR & W Panama	MD	Las Ventanas de Osa; Palmar Norte; Golfito
Spangled-cheeked Tanager	Mid- to high elevations of Cordillera Tilarán to W Panama	ME	Santa Elena Reserve; Vara Blanca; El Empalme; Tapantí
Blue-and-gold Tanager	Mainly foothills of E slope CR to C. Panama	MD	Tapantí; Quebrada Gonzales; Virgen del Socorro
Black-cheeked Ant-tanager	Only in lowlands near Golfito	M	Golfito; Esquinas Rainforest Lodge
Sooty-capped Bush-tanager	High elevations of Cordillera Tilarán south to W Panama	E	Monteverde; Póas; Cerro de La Muerte

Finches, Grosbeaks

Black-thighed Grosbeak	Mid-elevations of CR & W Panama	MD	Monteverde; Arenal Observatory; Vara Blanca
Pink-billed Seed-finch	Lowlands of SE Nicaragua to NW Panama	D	Los Chiles; Oro Verde; Puerto Viejo de Sarapiquí and Talamanca
Cocos Finch	Cocos Island	ME	Cocos Island
Peg-billed Finch	Mid- to high elevations of Cordillera Tilarán to W Panama	D	Póas; Finca el Jaular; Cerro de La Muerte
Slaty Flowerpiercer	Mid- to high elevations of CR and W Panama	ME	Monteverde; Póas; El Empalme
Large-footed Finch	High elevations of Cordillera Central to W Panama	E	Cerro de La Muerte; Hotel Georgina; Póas
Yellow-thighed Finch	High elevations of Cordillera Central to W Panama	ME	Póas; El Empalme; Cerro de La Muerte
Black-headed Brush-finch	Mid-elevations of SW CR to Colombia	D	Los Cusingos; San Vito
Sooty-faced Finch	Mainly E slope foothills of CR to E Panama	D	Arenal Observatory; Quebrada Gonzales; Hitoy-Cerere

Juncos

Volcano Junco	Very high elevations of Cordillera Central to E. Panama	E	Cerro de La Muerte

CR= Costa Rica; E=easy; M=moderate; MD=moderately difficult; ME=moderately easy; FD=fairly difficult; D=difficult; VD=very difficult

BIRD SPECIALTIES

E. Conger.

SIDE TRIPS

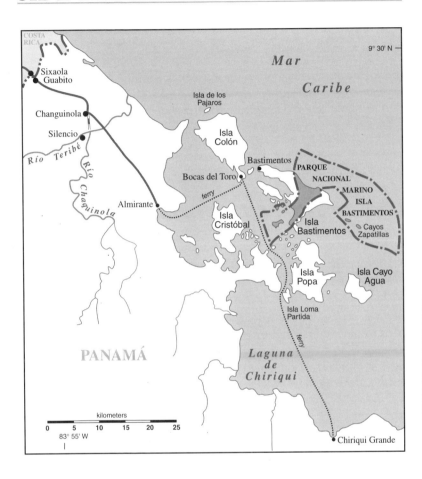

PANAMA

If you have birded Costa Rica and are anxious to start a Panama list, you can easily get to a little-visited area of Panama from Sixaola in southeastern Costa Rica. The Bocas del Toro region is in the extreme northwestern corner of Panama. While it shares a road system (and border crossing) with Costa Rica, it is isolated from the rest of Panama by the great Laguna de Chiriquí and all Panamanian traffic into the area is by boat.

Because of the relative ease of access, this region sees more tourists from Costa Rica than from those visiting the rest of Panama. The big draw is snorkeling and diving among the literally thousands of reefs and shallow islets that dot extensive areas of shallow water. Diving and tourism are based out of the small town of Bocas del Toro on Isla Colón, but birding in the area is also good. The region contains Panama's only marine park, Marino Isla Bastimentos, of more than 13,000 hectares (32,110 acres), which covers a substantial part of Bastimentos Island with its cover of secondary and primary forest. Terrain on the adjacent mainland is largely mountainous with the foothills of the Talamancas descending close to the sea, leaving few extensive flat lowland areas. The latter have long been developed as banana plantations.

The region has an interesting history, beginning with Columbus' visit to Almirante Bay in 1502 on his third voyage to the New World. The area was largely forgotten for hundreds of years until the massive development of banana plantations, in this part of the world by the United Fruit Company in the late 1800s. Today, bananas are still very important to the local economy and large plantations cover most flat areas of the mainland. But wander into the foothills of the Talamancas and you are in another world; one dotted with isolated small Indian villages where access is by foot or horse. Or investigate any of the hundreds of islands along the coast.

When birding in this region of Panama, you have opportunities to see considerable numbers of seabirds and water birds, some quite rare, such as the **Red-billed Tropicbird**. That's in addition to the multitudes of colorful tanagers, toucans, parrots, hummingbirds and trogons that are commonly associated with the tropics, in addition to the more obscure woodcreepers, antbirds and flycatchers. Panama has even more birds than Costa Rica, about 929 species, but you have to start somewhere!

If you want to get to this region of Panama from Costa Rica, it's fairly simple. MEPE Autotransportes (you can try 257-8129, but I've never had any luck getting someone to answer the phone) has three buses a day from San José (A11, C Central & 1) to Sixaola with the first one at 6 a.m. There are also more frequent buses to Sixaola from Limón. From the bus-stop in Sixaola, walk across the bridge over the river and you're in Panama, once you go through the Costa Rican and Panamanian border control offices on the bridge. Note that, to enter Panama, visas are necessary for citizens of most countries. They should be obtained in San José, but if you show up at the border without one you should be able to get through after the officer gets "upset" but then tells you to buy one at the Banco Nacional in Bocas del Toro at your first opportunity.

Get a bus or taxi from the Panama border town of Guabito to Changuinola or Almirante. A taxi costs $20 to Almirante; a bus about $4. Boys commonly try to grab your baggage as you're disembarking from the Sixaola bus and carry it across the bridge for you. They are not just being nice; they expect to be paid, which is all right, but they are also point men (boys) for the taxis.

The boys sometimes quote a cheap fare just to get you in the taxi. After you have arrived at your destination, you learn that the fare is more and the boy has no right to quote you a price! Check prices carefully with the driver and make sure the driver is the owner, or you know who is. At Almirante, there is a ferry service that leaves for Bocas del Toro every hour or so for $3.

There is also a direct daily bus from San José to Changuinola. It leaves from near the Hotel Cocori (C14; A 5&7) at 10 a.m. for about $7—talk about a bargain.

Bocas Del Toro

Bocas del Toro has run-down inexpensive hotels, but $20 does get you a private bath and hot water. I stayed at Brisis (507-757-9248; formerly known as the Hotel Thomas), which was quiet and cooled by the daily sea breeze. You can rent bicycles or small motorcycles to get around on the island, and taxis cost a few dollars. Two dollars will get you over to the village of Bastimentos on Isla Bastimentos.

When I went to Isla Bastimentos, I walked from the village across the island to its seaward side. My best bird of the day was a beautiful **Plumbeous Kite**, which sat in a tree for a considerable period of time while I admired it. **White-collared Manakins** and **Bay Wrens** were abundant in thickets a short distance from the sea. **Tawny-crested Tanagers, Great-crested Flycatchers** and **Olive-fronted Parakeets** were also present. The land portion of Bastimentos Marine Park is an obvious destination. I was told there is a considerable amount of primary forest in the park, as well as secondary growth and a freshwater lake. There are no maintained trails, but locals know some access paths.

Quite a number of seabirds can be spotted from Las Brisis and elsewhere along the coast—**Sandwich Terns, Royal Terns**, herons, egrets and some shorebirds, depending on the time of year. Isla de Las Pajaros (also known as Swan Cay) is a small rocky island near the northern end of Isla Colón. It is one of the very few known nesting sites of the **Red-billed Tropicbird** in this area of the world. **Brown Boobies**, as well as other seabirds, also nest on the island. There are no regular boats to Swan Cay, but rather costly charters can be arranged. When I wanted to go, asking price for a three-hour round trip in a dugout canoe was $60. I refused. It seemed a bit of a gouge, since all-day trips go for $70 or less. A possible economical alternative is to go on a group tour with Alex Salas of Happy Bocas Charters. They sometimes go out to the island on a day trip with a group (minimum of seven people) on a 13 metre (36 foot) sailboat for $16 per person. Also check with Alex for trips to other interesting areas.

If you do try to get out to Swan Cay, go quite early in the morning, as many birds leave the island on daily feeding excursions. The sea also gets rougher later in the day and small boats sometimes can't make it to the exposed island.

CHANGUINOLA

I had the fortunate experience of meeting Hector Montenegro, who drives a taxi in Changuinola. When he realized what I was doing, he arranged for a trip up the Changuinola River by dugout canoe. His brother-in-law, Juan Martinez, accompanied us and acted as a guide through the mixed forest, farmland, crops and cocoa plantations that small-scale farmers have developed in the region. We saw a number of birds, including a **White Hawk**, which is apparently quite common in the region, a **Snowy Cotinga**, a **Pale-vented Pigeon** and a **Cinnamon Woodpecker**. Although we didn't see any, **Red-rumped Woodpeckers** are also common in the area. This species is found in Costa Rica only in the Sixaola area, where they are quite uncommon, and in the Golfito Dulce area. It's one of the more difficult birds to add to your Costa Rica list, but considerably easier to find in Panama. Look for them in heavy foliage, especially in cocoa plantations.

This area was dripping with psittacids. **White-crowned Parrots** and **Mealy Parrots** were very common, but we also saw **Crimson-fronted Parakeets, Olive-fronted Parakeets, Red-lored Parrots, Orange-chinned Parakeets** and the more uncommon **Blue-headed Parrot**. In other words, just about every psittacid you would expect to see in the area, except for the **Brown-hooded Parrot**, which I'm sure also occurs in some numbers.

Aside from the birds, this trip was a great experience and quite inexpensive. The skill with which the men negotiated the heavy dugout up the clear, cool river, poling up shallows in some areas, was great to see. I also got a glimpse of the fascinating culture and way of life of the Ngobe-Bugla tribe as we stopped by two of their roadless villages. If you get to this area, try to contact Hector (758-7359 or 758-6033) if you are interested in such a trip. He is no expert on birds but he is very enthusiastic and knows the area and people well.

If you can't find Hector, take a bus or taxi for $6 to Silencio, a small community near where the Río Teribé empties into the Changuinola. Get a boat to ferry you across the river (there is lots of traffic) and bird the nearby woods and crop land. You will likely see many of the same species as further up the river, but you won't get the cultural experience. Numerous **Eastern Kingbirds** were in this region when I was there in late April.

LIST OF BIRDS SIGHTED IN BOCAS DEL TORO, AND CHANGUINOLA AREA

(a=abundant; c=common; u=uncommon; s=scarce; r=rare)

Species	Jan-Mar	Apr-Jun	Jul-Sep
Brown Pelican	c		
Olivaceous Cormorant	u		
Green-backed Heron	c		
Snowy Egret	u		
Great Egret	u		
Great Blue Heron	c		
Plumbeous Kite	r		
White Hawk	r		
Purple Gallinule	u		
Northern Jacana	u		
Semipalmated Plover	u		
Spotted Sandpiper	u		
Laughing Gull	c		
Royal Tern	a		
Sandwich Tern	c		
Pale-vented Pigeon	s		
Short-billed Pigeon	c		
Ruddy Ground-dove	c		
Blue Ground-dove	s		
Crimson-fronted Parakeet	u		
Olive-throated Parakeet	u		
Orange-chinned Parakeet	u		
White-crowned Parrot	c		
Blue-headed Parrot	s		
Red-lored Parrot	u		
Mealy Parrot	c		
Blue-chested Hummingbird	u		
Rufous-tailed Hummingbird	u		
Ringed Kingfisher	a		
Amazon Kingfisher	a		
Black-cheeked Woodpecker	c		
Cinnamon Woodpecker	u		

Species	Jan-Mar	Apr-Jun	Jul-Sep
Streaked-headed Woodcreeper	c		
Masked Tityra	u		
Snowy Cotinga	s		
White-collared Manakin	u		
Eastern Kingbird	c		
Tropical Kingbird	c		
Great Kiskadee	c		
Great-crested Flycatcher	u		
Eastern Wood-pewee	u		
Yellow-bellied Elaenia	u		
Gray-breasted Martin	a		
Barn Swallow	a		
Southern Rough -winged Swallow	a		
Brown Jay	u		
Bay Wren	u		
Clay-colored Robin	c		
Red-eyed Vireo	u		
Bananaquit	u		
Montezuma Oropendola	a		
Great-tailed Grackle	c		
Black-cowled Oriole	s		
Golden-hooded Tanager	u		
Blue-gray Tanager	c		
Scarlet-rumped Tanager	c		
Tawny-crested Tanager	u		
White-collared Seedeater	c		
Variable Seedeater	c		
Thick-billed Seed-finch	c		
Black-striped Sparrow	c		

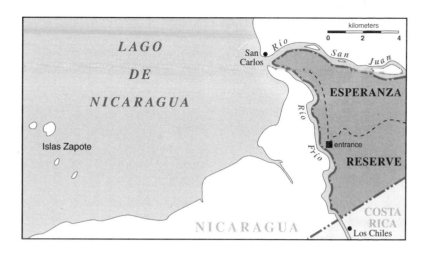

NICARAGUA

Although Nicaragua has undergone years of revolutionary war and strife, there are signs the country is returning to a more peaceful state since the elections of 1990. In addition, Nicaragua is now encouraging tourism and major airlines offer charter flights to Managua. All in all, this country may be a major tourist destination in future years if developments remain positive. If you want to beat the rush, now may be the time.

SAN CARLOS–ESPERANZA

A little-known back door to Nicaragua is via Los Chiles in north central Costa Rica to the small town of San Carlos on the southeastern shore of Lago de Nicaragua. Until a few years ago, this border crossing was closed, especially to foreigners. But now all you have to do is go through Costa Rican immigration in Los Chiles, hop on one of several daily public boats at the dock, go through the Nicaraguan control station at the border and continue on to San Carlos. There you will go through Nicaraguan immigration.

The trip costs about $7 per person and takes about 1.5 hours. A boat left Los Chiles at 8:30 a.m. when I took the trip, but check for current schedules when you get there. At the Nicaraguan consulate in San José, I was told Canadians need a visa to enter Nicaragua and that it costs $35. When I questioned them, they said it might be less expensive at border crossings. I crossed the border without a visa and there was a $7 charge in San Carlos.

If you go, you will see numerous water birds on the trip down the Río Frío and on the short expanse of Lago de Nicaragua that you cross to get to San Carlos. The sharp-eyed Oscar Rojas was with me and he was invaluable in pointing out all sorts of animal life along the river, as well as birds. He spotted a few **Limpkins** roosting in trees, which I could not really get a good look at as we passed by. But I did see **Anhingas, Olivaceous Cormorants, Ringed Kingfishers, Belted Kingfishers, Great Blue Herons, Great Egrets, Mangrove Swallows** and some beautifully patterned **Bare-necked Tiger-herons**.

The San Carlos region of Nicaragua has a long and colorful history. The town itself was ravaged by pirates several times in the mid-1700s, when they were on their way to sack the much-richer city of Granada. What was once a fairly prosperous town with neat and tidy streets and large, handsome wooden houses has been ravaged by fires and the recent long years of conflict with their accompanying conditions of impoverishment. The town now is a ramshackle collection of tin-roofed houses and huts, harboring about 7,000 people. But you can cash traveler's checks at the Banco Nacional, and the Leyko Cabinas, about four blocks west of the church, is a secure, clean, moderately priced place to stay.

A great place to bird near San Carlos is La Esperanza, which was once the 3,660 hectare (9,040 acre) farm/ranch of the Somosa family. This land is along the border of Costa Rica and the Río San Juan. It was purchased in 1994 by the non-profit organization, Cooperacion Austriaca, and then donated to the government. The conditions of the donation were that it be administered by a non-government organization whose objective is to use the land for conservation, education, research and eco-tourism, with strong involvement from local people. Since this land contains large tracts of primary lowland forest, a very scarce resource in adjacent Costa Rica, it could become a major birding as well as eco-tourism area in the near future.

Esperanza contains large areas of land subject to annual flooding, some pastures and crop land (most being allowed to revert to native vegetation) and areas of secondary and primary forest. Their present list of birds contains 176 species, but this is very preliminary and was compiled over a very short time. The region should harbor well over 250 to 300 species. Development plans for Esperanza include a modest research center and an equally small hotel for eco-tourists. Daily rates will likely be around $65–$85 per night, including three meals. When I visited in May 1996, there was no infrastructure and there probably won't be for a few years. I took day trips (about 20 minutes one way) to Esperanza from San Carlos for about $20 per day.

In the more open areas of Esperanza, I saw a few **Ruddy-breasted Seedeaters**, a species reported to be quite common in the area, as well as **Gray-crowned Yellowthroats, Common Ground-doves** and some of the more common flycatchers. One of the large trees left standing in a field held a raptor's nest, which may have been used by a pair of **Laughing Falcons**. One falcon flew by and perched on the opposite side of the tree from the nest and started calling. Its mate joined in soon after and they proceeded to duet for more than a minute, their calls rolling over the open field. I watched them closely through the telescope and admired their vivid markings, especially their black face masks. By the way, all the masks I've seen on **Laughing Falcons**, including those on museum specimens, are much broader than that illustrated in Stiles and Skutch (1989).

Roadside Hawks were very abundant in this area. An hour's birding in fairly open habitat yielded five or six. The open fields are also good places to see parrots, parakeets and water birds as they fly overhead. A flock of **Muscovy Ducks** was my high point in this regard.

Birding in second growth in Esperanza can vary from great to moderate, depending on weather conditions and bird activity. It wasn't great when I was there, but I did manage to see **Great Curassows, Slaty-tailed Trogons, Cinnamon Woodpeckers, Pale-billed Woodpeckers, Blue-black Grosbeaks** and **Black-faced Grosbeaks.** My best sightings in this habitat were a **White-winged Becard** and a **Yellow-billed Cuckoo.** The latter species may be sporadically common, but they are quite difficult to find. Most are in the area briefly only as migrants, on their way to and from major wintering areas in South America.

The only day I had to bird primary forest at Esperanza, we unfortunately picked a spot where there were no trails and my guide had to hack our way through some pretty heavy going. Between the commotion and the underbrush, we didn't see much. However, among stands of jungle are flat marshy areas, which can be nearly dry or contain water several feet deep, depending on the season.

These areas were just beginning to fill when I was there. Not only did they contain lots of water birds, they also harbored numerous raptors and seedeaters and were great for seeing ecotone species. Without moving more than 200 or 300 meters (650 or 1,000 feet), we saw **Limpkins, Muscovy Ducks, Black-bellied Whistling-ducks, Wood Storks,** a **Laughing Falcon,** three **Roadside Hawks,** a **Plumbeous Kite,** a **Black-shouldered Kite,** a small flock of **Gray-headed Chachalacas,** several flocks of **Crimson-fronted Parakeets** and **Orange-chinned Parakeets.** We also saw **Black-headed Trogons, Black-cheeked Woodpeckers, Hoffmann's Woodpeckers, Gray-crowned Yellowthroats, Montezuma Oropendolas,** lots of **Red-winged Blackbirds, Golden-hooded Tanagers,** nine species of flycatchers and many others. Birds were literally everywhere, and this was nearing midday.

Other good species reported on the property include **Slaty-breasted Tinamou, Reddish Egret, Lesser Yellow-headed Vulture, Bicolored Hawk, Crested Guan, Green-breasted Mango, Pale-billed Woodcreeper, Long-tailed Woodcreeper, Great Antshrike, Slaty Antshrike, White-flanked Antwren, Black-headed Tody-flycatcher** and **Rose-throated Becard.** Some rare sightings include **Barred Forest-falcon, Slaty-backed Forest-falcon** and even a **Crested Eagle.**

Esperanza at this time is not for the armchair birder. If you go, be prepared to get your feet—and possibly more—wet. As I mentioned, the area is just starting to be developed, so there is a lack of trails, *cabinas*, etc.

Because it's right on the border with Costa Rica, this is a region that was highly sensitive during the long years of conflict in Nicaragua. They are just starting to regain a sense of normalcy. A Nicaraguan border patrol accompanied us everywhere we went. They were nice fellows—some were even interested in birds—but birding with armed guards takes some getting used to. They are obviously going to have to change their policy when tourist traffic gets heavier.

If you want to bird Esperanza, contact Peter Kaltenegger in San Carlos (283-0354) or try the Managua office (266-8172). If you just show up, it may take a few days to make contact, since Peter also manages other projects in Nicaragua for Cooperacion Austriaca.

SOLENTINAME ISLANDS

The Solentiname Islands, located less than an hour away from San Carlos by fast launch, are other birding destinations. These islands have become a sort of mecca for poets, artists and writers, and the balsa wood carvings produced there are world renowned. It all started when a priest, himself a poet, founded a community on Mancarrón Island and helped develop the artistic talents of the local people.

One of the nearest islands to San Carlos is Isla de Zapote, which is a biological reserve because of the large numbers of nesting birds on the island. When I was there, I saw literally thousands of **Olivaceous Cormorants** balanced in what appeared to be precariously placed nests in many of the trees that lined the windward shore of the island. Many of the nests looked like little more than a few dry sticks wedged in forked branches, but some were fairly large platforms. Their strange grunts, often uttered when a mate was returning to a nest, were at first difficult to associate with a bird.

Scattered among the cormorants were nesting **Black-crowned Night-herons, White Ibises, Bare-throated Tiger-herons, Great Egrets** and a few **Wood Storks. Anhingas** were common, perched on the rocky shoreline of the lee side of the island. In the trees among the nesting birds were **Red-eyed Vireos, Great-crested Flycatchers** and several species of more common flycatchers and tanagers. A few **Yellow-green Vireos** were also present. The behavior of this species is unusual in that it winters in South America but comes to Central America to breed.

We also saw a **Yellow-headed Caracara**—probably scavenging dead nestlings on the island—and an **Osprey** as we were leaving. The whole trip cost about $35. If you want to go, talk to the people at the dock or inquire at the small shop in San Carlos that sells art from the Solentiname Islands; Griselda there was very helpful. Allow three to four hours for the trip.

LIST OF BIRDS SIGHTED IN ESPERANZA AND SOLENTINAME ISLANDS AREA
(a=abundant; c=common; u=uncommon; s=scarce; r= rare)

Species	Jan-Mar	Apr-Jun	Jul-Sep	Species	Jan-Mar	Apr-Jun	Jul-Sep
Olivaceous Cormorant	a			Amazon Kingfisher	c		
Anhinga	a			Green Kingfisher	c		
Bare-throated Tiger-heron	u			Black-cheeked Woodpecker	c		
Black-crowned Night-heron	c			Hoffmann's Woodpecker	c		
Green-backed Heron	a			Cinnamon Woodpecker	s		
Little Blue Heron	c			Pale-billed Woodpecker	u		
Snowy Egret	s			Barred Antshrike	u		
Great Egret	a			White-winged Becard	s		
Great Blue Heron	s			Masked Tityra	u		
Wood Stork	a			Tropical Kingbird	c		
White Ibis	c			Social Flycatcher	u		
Roseate Spoonbill	u			Great Kiskadee	c		
Black-bellied Whistling-duck	a			Brown-crested Flycatcher	u		
				Great-crested Flycatcher	s		
Muscovy Duck	c			Dusky-capped Flycatcher	u		
Turkey Vulture	c			Tropical Pewee	c		
Black Vulture	c			Yellow-bellied Elaenia	u		
Osprey	c			Southern Beardless Tyrannulet	r		
Black-shouldered Kite	c			Barn Swallow	c		
Plumbeous Kite	s			Northern Rough-winged Swallow	c		
Roadside Hawk	u			Mangrove Swallow	a		
Yellow-headed Caracara	u			Clay-colored Robin	c		
Laughing Falcon	c			Red-eyed Vireo	c		
Gray-headed Chachalaca	c			Yellow-green Vireo	u		
Great Curassow	u			Yellow Warbler	u		
Limpkin	u			Gray-crowned Yellowthroat	a		
Northern Jacana	c			Montezuma Oropendola	c		
Laughing Gull	c			Great-tailed Grackle	a		
Red-billed Pigeon	u			Red-winged Blackbird	a		
Short-billed Pigeon	c			Golden-hooded Tanager	s		
Common Ground-dove	s			Blue-gray Tanager	u		
Blue Ground-dove	u			Palm Tanager	u		
Crimson-fronted Parakeet	a			Scarlet-rumped Tanager	u		
Orange-chinned Parakeet	a			Black-faced Grosbeak	u		
Yellow-billed Cuckoo	r			Blue-black Grosbeak	u		
Squirrel Cuckoo	u			Yellow-faced Grassquit	c		
Groove-billed Ani	c			Variable Seedeater	c		
Common Pauraque	u			Ruddy-breasted Seedeater	c		
Slaty-tailed Trogon	c			Blue-black Grassquit	a		
Black-headed Trogon	c			Black-striped Sparrow	c		
Ringed Kingfisher	a			House Sparrow	c		
Belted Kingfisher	u						

APPENDIX I

DISTRIBUTION OF BIRDS IN COSTA RICA
(All lowland areas are <1,000 m (3,000 ft) in elevation)

Group	Main Area of Distribution.	Number of Species
1	Country-wide—except perhaps in the high mountains	275
2	Country-wide—except NW	101
3	Country-wide—except SW	8
4	Country-wide—except NE	0
5	Country-wide—except SE	1
6	Eastern lowlands —except dry areas south of Lago de Nicaragua	84
7	Northeastern Lowlands	9
8	Southeastern Lowlands	3
9	Western Lowlands	10
10	Northwestern Lowlands —includes dry areas south of Lago de Nicaragua	47
11	Southwestern Lowlands	39
12	Northern Lowlands	4
13	Southern Lowlands	5
14	Valle Central	4
15	Mountains—usually above 1,000 m (2–3,000 ft)	83
16	Highlands—greater than 1,700 m (5,000 ft)	40
17	Pacific Coast—oceanic	11
18	Both coasts—oceanic	4
19	Cocos Island	8
20	Northwest and Valle Central	15
21	Very rare, accidental, extinct in Costa Rica	75

*= species most commonly sighted during birding trips to Costa Rica; R=resident; M=migrant; WR=winter resident; SR=summer resident

GROUP 1
Countrywide-except perhaps in high mountains

Species	Comments
Little Tinimou	locally common; to 1,500 m
Pied-billed Grebe	uncommon; mainly in NW
Least Grebe	uncommon; lowlands to 1,500 m
*Brown Pelican	mostly coastal
*Olivaceous Cormorant	to 1,500 m
*Anhinga	lowlands
*Magnificent Frigatebird	mainly coastal
Pinnated Bittern	Tempisque, Río Frío, to 600 m
Least Bittern	uncommon; Tempisque, Río Frío, to 1,400 m
*Bare-throated Tiger-heron	lowlands to 1,100 m
*Black-crowned Night-heron	lowlands, rare in Valle Central

Species	Comments
Yellow-crowned Night-heron	uncommon; lowlands, large rivers
Boat-billed Heron	uncommon; lowlands to 300 m; Río Frío, Tortuguero, Tempisque
*Cattle Egret	abundant; to 2,000 m
*Green-backed Heron	abundant; to 1,800 m
*Little Blue Heron	abundant; lowlands to 1,500 m
Tricolored Heron	scarce; lowlands to 1,500 m mostly as WR
Reddish Egret	scarce; lowlands, uncommon
*Snowy Egret	common usually as WR; lowlands to 700 m
*Great Egret	abundant usually as WR; to mid-elevations
*Great Blue Heron	common; usually WR
*Wood Stork	locally common; Tempisque, Río Frío
*White Ibis	common; lowlands, Tempisque, Río Frío, Golfo de Nicoya
*Roseate Spoonbill	common on Pacific slope; scattered on Caribbean
Black-bellied Whistling-duck	widespread in lowlands; to Valle Central
Muscovy Duck	lowlands, uncommon
*Blue-winged Teal	lowlands mainly; common in Tempisque, Río Frío
Northern Shoveller	scarce; to mid-elevations, Tempisque mainly
Ring-necked Duck	locally common Tempisque, rare elsewhere
Lesser Scaup	uncommon; regular only in Tempisque
Masked Duck	scarce; Cartago, Tempisque
*Turkey Vulture	abundant
*Black Vulture	abundant
King Vulture	uncommon
*Osprey	M, WR, rare SR
Gray-headed Kite	lowlands to 2,500 m
Hook-billed Kite	lowlands to foothills, rare in Valle Central
*Black-shouldered Kite	lowlands to 1,500 m; especially common in NE
Snail Kite	locally common only in Río Frío, Tempisque
Double-toothed Kite	lowlands to 1,500 m, rare in NW
Plumbeous Kite	locally common R and M
Mississippi Kite	M mostly along E slope
Crane Hawk	uncommon; lowlands to 500 m
Northern Harrier	uncommon M, WR
Sharp-shinned Hawk	uncommon M, WR; mostly 500–2,500 m
Common Black-hawk	common, especially along coasts

Species	Comments
Great Black-hawk	scarce; to 1,200 m
Black-collared Hawk	scarce; locally common; Río Frío, Tempisque, Osa
Gray Hawk	most common in NW
*Roadside Hawk	common; to 2,000 m
*Broad-winged Hawk	abundant M, WR; to 1,200 m
Short-tailed Hawk	R, M and WR; uncommon
*Swainson's Hawk	abundant M, rare WR
Group-tailed Hawk	sporadic; foothills of Cordillera de Guanacaste
Ornate Hawk-eagle	scarce; usually to 1,500 m
*Crested Caracara	common in NW, increasing elsewhere
Laughing Falcon	fairly common; lowlands; rarely to 1,800 m
Collared Forest-falcon	scarce; lowlands to 1,500 m; most common in NW, especially Río Frío
American Kestrel	sporadic, M and WR
Merlin	uncommon fall M and WR; Río Frío, Valle Central
*Bat Falcon	uncommon; lowlands to 1,700 m; rare in NW
Peregrine Falcon	uncommon M, WR; Tempisque, Golfo de Nicoya, Tárcoles
Crested Guan	decreasing; forested lowlands; Santa Rosa
Great Currasow	lowlands to 1,200 m; decreasing; Santa Rosa
Limpkin	most abundant Tempisque, Río Frío, rare elsewhere
Spotted Rail	rarely seen; Tempisque, Río Frío, Cartago, Turrialba
Gray-necked Wood-rail	locally common to 1,400 m
Sora	locally common M, WR; Tempisque, Río Frío
Black Rail	Tempisque, Río Frío, Osa, elsewhere?
White-throated Crake	common, but rare in NW
Common Gallinule	sporadic; lowlands to 1,500 m
*Purple Gallinule	lowlands to 1,500 m
American Coot	mainly M, WR; to 1,500 m; common in Tempisque
*Northern Jacana	abundant; lowlands to 1,500 m
*American Oystercatcher	R on Pacific; M both coasts
*Black-necked Stilt	abundant; R in Golfo de Nicoya; M, WR both coasts
Lesser Golden-plover	scarce; M, WR, SR
*Black-bellied Plover	abundant M, WR, uncommon SR; less common E coast
*Semipalmated Plover	abundant M, WR; less common E coast
Wilson's Plover	uncommon; R Golfo de Nicoya; M, WR on both coasts
Killdeer	scarce but widespread M, WR; R in Cartago area
Collared Plover	uncommon R; lowlands
*Whimbrel	abundant M, WR; fairly common SR; scarce on E coast
Upland Sandpiper	uncommon M; mainly Valle Central, Pacific
Greater Yellowlegs	common M, WR, uncommon SR; lowlands to mid-elevations
Lesser Yellowlegs	common M, WR, rare SR

APPENDIX I

Species	Comments
Solitary Sandpiper	uncommon M, WR, SR to 2,000 m or 3,000 m during M
*Willet	abundant M, WR; common SR
*Spotted Sandpiper	abundant M, WR, rare SR
*Ruddy Turnstone	common M, WR, uncommon SR
Common Snipe	scarce M, WR; to 3,000 m during migration
*Short-billed Dowitcher	abundant M, WR, uncommon SR; scarce on E coast
Long-billed Dowitcher	scarce M, WR
Sanderling	common M, uncommon WR
*Western Sandpiper	abundant M, WR, locally common SR; to 1,500 m
*Semipalmated Sandpiper	abundant M, WR, occasional SR; less common E coast
*Least Sandpiper	locally common M, WR, rare SR; to 1,500 m; less common E coast
Baird's Sandpiper	uncommon M chiefly through Valle Central
Pectoral Sandpiper	locally common M to 1,600 m
Ring-billed Gull	uncommon coastal WR; scarce on E coast; increasing
Herring Gull	uncommon coastal WR; scarce on E coast; increasing
*Laughing Gull	locally abundant; coastal M, WR, SR; less common on E coast
Black Tern	abundant; coastal M, WR; Golfos de Nicoya, Dulce; rare SR
Gull-billed Tern	locally common M, WR, SR; coastal; scarce on E coast
Common Tern	common M, WR, SR both coasts
Bridled Tern	fairly common; coastal NW; breeds on islands; uncommon elsewhere
*Least Tern	sporadically common coastal M, uncommon WR, SR; scarce on E coast
*Royal Tern	common coastal year-round
*Sandwich Tern	common coastal M, WR, fairly common SR
Elegant Tern	uncommon coastal M, WR, very uncommon SR, rare on E coast
*Rock Dove	common in cities
Scaled Pigeon	locally common; lowlands, especially common Río Frío and lowlands to W
*Red-billed Pigeon	abundant; to 2,100 m
Mourning Dove	R in Valle Central, Cartago; M, WR abundant in NW
*Ruddy Ground-dove	abundant
*Blue Ground-dove	common; to 1,200 m; less common in NW
*Crimson-fronted Parakeet	common in deforested areas
*Orange-chinned Parakeet	abundant; to 1,200 m
Black-billed Cuckoo	scarce M
Yellow-billed Cuckoo	locally common but sporadic M, WR; especially in NW as WR
*Squirrel Cuckoo	common; lowlands to 2,500 m
Striped Cuckoo	increasing

Species	Comments
Common Barn-owl	lowlands to 1,850; most common in NW, Valle Central
Crested Owl	locally common; lowlands to 1,500
Spectacled Owl	common; to 1,500 m
Mottled Owl	uncommon; to 1,500 m; scarce in NW
Black-and-white Owl	uncommon; to 1,500 m
Common Potoo	uncommon; lowlands to 1,200 m
Common Nighthawk	uncommon R, M
Lesser Nighthawk	locally common R, M, WR
*Common Pauraque	common; to 1,700 m
Chuck-will's-widow	scarce M, WR
White-tailed Nightjar	locally common; scarce on E slope
*White-collared Swift	common R
*Vaux's Swift	common R
*Long-tailed Hermit	common to 100 m; usually restricted to gallery forest in NW
*Little Hermit	abundant to 1,500 m; only in gallery forest in NW
Scaly-breasted Hummingbird	locally common to 1,200 m; sporadic on E coast
Brown Violet-ear	uncommon; foothills
Blue-throated Goldentail	uncommon, but common in Río Frío
*Rufous-tailed Hummingbird	abundant; to 1,800 m; least common in NW
*Violaceous Trogon	fairly common to 1,200 m; uncommon in NW
*Ringed Kingfisher	fairly common to 900 m
*Belted Kingfisher	fairly common M, WR
*Amazon Kingfisher	common to 900 m
*Green Kingfisher	common to 1,200 m
American Pygmy Kingfisher	scarce; to 600 m
*Blue-crowned Motmot	common, but absent in Caribbean lowlands
White-necked Puffbird	scarce; to 600 m
*Lineated Woodpecker	common, increasing; to 1,100 m
*Pale-billed Woodpecker	decreasing; to 1,500 m
Ruddy Woodcreeper	uncommon ; most numerous in hills Peninsula de Nicoya
Olivaceous Woodcreeper	scarce; lowlands to 1,500 m
Barred Woodcreeper	uncommon; lowlands to 1,300 m
Buff-throated Woodcreeper	uncommon; lowlands to 900 m; uncommon in NW
Spotted Woodcreeper	scarce; most common in foothills 700–1,400 m
*Streaked-headed Woodcreeper	common; lowlands to 1,500 m
Brown-billed Scythebill	scarce; foothills 300-1,700 m; south from Cordillera de Tilarán
Plain Xenops	locally common; rare in NW where confined to gallery forest
*Barred Antshrike	common; lowlands to 1,400 m; uncommon in humid regions
Slaty Antwren	common; to 2,300 m; wetter forests

Species	Comments
Dusky Antbird	common; lowlands to 1,200 m; uncommon in S part of NW
White-winged Becard	locally common, to 1,200 m; uncommon in NW
*Masked Tityra	common; lowlands to 2,300 m
*Black-crowned Tityra	uncommon; lowlands to 1,200 m
Black Phoebe	uncommon; to 1,800 m
Eastern Kingbird	common M
*Tropical Kingbird	abundant; to 2,400 m
Piratic Flycatcher	common; to 1,800 m; arrives Jan, departs Sep–Oct
*Boat-billed Flycatcher	common; to 2,000 m
Bright-rumped Attila	uncommon; to 1,800 m
*Sulphur-bellied Flycatcher	locally common M; to 200 m
*Social Flycatcher	common; to 1,700 m
*Great Kiskadee	abundant, increasing; to 1,500 m
Great-crested Flycatcher	common M, common WR on Pacific; uncommon on Caribbean slope
*Dusky-capped Flycatcher	common; to 1,800 m
Olive-sided Flycatcher	common M, rare WR to 2,300 m
*Western Wood-pewee	abundant M; rare WR; mostly above 700 m
*Eastern Wood-pewee	abundant M; rare WR; mostly below 1,500 m
Yellow-bellied Flycatcher	scarce M; locally common WR, to 1,500 m
Acadian Flycatcher	common M; uncommon WR; most common on E slope
*Alder Flycatcher	abundant M; no definite WR; most common on E slope
Willow Flycatcher	common M; uncommon WR; mostly in Pacific lowlands
Sulphur-rumped Flycatcher	uncommon; lowlands to 1,200 m
Golden-crowned Spadebill	uncommon; to 1,200 m
Yellow-olive Flycatcher	locally common; to 1,400 m; less common on E slope
*Common Tody-flycatcher	common; lowlands to 1,100 m
Slate-headed Tody-flycatcher	uncommon, most abundant in SW; to 900 m
Northern Bentbill	uncommon; to 1,200 m; rare in NW
*Torrent Tyrannulet	locally common along streams south from Cordillera de Tilarán
*Yellow-bellied Elaenia	common; increasing; to 1,800 m
Mistletoe Tyrannulet	uncommon; to 3,000 m; but absent in extreme NW
Brown-capped Tyrannulet	scarce; lowlands of E slope to Tortuguero, south from foothills of Cordillera Central
Ochre-bellied Flycatcher	uncommon, scarce; to 1,200 m
Purple Martin	irregularly common M; most common on E slope
*Gray-breasted Martin	locally common; to 1,700 m
Cliff Swallow	common M; mostly coastal; rare WR
*Barn Swallow	abundant M; locally abundant WR
*Northern Rough-winged Swallow	common M, R, WR

Species	Comments
*Blue-and-white Swallow	common; 400–3,000 m; rare in NW
*Bank Swallow	abundant M; rare WR
Tree Swallow	irregularly common; to 1,500 m
*Mangrove Swallow	locally abundant; lowlands to 1,000 m
*Brown Jay	common in N; increasing in S
*Plain Wren	common; to 2,000 m
*House Wren	abundant; to 2,700 m
*Clay-colored Robin	abundant; to 2,400 m; less common in NW
Wood Thrush	locally common M, WR; to 1,700 m
*Swainson's Thrush	abundant M, rare WR
Gray-cheeked Thrush	uncommon fall M; casual WR
*Orange-billed Nightingale-thrush	locally common; 400–2,300 m; patchy distribution
*Tropical Gnatcatcher	common; to 1,500 m; rare in north NW
*Long-billed Gnatwren	uncommon; to 1,200 m; local in NW
Cedar Waxwing	sporadic M, WR
Rufous-browed Peppershrike	uncommon; patchy distribution
Green Shrike-vireo	locally common; lowlands to 1,000 m
*Yellow-throated Vireo	common M, WR; to 2,000 m
*Red-eyed Vireo	abundant M, to 1,300 m
*Yellow-green Vireo	abundant Pacific; scarce on Caribbean slope
*Philadelphia Vireo	common M, WR on Pacific slope; less numerous on Caribbean slope; to 1,600 m
*Lesser Greenlet	common; to 900 m
*Bananaquit	common; to 1,200 m
*Black-and-white Warbler	abundant M; uncommon WR
Prothonotary Warbler	common M, locally common WR, to 1,500 m
Worm-eating Warbler	uncommon, M, WR, to 1,500 m
Golden-winged Warbler	locally common M, uncommon WR; patchy distribution
Blue-winged Warbler	uncommon M, WR; lowlands
*Tennessee Warbler	abundant M, WR; most numerous in foothills
Tropical Parula	common; foothills 600–1,800 m
*Yellow Warbler	abundant M, WR; to 1,500 m
Magnolia Warbler	scarce M, WR; lowlands to 1,500 m
Yellow-rumped Warbler	uncommon M, WR, to 1,500 m
*Black-throated green Warbler	common M, WR in highlands, above 1,000 m
Blackburnian Warbler	uncommon M, WR
*Chestnut-sided Warbler	abundant M, WR; uncommon in NW; to 1,800 m
Bay-breasted Warbler	scarce M, WR; to 1,800 m
Palm Warbler	scarce M, rare WR; to 800 m
Ovenbird	uncommon M, WR, to 1,500 m
*Northern Waterthrush	common M, WR, to 1,500 m

Species	Comments
Louisiana Waterthrush	locally common M, WR; less common on Pacific coast
Kentucky Warbler	locally common M, WR; to 1,800 m
Mourning Warbler	uncommon M, WR, to 1,400 m
MacGillivray's Warbler	scarce M, WR; to 2,000 m
Common Yellowthroat	locally common M, WR; lowlands to foothills
*Gray-crowned Yellowthroat	common, increasing; to 1,500 m
Yellow-breasted Chat	uncommon M, WR
Hooded Warbler	very uncommon M, WR; to 1,200 m
*Wilson's Warbler	common M, WR; only migrant Warbler found regularly in *páramo*
Canada Warbler	common M, very rare WR
American Redstart	uncommon M, WR; to 1,500 m
Golden-crowned Warbler	uncommon; 300–2,100 m
Buff-rumped Warbler	common along streams; to 1,500 m
*Yellow-billed Cacique	locally common; rare in extreme dry NW
*Bronzed Cowbird	common; increasing
*Great-tailed Grackle	abundant in cleared land; increasing
*Orchard Oriole	common M, uncommon WR
*Northern Oriole	common M, WR; to 2,000 m
*Eastern Meadowlark	R, cleared land to 2,500 m; increasing
Bobolink	rare; fall M only
Dickcissel	common M; sporadically abundant WR in rice fields
*Silver-throated Tanager	locally common, 600–1,700 m; lowlands in wet season
*Red-legged Honeycreeper	common; to 1,200 m; decreasing
*Blue-gray Tanager	abundant, to 2,300 m
*Palm Tanager	common; to 1,500 m; scarce in NW
*Summer Tanager	common M, WR; to 2,500 m
Scarlet Tanager	locally common M; to 1,500 m
*Common Bush-tanager	abundant; wet forests 400–2,300 m
*Buff-throated Saltator	common except local in NW
*Rose-breasted Grosbeak	locally common M, WR; to 1,500 m
Blue-black Grosbeak	locally common; to 1,200 m
Indigo Bunting	scarce M, WR; to 1,500 m
White-collared Seedeater	common, expanding; to 1,500 m
*Blue-black Grassquit	common; to 1,700 m
*Rufous-collared Sparrow	abundant; mainly 600–3,000 m
*House Sparrow	common in cities

GROUP 2
Countrywide except NW slope

Species	Comments
*Great Tinimou	common; lowlands and foothills to 1,700 m
Chestnut-bellied Heron	scarce; only known breeding colony at Westfalia
*American Swallow-tailed Kite	common
Tiny Hawk	scarce; humid lowlands
Bicolored Hawk	uncommon; humid lowlands to 1,800 m
Black-chested Hawk	uncommon; usually 400–1,600 m on E slope, higher SW slope
White Hawk	uncommon; to 1,400 m, scarce in flat lowlands
Solitary Eagle	scarce; to 1,700 m; most common on E slope
Black-and-white Hawk-eagle	scarce; uncommon; lowlands usually to 1,000 m
Black Hawk-eagle	scarce; usually to 1,000 m, sometimes 2,000 m
Barred Forest-falcon	uncommon; lowlands to 1,800 m
*Grey-headed Chachalaca	fairly common; lowlands to 1,100 m
Uniform Crake	uncommon; lowlands to 1,000 m; rarely seen
Gray-breasted Crake	uncommon; lowlands
Sungrebe	fairly common; lowlands, quiet streams
Sunbittern	uncommon, decreasing, 100–1,200 m
Pale-vented Pigeon	uncommon; lowlands to 600 m
*Short-billed Pigeon	common; lowlands to 1,400 m
*Gray-chested Dove	common; to 1,200 m
Ruddy Quail-dove	uncommon; common; lowlands to 1,200 m
Brown-hooded Parrot	uncommon, decreasing; lowlands to 1,600 m
*White-crowned Parrot	abundant; to 1,600 m
Blue-headed Parrot	increasing; to 1,200 m
*Red-lored Parrot	common; increasing; to 1,000 m
Mealy Parrot	uncommon, decreasing; to 500 m
Vermiculated Screech-owl	locally common; to 1,100 m
Great Potoo	locally common; lowland wet forest
Short-tailed Nighthawk	common; lowlands to 1,000 m
Lesser Swallow-tailed Swift	common to 1,000 m
White-tipped Sicklebill	uncommon; to 1,200 m
*Bronzy Hermit	locally common; to 700 m
*Band-tailed Barbthroat	common; to 1,200 m
White-necked Jacobin	uncommon; to 700 m
Violet-headed Hummingbird	uncommon; to 1,000 m
*Crowned Woodnymph	common; lowlands to 1,200 m
*Purple-crowned	fairly common; lowlands to 1,700 m
Long-billed Starthroat	common only in SW; lowlands to 1,200 m
*Slaty-tailed Trogon	common; lowlands to 1,200 m
Black-throated Trogon	common; lowlands; strays in NW
*Rufous-tailed Jacamar	fairly common; lowlands to 700 m, rarely to 1,200 m

Species	Comments
White-whiskered Puffbird	uncommon; to 1,200 m
Red-headed Barbet	uncommon; foothills 300–1,600 m; from Cordillera de Tilarán south
*Chestnut-mandibled Toucan	common; lowlands to 1,800 m
Smoky-brown Woodpecker	locally common; to 1,800 m; absent in wet SW
Rufous-winged Woodpecker	locally common; to 900 m
Long-tailed Woodcreeper	uncommon to rare; foothills 400–1,300 m
*Wedge-billed Woodcreeper	common; lowlands to 1,500 m
Black-striped Woodcreeper	scarce; lowlands to 1,200 m
*Slaty Spinetail	common; lowlands to 1,500 m
Striped Foliage-gleaner	scarce; lowlands to 600 m
Buff-throated Foliage-gleaner	common; lowlands to 1,200 m
Scaly-throated Leaftosser	uncommon
Great Antshrike	locally common; lowlands to 1,000 m
Russet Antshrike	locally common; higher lowlands and foothills
Dotted-winged Antwren	uncommon; lowlands to 1,000 m
Bare-crowned Antbird	scarce; lowlands to 1,200 m
*Chestnut-backed Antbird	common; lowlands to 900 m
Immaculate Antbird	locally common; foothills 300–1,700 m
Bicolored Antbird	scarce; lowlands to 1,700 m
Black-faced Antthrush	scarce; lowlands to 1,500 m
Spectacled Antpitta	locally common; foothills to 1,200 m
Cinnamon Becard	uncommon; lowlands to 700 m; less common in SW
Rufous Piha	uncommon; lowlands 1,200 m
Speckled Mourner	rare, wet lowlands and foothills to 700 m
*Red-capped Manakin	common lowlands to 1,000 m
White-ruffed Manakin	locally common; 400–1,500 m
Thrushlike Manakin	scarce; to 1,700 m; very uncommon in lowlands
*Gray-capped Flycatcher	locally common; to 1,600 m
Rufous Mourner	uncommon; to 1,200 m; absent in Valle Central
*Tropical Pewee	common; to 1,500 m; rare in mangroves in NW
Ruddy-tailed Flycatcher	scarce; wet lowlands to 1,200 m
Eye-ringed Flatbill	scarce; lowlands to 2,100 m
Scale-crested Pygmy-tyrant	common; foothills, 300–1,700 m
Yellow Tyrannulet	locally common; lowlands to 1,200 m
Slaty-capped Flycatcher	scarce; foothills
*Southern Rough-winged Swallow	abundant
White-breasted Wood-wren	common; lowlands to 1,800 m; rare in lowlands of SW
Gray Catbird	scarce; M, WR; patchy distribution
Tawny-crowned Greenlet	scarce; to 1,200 m
Chestnut-headed Oropendola	locally common especially in foothills
*Scarlet-rumped Cacique	uncommon; lowlands to 1,100 m
Giant Cowbird	scarce; lowlands to 1,700 m

Species	Comments
White-vented Euphonia	scarce; to 1,500 m
*Yellow-crowned Euphonia	common; to 1,200 m
Speckled Tanager	locally common; foothills, 400–1,400 m
*Golden-hooded Tanager	common; to 1,500 m
Bay-headed Tanager	uncommon; 600–1,500 m; lower in wet season
*Green Honeycreeper	uncommon; to 1,200 m
Shining Honeycreeper	locally common; to 1,200 m
Blue Dacnis	locally common; to 900 m
*Scarlet-thighed Dacnis	locally common; 500–1,500 m; lower in wet season
*Scarlet-rumped Tanager	abundant, to 1,700 m; in humid areas in NW
*Hepatic Tanager	uncommon; to 1,700 m; also on slopes above 1,100 m of Cordillera de Guanacaste
White-throated Shrike-tanager	scarce; to 700 m
White-lined Tanager	locally common; to 1,400 m
White-shouldered Tanager	locally common; to 700 m
*Yellow-faced Grassquit	common in clearings; to 2,000 m
*Variable Seedeater	abundant; absent in Valle Central; to 1,500 m
Thick-billed Seed-finch	common; to 1,100 m
*Orange-billed Sparrow	common; to 1,200 m
*Black-striped Sparrow	common; to 1,500 m

GROUP 3
Countrywide except SW slope

Species	Comments
Violaceous Quail-dove	scarce; lowlands to 1,200 m
*Collared Aracari	common; lowlands to 1,200 m; rare in dry NW
*Keel-billed Toucan	common; lowlands to 1,200 m; uncommon in NW
Spotted Antbird	locally common; lowlands to 1,200 m; 600–750 m in extreme NW
*Groove-billed Ani	lowlands to 2,300 m
Black-headed Nightingale-thrush	common foothills; 300–1,300 m
*Montezuma Oropendola	common; to 800 m; scarce in NW
Blue Grosbeak	local R in NW; uncommon M, WR on E slope

GROUP 5
Countrywide except SE slope

Species	Comments
Fork-tailed Emerald	uncommon; lowlands to 1,500 m

GROUP 6
Eastern Lowlands (except dry areas S of Lago de Nicaragua)

Species	Comments
Rufescent Tiger-heron	scarce; lowlands to 500 m
Fasciated Tiger-heron	scarce; foothills, 200–800 m, mountain streams to 2,400 m with trout
Green Ibis	uncommon; lowlands, also Río Frío

Species	Comments
Semiplumbeous Hawk	locally common; lowlands to 800 m
Slaty-backed Forest-falcon	uncommon; lowlands
Rufous-fronted Wood-quail	locally common; to 1,000 m
Purplish-backed Quail-dove	locally common; 400–1,000 m
Olive-backed Quail-dove	uncommon; forested lowlands to 400 m
Great Green Macaw	decreasing, scarce; lowlands to 600 m
Olive-throated Parakeet	decreasing; to 700 m; scarce in SE
Red-fronted Parrotlet	extensive altitudinal movements; uncommon
Rufous-vented Ground-cuckoo	scarce; lowlands to 900 m
Least Pygmy-owl	locally common; to 800 m
Chimney Swift	abundant M; usually near coast
*Gray-rumped Swift	common R; to 600 m
Black-crested Coquette	scarce; foothills 300–1,200 m; occasional in Valle Central
Green Thorntail	scarce; foothills 700–1,400 m
Blue-chested Hummingbird	locally common; to 500 m
Black-bellied Hummingbird	scarce; slopes 600–2,000 m
Snowcap	scarce; slopes 300–1,000 m
Red-footed Plumeleteer	uncommon; lowlands to 700 m
White-bellied Mountain-gem	locally common; slopes 700–1,400 m; absent in extreme N
Lattice-tailed Trogon	locally common; N to Volcan Miravalles; 100–1,100 m
Green-and-rufous Kingfisher	scarce; lowlands
*Broad-billed Motmot	fairly common; lowlands to 1,500 m
*Rufous Motmot	common; lowlands to 1,400 m
Great Jacamar	very scarce; lowlands to 500 m
Pied Puffbird	scarce; lowland forest to 300 m
Lanceolated Monklet	fairly rare; foothills 400–1,300 m; from Cordillera Central south
White-fronted Nunbird	uncommon; to 700 m
*Yellow-eared Toucanet	locally common; foothills 300–1,200 m
*Black-cheeked Woodpecker	abundant in forest; to 900 m
Chestnut-colored Woodpecker	scarce; to 700 m
*Cinnamon Woodpecker	locally common; to 700 m
*Plain-brown Woodcreeper	locally common; to 700 m
Fasciated Antshrike	locally common; lowlands to 1,200 m
Slaty Antshrike	uncommon; lowlands to 1,000 m
Checker-throated Antwren	uncommon; lowlands to 700 m
*White-flanked Antwren	locally common; lowlands to 700 m
Rufous-rumped Antwren	scarce; 750–1,100 m; from S end Cordillera de Tilarán
Dull-mantled Antbird	locally common; only in 300–1,000 m zone
Ocellated Antbird	scarce; lowlands to 1,200 m
Black-headed Antthrush	locally common; foothills 400–1,200 m

Species	Comments
Rufous-breasted Antthrush	locally common; 800–1,800 m
Black-crowned Antpitta	locally common; 300–1,000 m; south from Cordillera de Tilarán
Fulvous-bellied Antpitta	common but seldom seen; lowlands to 900 m
Lovely Cotinga	rare, decreasing; usually 300–1,700 m
Snowy Cotinga	scarce; lowlands to 700 m
Purple-throated Fruitcrow	locally common; lowlands to 600 m
Bare-necked Umbrellabird	scarce; lowlands to 2,000 m
*White-collared Manakin	common; to 700 m
Gray-headed Manakin	scarce; to 750 m; most common in N
*Long-tailed Tyrant	common; to 600 m
*White-ringed Flycatcher	locally common; to 600 m
Yellow-margined Flycatcher	common; to 1,000 m
Black-headed Tody-flycatcher	uncommon; lowlands to 700 m
Black-capped Pygmy-tyrant	uncommon; lowlands to 600 m
*Banded-backed Wren	common; lowlands to 1,700 m
Striped-breasted Wren	uncommon; to 1,000 m
*Bay Wren	common; to 1,000 m
Black-throated Wren	locally common; to 1,100 m
Song Wren	scarce; lowlands to 1,000 m
Veery	uncommon M; rare in spring, no winter records.
Tawny-faced Gnatwren	locally common; to 1,200 m
Cerulean Warbler	sporadically common M, to 500 m
*Olive-crowned Yellowthroat	common; lowlands to 1,000 m
*Black-cowled Oriole	common; to 700 m
Yellow-tailed Oriole	uncommon; lowlands to 300 m
*Tawny-capped Euphonia	common; 600-1,700 m
*Olive-backed Euphonia	common; to 700 m
*Emerald Tanager	locally common; foothills, 300–1,100 m
Plain-coloured Tanager	scarce; from La Selva south
Rufous-winged Tanager	scarce; 200–700 m; lower in wet season
*Crimson-collared Tanager	locally common; to 1,100 m
Olive Tanager	uncommon; to 1,000 m
Red-throated Ant-thrush	uncommon; to 600 m
*Tawny-crested Tanager	common; to 1,000 m
Dusky-faced Tanager	uncommon; to 600 m
Black-and-yellow Tanager	locally common; foothills 600–1,200 m
*Black-headed Saltator	common; to 1,300 m
*Black-faced Grosbeak	locally common; to 900 m
Slate-colored Grosbeak	scarce; to 1,200 m
Pink-billed Seed-finch	scarce; to 900 m
Sooty-faced Finch	locally common especially in SE; 600-1,500 m; also in Dota

APPENDIX I

GROUP 7
Northeastern Lowlands

Species	Comments
Slaty-breasted Tinimou	uncommon; lowlands to 700m
*Coppery-headed Emerald	common; slopes 300–1,500 m
Keel-billed Motmot	scarce; foothills Cordillera Guanacaste, Tilarán; 300–900 m
Streaked-crowned Antvireo	uncommon; lowlands to 800 m
Tawny-chested Flycatcher	locally common; lowlands to 800 m
Sepia-capped Flycatcher	rare; also in Terraba–Coto Brus area
Nightingale Wren	locally common; lowlands to 1,400 m
*Blue-and-gold Tanager	locally common; foothills 400–1,200 m
Ashy-throated Bush-tanager	uncommon; patchy distribution; 400–1,200 m from Poas to Turrialba

GROUP 8
Southeastern Lowlands

Spotted-crowned Antvireo	lowlands to 800 m; only common near Panama border
Black-chested Jay	very local in extreme SE; north to Río Estrella
Sulphur-rumped Tanager	uncommon; to 700 m

GROUP 9
Western Lowlands

Lesser Yellow-headed Vulture	common only in Río Frío
White-tailed Hawk	very uncommon; foothills of Cordillera de Guanacaste
*Marbled Godwit	common M, WR, rare SR
Wandering Tattler	common M, uncommon WR, SR; mainly offshore islands
Surfbird	uncommon M outer coast; WR occasional Golfo de Nicoya
*Red Knot	common M, WR in Golfo de Nicoya, uncommon elsewhere
*Stilt Sandpiper	common M; locally common WR Golfo de Nicoya
*Wilson's Phalarope	common M, rare WR, SR Golfo de Nicoya; scarce elsewhere
Pomarine Jaeger	very uncommon; Golfo de Nicoya, Dulce
Parasitic Jaeger	rare in Golfo de Nicoya, more common offshore
Franklin's Gull	common coastal M, uncommon WR, rare SR
*Black Skimmer	common M, WR, rare SR
*Plain-breasted Ground-dove	locally common; Río Frío, savannas of Térraba, Coto
*White-tipped Dove	common
Gray-fronted Dove	uncommon; to 1,000 m
*Scarlet Macaw	decreasing, scarce in NW; more common Carara, Osa
Mangrove Cuckoo	scarce WR, may breed in NW
Pheasant Cuckoo	scarce; lowlands to 800 m

Species	Comments
Striped Owl	increasing, locally common; to 1,400 m
Whip-poor-will	casual WR; to 1,200 m
Black Swift	common R, M
Mangrove Hummingbird	scarce; restricted to mangroves
Olivaceous Piculet	scarce; to 1,400 m
*Fork-tailed Flycatcher	common in Térraba–Golfo Dulce region
Western Kingbird	sporadic WR south to Térraba
*Streaked Flycatcher	common M
*Panama Flycatcher	common only in mangroves
Royal Flycatcher	scarce; to 700 m; rarely on Caribbean slope
Greenish Elaenia	locally common; to 1,500 m; least common in extreme SW
Lesser Elaenia	uncommon; disjunct populations
Yellow-bellied Tyrannulet	uncommon; disjunct distribution
Violet-green Swallow	sporadic; uncommon M, WR; to 1,200 m
Rufous-and-white Wren	uncommon; increasing southward; to 1,100 m
Rufous-breasted Wren	common in SW; decreasing northward
Mangrove Warbler	common in mangroves; small populations near Limón
*Rufous-capped Warbler	common; to 1,200 m
Red-crowned Ant-tanager	uncommon; mainly in foothills
*Gray-headed Tanager	locally common; rarer in dry NW; to 1,200 m
Painted Bunting	scarce M, WR; mainly in Tempisque, Térraba
Ruddy-breasted Seedeater	locally common; disjunct distributions, Térraba, Río Frío, Coto

GROUP 10
Northwestern Lowlands (includes dry areas S of Lago de Nicaragua E to Caño Negro)

Species	Comments
*Thicket Tinimou	common
*Jabiru	uncommon; breeds only in Tempisque, visits Río Frío
Glossy Ibis	scarce; Tempisque
Fulvous Whistling-duck	Tempisque only, increasing
American Wigeon	uncommon but regular, Tempisque
Northern Pintail	sporadic, Tempisque
Cinnamon Teal	casual, Tempisque only
Bay-winged Hawk	locally common Tempisque
*Plain Chachalaca	most common in hills of Peninsula de Nicoya
Rufous-necked Wood-rail	locally common; mangroves of Golfo de Nicoya
Yellow-breasted Crake	Tempisque, Río Frío, elsewhere in Costa Rica? seldom seen
*Double-striped Thick-knee	common in open pastures and savannas
Caspian Tern	uncommon year-round; Golfo de Nicoya
Forster's Tern	casual coastal WR, Golfo de Nicoya
*White-winged Dove	common; strays to Valle Central

Species	Comments
*White-fronted Parrot	common; to 1,100 m
Yellow-naped Parrot	uncommon, decreasing
Ocellated Poorwill	restricted to small colony near Brasilia
Green-breasted Mango	spreading, scattered sightings in NE
Ruby-throated Hummingbird	uncommon WR; very rare elsewhere
*Black-headed Trogon	common; lowlands; strays in SW and Valle Central
Elegant Trogon	scarce; to 700 m
Tody Motmot	very uncommon; 500–1,000 m
*Turquoise-browed Motmot	common; lowlands to 800 m
Ivory-billed Woodcreeper	uncommon; most common in higher foothills 400–900 m
Rose-throated Becard	locally common; to 300 m; scattered records elsewhere
*Brown-crested Flycatcher	common; to 900 m
*Nutting's Flycatcher	locally common; to 1,200 m
Stub-tailed Spadebill	scarce; lowlands to 1,300 m
Scrub Flycatcher	locally common only around Golfo de Nicoya; rarely in mangroves in SW
Northern Beardless-tyrannulet	scarce; to 800 m; common Río Frío
*White-throated Magpie-jay	abundant; to 1,200 m
*Rufous-naped Wren	abundant; to 800 m
Spotted-breasted Wren	very local; Río Frío west to Upala, Canalete; to 200 m
Rock Wren	locally common on west slope of Cordillera de Guanacaste only
White-lored Gnatcatcher	common; to 700 m; scarce in S part of range
Mangrove Vireo	locally common in mangroves
Nicaraguan Grackle	locally common only in Río Frío
Spotted-breasted Oriole	uncommon; to 500 m
*Streaked-backed Oriole	locally common; to 400 m
Yellow-headed Blackbird	casual WR
Scrub Euphonia	locally common; to 1,100 m
*Yellow-throated Euphonia	locally common; rare in SW
Western Tanager	scarce WR; rare in Valle Central and SW
*Striped-headed Sparrow	common; to 800 m
Rusty Sparrow	scarce R; 600–900 m
Botteri's Sparrow	rare, local; 400-1,100 m

GROUP 11
Southwestern Lowlands

Red-throated Caracara	decreasing, regular only in Golfo Dulce lowlands
*Yellow-headed Caracara	common; expanding range rapidly
Crested Bobwhite	invader from Panama; increasing
Marbled Wood-quail	uncommon; forested lowlands; Golfo Dulce
*Smooth-billed Ani	abundant, increasing; some sightings N to Cañas

Species	Comments
*Band-rumped Swift	abundant R; to 1,200 m
White-crested Coquette	scarce; foothills 300–1,200 m; occasional in SE
Beryl-crowned Hummingbird	locally common; to 1,200 m
Snowy-bellied Hummingbird	scarce; foothills 300–1,600 m; absent lowlands
White-tailed Emerald	common; slopes 750–2,000 m
*Baird's Trogon	fairly common; to 1,200 m
*Fiery-billed Aracari	abundant; lowlands to 1,500 m
*Golden-naped Woodpecker	common in forest; to 1,500 m
*Red-crowned Woodpecker	abundant, expanding because of deforestation
Tawny-winged Woodcreeper	uncommon; to 1,500 m
Pale-breasted Spinetail	increasing; common in savannas
Ruddy Foliage-gleaner	locally common in Coto Brus valley
*Black-hooded Antshrike	common; lowlands to 1,100 m
Turquoise Cotinga	scarce; lowlands to 1,800 m
Yellow-billed Cotinga	uncommon; mainly in mangroves
Lance-tailed Manakin	locally common only in Coto Brus
*Orange-collared Manakin	common; to 1,100 m
Black-tailed Flycatcher	scarce; to 900 m
Bran-colored Flycatcher	very local, most common General-Térraba; 900–1,200 m
Southern Beardless-tyrannulet	scarce; to 700 m; rarely in gallery forest of Tempisque
Yellow-crowned Tyrannulet	uncommon, increasing
*Riverside Wren	locally common; to 1,200 m
Black-bellied Wren	locally common north to Térraba valley; rare northward
Scrub Greenlet	uncomon; to 900 m
Masked Yellowthroat	locally common R near San Vito; 900–1,200 m
*Red-breasted Blackbird	increasing; most common south of Palmar Norte
Thick-billed Euphonia	uncommon
Spotted-crowned Euphonia	locally common; to 1,400 m
Black-cheeked Ant-tanager	locally common; only in lowlands around Osa, Golfito
Rosy Thrush-tanager	very local, uncommon; General, Térraba, Coto Brus, Coto
*Streaked Saltator	increasing; scattered records in SE
Yellow-bellied Seedeater	nomadic or permanent R; patchy distribution
Black-headed Brush-finch	locally common; foothills, 300–1,200 m
Wedge-tailed Grass-finch	scarce, local; Térraba

GROUP 12
Northern Lowlands

Species	Comments
Tawny-faced Quail	uncommon? low foothills
*Hoffman's Woodpecker	expanding because of deforestation
*Grayish Saltator	increasing from Valle Central
*Red-winged Blackbird	common, increasing

GROUP 13
Southern Lowlands

Rufous Nightjar	uncommon; to 1,000 m
Red-rumped Woodpecker	uncommon; only near Panama border
Blue-crowned Manakin	common in SW; to 1,300 m; only in extreme SE near Panama border
Whistling Wren	fairly common; wet lowlands to 1,700 m
Slate-colored Seedeater	nomadic, increasing; to 1,000 m

GROUP 14
Valle Central

Species	Comments
Buff-breasted Sandpiper	very uncommon M, fall only
*White-throated Flycatcher	locally common only in Valle de Guarco
*Sedge Wren	locally abundant near Cartago, Ochomogo
Prevost's Ground-sparrow	locally common; 600–1,600 m

GROUP 15
Mountains—between 800–1,000 m and 1,600–2,000 m (2,500–3,000 and 5,000–6,000 ft)

Highland Tinimou	uncommon
Red-tailed Hawk	uncommon R; some M at lower elevations
Black Guan	uncommon
Spotted Wood-quail	uncommon
Buffy-crowned Wood-partridge	uncommon
Black-breasted Wood-quail	rare or absent in SW mountains
*Band-tailed Pigeon	abundant
Ruddy Pigeon	widespread uncommon; breeds above 1,500 m
Maroon-chested Ground-dove	infrequent sightings; nomadic
Buff-fronted Quail-dove	uncommon; wet forests
Chiriquí Quail-dove	foothills to mountains 600–2,500 m; drier forests
*Sulfur-winged Parakeet	only in Talamancas; 750–3,000 m
Barred Parakeet	most abundant in Talamancas; 750–3,000 m
Tropical Screech-owl	foothills to 1,500 m; from Cordillera de Tilarán south
Bare-shanked Screech-owl	uncommon; above 900 m to timberline
Andean Pygmy-owl	locally common; south from Cordillera Central
White-chinned Swift	uncommon R?
Spot-fronted Swift	uncommon R?; absent from E slope?

Species	Comments
*Chestnut-collared Swift	common R; may forage to sea level
*Green Hermit	common
Green-fronted Lancebill	scarce; most common on wet Caribbean slope
*Violet Sabrewing	common; may descend to 400 m after breeding
*Green-crowned Brilliant	common; mostly on Caribbean slope
Striped-tailed Hummingbird	common; breeds 800–2,000 m
*Purple-throated Mountain-gem	locally common; absent from most of Talamancas
Magenta-throated Woodstar	locally common; W slope
Scintillant Hummingbird	locally common; mostly on Pacific slopes
*Resplendent Quetzal	common; over 1,200
Collared Trogon	common
Orange-bellied Trogon	uncommon; above 700 m in N; higher and rarer in S
Prong-billed Barbet	common; to 2,500 m; from Cordillera de Tilarán south
*Emerald Toucanet	common
*Acorn Woodpecker	locally common; from Cordillera Central south
Yellow-bellied Sapsucker	scarce M, WR
Golden-olive Woodpecker	uncommon; most abundant south of Cordillera de Tilarán
Black-banded Woodcreeper	uncommon; south from NE Cordillera Central; 900–2,000 m
*Spotted-crowned Woodcreeper	locally common; 1,000 m to timberline
Strong-billed Woodcreeper	scarce
Red-faced Spinetail	uncommon
Spotted Barbtail	uncommon
Lineated Foliage-gleaner	uncommon; 600–2,300 m
Spectacled Foliage-gleaner	scarce; 800–2,000 m
Buff-fronted Foliage-gleaner	uncommon; 800–2,500 m
Streaked-breasted Treehunter	scarce; 700–2,500 m; rarely 3,000 m
Tawny-throated Leaftosser	scarce; 700–1,800 m
Gray-throated Leaftosser	scarce; 600–1,500 m; not reported from Talamancas
Streaked Xenops	uncommon; 800–2,400 m; from E side Cordillera Central south
Plain Antvireo	uncommon; 700–2,500 m; wet forests
Scaled Antpitta	scarce; not reported on SW slopes of Talamancas
Ochre-breasted Antpitta	scarce; 700–1,300 m
Silvery-fronted Tapaculo	locally common; from 1,000 m to timberline
Black-and-white Becard	uncommon; mainly on E slope
*Three-wattled Bellbird	fairly common; lower elevations Jul-Dec
Sharpbill	scarce; lower elevations after breeding
White-crowned Manakin	uncommon; south from Cordillera Central
Dark Pewee	scarce; south from Cordillera de Tilarán
Golden-bellied Flycatcher	scarce; 700–2,300 m

Species	Comments
Yellowish Flycatcher	uncommon; 800–2,400 m
*Tufted Flycatcher	common; rarely down to 400 m
White-throated Spadebill	locally common; 700–2,100 m
Rufous-browed Tyrannulet	locally common in Cordillera Central; scarce elsewhere
*Mountain Elaenia	common
Zeledon's Tyrannulet	scarce; most common on Caribbean slope
Olive-striped Flycatcher	uncommon
Azure-hooded Jay	uncommon; absent in Cordillera de Guanacaste
American Dipper	locally common
Ochraceous Wren	locally common; south from Cordillera de Tilarán
*Gray-breasted Wood-wren	common
*White-throated Robin	common on Pacific slope; uncommon on Caribbean slope
*Pale-vented Robin	lower in non-breeding season; east slope only
*Mountain Robin	common
Black-faced Solitaire	scarce; lower after breeding
Slaty-backed Nightingale-thrush	uncommon
*Slate-throated Redstart	common
Three-striped Warbler	uncommon
*Golden-browed Chlorophonia	common; lower in wet season
Blue-hooded Euphonia	uncommon; breeds on Pacific slope; mostly on Caribbean slope thereafter
*Spangled-cheeked Tanager	uncommon; 1,200–2,700 m
*White-winged Tanager	uncommon
*Yellow-throated Brush-finch	common, especially in upper reaches of Valle Central
Chestnut-capped Brush-finch	uncommon
White-eared Ground-sparrow	uncommon; not found in Talamancas
Lincoln's Sparrow	very uncommon fall M, WR; mainly in western highlands, Valle Central

GROUP 16
Highlands—greater than 1,600–2,000 m

Unspotted Saw-whet Owl	uncommon; from Cordillera Central south
Dusky Nightjar	locally common R; from Cordillera Central south
Green Violet-ear	uncommon; from Cordillera de Tilarán south
*Fiery-throated Hummingbird	abundant
Gray-tailed Mountain-gem	uncommon; oak forests of Talamancas only
*Magnificent Hummingbird	common
*Volcano Hummingbird	abundant
*Hairy Woodpecker	common
Ruddy Treerunner	uncommon; but lower in Cordillera de Guanacaste
*Buffy Tuftedcheek	locally common

Species	Comments
Barred Becard	scarce; most common south of Cordillera de Tilarán
Ochraceous Pewee	scarce
*Black-capped Flycatcher	common
Silvery-throated Jay	scarce; south from south end Cordillera Central
Timberline Wren	common; mostly above timberline
*Sooty Robin	abundant; south from Cordillera Central
*Ruddy-capped Nightingale-thrush	locally common
*Black-billed Nightingale-thrush	abundant; uncommon in *páramo*
*Long-tailed Silky-flycatcher	common
*Black-and-yellow Silky-flycatcher	locally common; usually above 1,200 m
Yellow-winged Vireo	uncommon
Brown-capped Vireo	scarce
*Flame-throated Warbler	common
Hermit Warbler	casual WR
Townsend's Warbler	rare but regular M, WR; above 1,300 m
*Collared Redstart	common
Black-cheeked Warbler	widespread but uncommon
Zeledonia	common, but rarely seen
Flame-colored Tanager	locally common
*Sooty-capped Bush-tanager	abundant; also in *páramo*
Black-thighed Grosbeak	locally common
Blue Seedeater	scarce
Slaty Finch	scarce to rare
Peg-billed Finch	locally common
*Slaty flowerpiercer	common; also in *páramo*
*Large-footed Finch	abundant; from 2,100 m into *páramo*
*Yellow-thighed Finch	common; lower after breeding
*Volcano Junco	locally common; especially in *páramo*
Lesser Goldfinch	scarce; upper slopes of Valle Central and SW Talamancas
Yellow-bellied Siskin	scarce, nomadic; south from Cordillera Central

GROUP 17
Pacific Coast—Oceanic

Wedge-tailed Shearwater	sporadic in Golfo de Nicoya
Sooty Shearwater	sporadic in Golfo de Nicoya
Least Storm-petrel	common WR, Golfo de Nicoya, Dec–Jun
Wedge-rumped Storm-petrel	regular offshore, Jul–Nov
Leach's Storm-petrel	uncommon offshore, rare inshore, Golfo de Nicoya
Black Storm-petrel	uncommon offshore, concentrations of WR in Golfo de Nicoya
Red-billed Tropicbird	uncommon; possibly Caribbean as well
Blue-footed Booby	irregular, uncommon; Golfo de Nicoya

APPENDIX I

Species	Comments
Red Phalarope	scattered records
Red-necked Phalarope	common fall M, scarce spring M; occasionally inshore
Sabine's Gull	moderately common M; rarely Golfos de Nicoya, Dulce

GROUP 18
Both Coasts—Oceanic

Audubon's Shearwater	uncommon; sporadically in Golfo de Nicoya
Wilson's Storm-petrel	infrequently in Golfo de Nicoya, Apr–Aug
Brown Booby	locally common breeding resident
Masked Booby	uncommon visitor

GROUP 19
Cocos Island

Red-footed Booby	breeds on Cocos Island
Great Frigatebird	abundant breeder
Brown Noddy	breeds sporadically
Black Noddy	breeds regularly
White Tern	breeds regularly
Cocos Cuckoo	
Cocos Flycatcher	common
Cocos Finch	common

GROUP 20
Northwest Lowlands and Valle Central

Spotted-bellied Bobwhite	locally common
*Common Ground-dove	common
*Inca Dove	abundant, increasing
*Orange-fronted Parakeet	decreasing; to 1,000 m
Lesser Ground-cuckoo	scarce
Pacific Screech-owl	common; lowlands to 1,000 m
*Ferruginous Pygmy-owl	common; to 1,500 m
*Steely-vented Hummingbird	common; lowlands to 1,800 m
Cinnamon Hummingbird	locally common; lowlands to 1,000 m
Plain-capped Starthroat	locally common; rarely in SW
*Long-tailed Manakin	locally common; lowlands to 1,500 m
*Scissor-tailed Flycatcher	abundant; uncommon in Valle Central
*Banded Wren	locally common in dry lowlands, to 800 m
Olive Sparrow	scarce; to 900 m
Grasshopper Sparrow	scarce R and WR; patchy distribution

GROUP 21
very rare, accidental, extinct in Costa Rica

Species	Comments
Eared Grebe	1 record
Black-capped Petrel	1 record
Dark-rumped Petrel	
Parkinson's Petrel	
Pink-footed Shearwater	
Short-tailed Shearwater	1 record
White-faced Storm-petrel	1 record
Band-rumped Storm-petrel	
Markham's Storm-petrel	
American White Pelican	1 record
American Bittern	extinct?
White-faced Ibis	1 record
White-faced Whistling-duck	Tempisque only, extremely rare
Green-winged Teal	Tempisque, rare
Mallard	no recent records
Greater Scaup	1 record
Cooper's Hawk	M, WR, very rare but regular
Crested Eagle	very rare R, La Silva, Osa
Harpy Eagle	very rare, decreasing; Osa, Llanura de San Carlos
Aplomado Falcon	1 record
Orange-breasted Falcon	extinct?
Ruddy Crake	3 records in N. Guanacaste
Painted-billed Crake	1 or 2 records
Ocellated Crake	1 record
Wattled Jacana	1 record near Panama
American Avocet	4 records, all in NW Tempisque area
Snowy Plover	scattered records during migration
Hudsonian Godwit	1 record
Long-billed Curlew	very rare Golfo de Nicoya
White-rumped Sandpiper	very rare M both coasts
Dunlin	5 records
Curlew Sandpiper	1 record
Ruff	1 record
South Polar Skua	sporadic both coasts
Long-tailed Jaeger	1 record
Bonaparte's Gull	3 sightings on W coast
Gray Gull	1 record at Cocos Island
Heermann's Gull	1 possible sighting, Chomes 1985
Sooty Tern	accidental after storms
White-crowned Pigeon	1 record on NE coast
Great Horned Owl	most sightings in Valle Central

Species	Comments
Burrowing Owl	2 records
Short-eared Owl	1 record
Oilbird	1 record
Great Swallow-tailed Swift	5 records
Rufous-crested Coquette	4 records
Sapphire-throated Hummingbird	2 records
White-bellied Emerald	few old sightings; none recent
Indigo-capped Hummingbird	extremely rare; Cordillera de Guanacaste
Wing-banded Antbird	possibly 1 Costa Rica record
Blue-tailed Hummingbird	2 records
Gray Kingbird	very rare M along E coast
Ash-throated Flycatcher	1 definite record
Least Flycatcher	very rare M, WR
Brown-chested Martin	3 records
Cave Swallow	one old report, possibly migrant
White-eyed Vireo	2 records of fall migrants
Solitary Vireo	very rare WR
Black-whiskered Vireo	accidental
Warbling Vireo	6 sightings
Orange-crowned Warbler	accidental fall M; 1 record
Nashville Warbler	casual winter visitor; 2 records
Northern Parula	very rare M, WR
Cape May Warbler	rare WR, to 1,300 m
Black-throated Blue Warbler	rare M, WR; 6 sightings
Yellow-throated Warbler	scattered records both coasts; M, WR
Blackpoll Warbler	very rare fall M; 10 sightings
Pine Warbler	accidental fall M; 10 sightings
Prairie Warbler	very occasional fall M, WR
Connecticut Warbler	3 sightings
Melodious Blackbird	1 record
Black-headed Grosbeak	2 records
Grassland Yellow-finch	1 record
Savannah Sparrow	1 sighting
Chipping Sparrow	1 record

CHECKLIST FOR BIRDS OF COSTA RICA

Name: _____

1) _____
   Date   Location

2) _____
   Date   Location

3) _____
   Date   Location

4) _____
   Date   Location

5) _____
   Date   Location

6) _____
   Date   Location

7) _____
   Date   Location

	1	2	3	4	5	6	7
Tinamous							
Great Tinamou							
Highland Tinamou							
Little Tinamou							
Thicket Tinamou							
Slaty-breasted Tinamou							
Grebes							
Pied-billed Grebe							
Least Grebe							
Eared Grebe							
Shearwaters and Petrels							
Black-capped Petrel							
Dark-rumped Petrel							
Parkinson's Petrel							
Pink-footed Shearwater							
Wedge-tailed Shearwater							
Sooty Shearwater							
Short-tailed Shearwater							
Audubon's Shearwater							

	1	2	3	4	5	6	7
Wilson's Storm-petrel							
White-faced Storm-petrel							
Least Storm-petrel							
Wedge-rumped Storm-petrel							
Band-rumped Storm-petrel							
Leach's Storm-petrel							
Markham's Storm-petrel							
Black Storm-petrel							
Tropicbirds							
Red-billed Tropicbird							
Pelicans							
American White Pelican							
Brown Pelican							
Boobies							
Blue-footed Booby							
Brown Booby							
Masked Booby							
Red-footed Booby							
Cormorants							
Olivaceous Cormorant							
Anhingas							
Anhinga							
Frigatebirds							
Magnificent Frigatebird							
Great Frigatebird							
Herons, Egrets, Bitterns							
American Bittern							
Pinnated Bittern							
Least Bittern							
Rufescent Tiger-heron							
Fasciated Tiger-heron							
Bare-throated Tiger-heron							
Black-crowned Night-heron							
Yellow-crowned Night-heron							
Boat-billed Heron							
Cattle Egret							

CHECKLIST

	1	2	3	4	5	6	7
Green-backed Heron							
Little Blue Heron							
Tricolored Heron							
Reddish Egret							
Snowy Egret							
Great Egret							
Great Blue Heron							
Chestnut-bellied Heron							

Storks

	1	2	3	4	5	6	7
Wood Stork							
Jabiru							

Ibises and Spoonbills

	1	2	3	4	5	6	7
Green Ibis							
White Ibis							
Glossy Ibis							
White-faced Ibis							
Roseate Spoonbill							

Ducks, Geese and Swans

	1	2	3	4	5	6	7
Black-bellied Whistling-duck							
Fulvous Whistling-duck							
White-faced Whistling-duck							
Muscovy Duck							
American Wigeon							
Green-winged Teal							
Mallard							
Northern Pintail							
Blue-winged Teal							
Cinnamon Teal							
Northern Shoveller							
Ring-necked Duck							
Lesser Scaup							
Greater Scaup							
Masked Duck							

American Vultures

	1	2	3	4	5	6	7
Turkey Vulture							
Lesser Yellow-headed Vulture							
Black Vulture							
King Vulture							

Osprey

	1	2	3	4	5	6	7
Osprey							

Hawks, Kites and Eagles

	1	2	3	4	5	6	7
Gray-headed Kite							
Hook-billed Kite							
American Swallow-tailed Kite							
Black-shouldered Kite							
Snail Kite							
Double-toothed Kite							
Plumbeous Kite							
Mississippi Kite							
Crane Hawk							
Northern Harrier							
Sharp-shinned Hawk							
Tiny Hawk							
Cooper's Hawk							
Bicolored Hawk							
Black-chested Hawk							
Semiplumbeous Hawk							
White Hawk							
Common Black-hawk							
Great Black-hawk							
Solitary Eagle							
Black-collared Hawk							
Bay-winged Hawk							
Gray Hawk							
Roadside Hawk							
Broad-winged Hawk							
Short-tailed Hawk							
Swainson's Hawk							
White-tailed Hawk							
Zone-tailed Hawk							
Red-tailed Hawk							
Crested Eagle							
Harpy Eagle							
Black-and-white Hawk-eagle							
Ornate Hawk-eagle							
Black Hawk-eagle							

Falcons and Caracaras

	1	2	3	4	5	6	7
Red-throated Caracara							
Crested Caracara							

	1	2	3	4	5	6	7
Yellow-headed Caracara							
Laughing Falcon							
Barred Forest-falcon							
Slaty-backed Forest-falcon							
Collared Forest-falcon							
American Kestrel							
Merlin							
Bat Falcon							
Aplomado Falcon							
Orange-breasted Falcon							
Peregrine Falcon							

Curassows, Guans and Chachalacas

	1	2	3	4	5	6	7
Plain Chachalaca							
Gray-headed Chachalaca							
Crested Guan							
Black Guan							
Great Curassow							

Pheasants, Quails, etc.

	1	2	3	4	5	6	7
Buffy-crowned Wood-partridge							
Spotted-bellied Bobwhite							
Marbled Wood-quail							
Rufous-fronted Wood-quail							
Spotted Wood-quail							
Black-breasted Wood-quail							
Tawny-faced Quail							
Crested Bobwhite							

Limpkins

	1	2	3	4	5	6	7
Limpkin							

Rails, Coots and Gallinules

	1	2	3	4	5	6	7
Spotted Rail							
Uniform Crake							
Gray-necked Wood-rail							
Rufous-necked Wood-rail							
Sora							
Yellow-breasted Crake							
Black Rail							
White-throated Crake							
Gray-breasted Crake							
Ruddy Crake							
Painted-billed Crake							
Ocellated Crake							
Common Gallinule							
Purple Gallinule							
American Coot							

Sungrebes

	1	2	3	4	5	6	7
Sungrebe							

Sunbittern

	1	2	3	4	5	6	7
Sunbittern							

Shorebirds, Gulls, Auks, etc.

	1	2	3	4	5	6	7
Northern Jacana							
Wattled Jacana							
American Oystercatcher							
Black-necked Stilt							
American Avocet							
Double-striped Thick-knee							

Plovers

	1	2	3	4	5	6	7
Lesser Golden-plover							
Black-bellied Plover							
Semipalmated Plover							
Wilson's Plover							
Killdeer							
Snowy Plover							
Collared Plover							

Sandpipers, etc.

	1	2	3	4	5	6	7
Hudsonian Godwit							
Marbled Godwit							
Whimbrel							
Long-billed Curlew							
Upland Sandpiper							
Greater Yellowlegs							
Lesser Sandpiper							
Solitary Sandpiper							
Willet							
Spotted Sandpiper							
Wandering Tattler							
Ruddy Turnstone							
Common Snipe							
Short-billed Dowitcher							
Long-billed Dowitcher							

CHECKLIST

Appendix II: Checklist for Birds of Costa Rica **241**

	1	2	3	4	5	6	7
Surfbird							
Red Knot							
Sanderling							
Western Sandpiper							
Semipalmated Sandpiper							
Least Sandpiper							
White-rumped Sandpiper							
Baird's Sandpiper							
Pectoral Sandpiper							
Dunlin							
Curlew Sandpiper							
Stilt Sandpiper							
Buff-breasted Sandpiper							
Ruff							

Phalaropes

	1	2	3	4	5	6	7
Red Phalarope							
Red-necked Phalarope							
Wilson's Phalarope							

Skuas and Jaegers

	1	2	3	4	5	6	7
South Polar Skua							
Pomarine Jaeger							
Parasitic Jaeger							
Long-tailed Jaeger							

Gulls and Terns

	1	2	3	4	5	6	7
Ring-billed Gull							
Herring Gull							
Laughing Gull							
Franklin's Gull							
Bonaparte's Gull							
Gray Gull							
Heermann's Gull							
Sabine's Gull							
Black Tern							
Gull-billed Tern							
Caspian Tern							
Common Tern							
Forster's Tern							
Bridled Tern							
Sooty Tern							
Least Tern							
Royal Tern							
Sandwich Tern							
Elegant Tern							
Brown Noddy							
Black Noddy							
White Tern							

Skimmers

	1	2	3	4	5	6	7
Black Skimmer							

Pigeons and Doves

	1	2	3	4	5	6	7
Rock Dove							
White-crowned Pigeon							
Scaled Pigeon							
Band-tailed Pigeon							
Pale-vented Pigeon							
Red-billed Pigeon							
Ruddy Pigeon							
Short-billed Pigeon							
Mourning Dove							
White-winged Dove							
Common Ground-dove							
Plain-breasted Ground-dove							
Ruddy Ground-dove							
Inca Dove							
Blue Ground-dove							
Maroon-chested Ground-dove							
White-tipped Dove							
Gray-fronted Dove							
Gray-chested Dove							
Buff-fronted Quail-dove							
Purplish-backed Quail-dove							
Chiriquí Quail-dove							
Olive-backed Quail-dove							
Violaceous Quail-dove							
Ruddy Quail-dove							

Parrots

	1	2	3	4	5	6	7
Scarlet Macaw							
Great Green Macaw							
Crimson-fronted Parakeet							
Olive-throated Parakeet							
Orange-fronted Parakeet							
Sulfur-winged Parakeet							
Barred Parakeet							
Orange-chinned Parakeet							
Red-fronted Parrotlet							
Brown-hooded Parrot							
White-crowned Parrot							
Blue-headed Parrot							
White-fronted Parrot							
Red-lored Parrot							
Yellow-naped Parrot							
Mealy Parrot							

	1	2	3	4	5	6	7

Cuckoos

	1	2	3	4	5	6	7
Black-billed Cuckoo							
Yellow-billed Cuckoo							
Mangrove Cuckoo							
Cocos Cuckoo							
Squirrel Cuckoo							
Groove-billed Ani							
Smooth-billed Ani							
Striped Cuckoo							
Lesser Ground-cuckoo							
Pheasant Cuckoo							
Rufous-vented Ground-cuckoo							

Owls

	1	2	3	4	5	6	7
Common Barn-owl							
Tropical Screech-owl							
Pacific Screech-owl							
Vermiculated Screech-owl							
Bare-shanked Screech-owl							
Crested Owl							
Great Horned Owl							
Spectacled Owl							
Least Pygmy-owl							
Andean Pygmy-owl							
Ferruginous Pygmy-owl							
Burrowing Owl							
Mottled Owl							
Black-and-white Owl							
Striped Owl							
Short-eared Owl							
Unspotted Saw-whet Owl							

Oilbird

	1	2	3	4	5	6	7
Oilbird							

Potoos and Nightjars

	1	2	3	4	5	6	7
Great Potoo							
Common Potoo							

Nightjars

	1	2	3	4	5	6	7
Short-tailed Nighthawk							
Common Nighthawk							
Lesser Nighthawk							
Common Pauraque							
Ocellated Poorwill				.			

	1	2	3	4	5	6	7
Chuck-will's-widow							
Rufous Nightjar							
Whip-poor-will							
Dusky Nightjar							
White-tailed Nightjar							

Swifts

	1	2	3	4	5	6	7
Black Swift							
White-chinned Swift							
Spot-fronted Swift							
Chestnut-collared Swift							
White-collared Swift							
Chimney Swift							
Vaux's Swift							
Band-rumped Swift							
Gray-rumped Swift							
Lesser Swallow-tailed Swift							
Great Swallow-tailed Swift							

Hummingbirds

	1	2	3	4	5	6	7
White-tipped Sicklebill							
Bronzy Hermit							
Band-tailed Barbthroat							
Long-tailed Hermit							
Green Hermit							
Little Hermit							
Green-fronted Lancebill							
Scaly-breasted Hummingbird							
Violet Sabrewing							
White-necked Jacobin							
Brown Violet-ear							
Green Violet-ear							
Green-breasted Mango							
Violet-headed Hummingbird							
White-crested Coquette							
Black-crested Coquette							
Rufous-crested Coquette							
Green Thorntail							
Fork-tailed Emerald							
Crowned Woodnymph							
Fiery-throated Hummingbird							
Sapphire-throated Hummingbird							
Blue-throated Goldentail							
White-bellied Emerald							
Beryl-crowned Hummingbird							
Blue-chested Hummingbird							

CHECKLIST

	1	2	3	4	5	6	7
Mangrove Hummingbird							
Steely-vented Hummingbird							
Indigo-capped Hummingbird							
Blue-tailed Hummingbird							
Snowy-bellied Hummingbird							
Cinnamon Hummingbird							
Rufous-tailed Hummingbird							
Striped-tailed Hummingbird							
Black-bellied Hummingbird							
White-tailed Emerald							
Coppery-headed Emerald							
Snowcap							
Red-footed Plumeleteer							
White-bellied Mountain-gem							
Purple-throated Mountain-gem							
Gray-tailed Mountain-gem							
Green-crowned Brilliant							
Magnificent Hummingbird							
Purple-crowned Fairy							
Plain-capped Starthroat							
Long-billed Starthroat							
Magenta-throated Woodstar							
Ruby-throated Hummingbird							
Scintillant Hummingbird							
Volcano Hummingbird							

Trogons

	1	2	3	4	5	6	7
Resplendent Quetzal							
Slaty-tailed Trogon							
Lattice-tailed Trogon							
Baird's Trogon							
Black-headed Trogon							
Elegant Trogon							
Collared Trogon							
Orange-bellied Trogon							
Black-throated Trogon							
Violaceous Trogon							

Kingfishers, Motmots, etc.

	1	2	3	4	5	6	7
Ringed Kingfisher							
Belted Kingfisher							
Amazon Kingfisher							
Green Kingfisher							
Green-and-rufous Kingfisher							

	1	2	3	4	5	6	7
American Pygmy Kingfisher							
Tody Motmot							
Broad-billed Motmot							
Keel-billed Motmot							
Turquoise-browed Motmot							
Rufous Motmot							
Blue-crowned Motmot							

Woodpeckers and Allies

Jacamars

	1	2	3	4	5	6	7
Rufous-tailed Jacamar							
Great Jacamar							

Puffbirds

	1	2	3	4	5	6	7
White-necked Puffbird							
Pied Puffbird							
White-whiskered Puffbird							
Lanceolated Monklet							
White-fronted Nunbird							

Barbets

	1	2	3	4	5	6	7
Red-headed Barbet							
Prong-billed Barbet							

Toucans

	1	2	3	4	5	6	7
Emerald Toucanet							
Collared Aracari							
Fiery-billed Aracari							
Yellow-eared Toucanet							
Keel-billed Toucan							
Chestnut-mandibled Toucan							

Woodpeckers

	1	2	3	4	5	6	7
Olivaceous Piculet							
Acorn Woodpecker							
Golden-naped Woodpecker							
Black-cheeked Woodpecker							
Hoffmann's Woodpecker							
Red-crowned Woodpecker							
Yellow-bellied Sapsucker							
Hairy Woodpecker							
Smoky-brown Woodpecker							
Red-rumped Woodpecker							
Golden-olive Woodpecker							
Rufous-winged Woodpecker							
Chestnut-colored Woodpecker							

	1	2	3	4	5	6	7
Cinnamon Woodpecker							
Lineated Woodpecker							
Pale-billed Woodpecker							

Woodcreepers

	1	2	3	4	5	6	7
Plain-brown Woodcreeper							
Tawny-winged Woodcreeper							
Ruddy Woodcreeper							
Long-tailed Woodcreeper							
Olivaceous Woodcreeper							
Wedge-billed Woodcreeper							
Strong-billed Woodcreeper							
Barred Woodcreeper							
Black-banded Woodcreeper							
Buff-throated Woodcreeper							
Ivory-billed Woodcreeper							
Black-striped Woodcreeper							
Spotted Woodcreeper							
Streaked-headed Woodcreeper							
Spotted-crowned Woodcreeper							
Brown-billed Scythebill							

Ovenbirds

	1	2	3	4	5	6	7
Pale-breasted Spinetail							
Slaty Spinetail							
Red-faced Spinetail							
Spotted Barbtail							
Ruddy Treerunner							
Buffy Tuftedcheek							
Striped Foliage-gleaner							
Lineated Foliage-gleaner							
Spectacled Foliage-gleaner							
Buff-fronted Foliage-gleaner							
Streaked-breasted Treehunter							
Buff-throated Foliage-gleaner							
Ruddy Foliage-gleaner							
Tawny-throated Leaftosser							
Gray-throated Leaftosser							
Scaly-throated Leaftosser							
Plain Xenops							
Streaked Xenops							

Antbirds

	1	2	3	4	5	6	7
Fasciated Antshrike							
Great Antshrike							

	1	2	3	4	5	6	7
Barred Antshrike							
Black-hooded Antshrike							
Slaty Antshrike							
Russet Antshrike							
Plain Antvireo							
Streaked-crowned Antvireo							
Spotted-crowned Antvireo							
Checker-throated Antwren							
White-flanked Antwren							
Slaty Antwren							
Rufous-rumped Antwren							
Dotted-winged Antwren							
Dusky Antbird							
Bare-crowned Antbird							
Chestnut-backed Antbird							
Dull-mantled Antbird							
Immaculate Antbird							
Bicolored Antbird							
Spotted Antbird							
Ocellated Antbird							
Black-faced Antthrush							
Wing-banded Antbird							
Black-headed Antthrush							
Rufous-breasted Antthrush							
Black-crowned Antpitta							
Scaled Antpitta							
Spectacled Antpitta							
Fulvous-bellied Antpitta							
Ochre-breasted Antpitta							

Tapaculos

	1	2	3	4	5	6	7
Silvery-fronted Tapaculo							

Tityras and Becards

	1	2	3	4	5	6	7
Barred Becard							
Cinnamon Becard							
White-winged Becard							
Black-and-white Becard							
Rose-throated Becard							
Masked Tityra							
Black-crowned Tityra							

Cotingas

	1	2	3	4	5	6	7
Rufous Piha							
Speckled Mourner							

CHECKLIST

	1	2	3	4	5	6	7
Lovely Cotinga							
Turquoise Cotinga							
Snowy Cotinga							
Yellow-billed Cotinga							
Purple-throated Fruitcrow							
Bare-necked Umbrellabird							
Three-wattled Bellbird							
Sharpbill							

Manakins

	1	2	3	4	5	6	7
Red-capped Manakin							
Blue-crowned Manakin							
White-crowned Manakin							
Long-tailed Manakin							
Lance-tailed Manakin							
White-ruffed Manakin							
Orange-collared Manakin							
White-collared Manakin							
Gray-headed Manakin							
Thrushlike Manakin							

American or Tyrant Flycatchers

	1	2	3	4	5	6	7
Black Phoebe							
Long-tailed Tyrant							
Scissor-tailed Flycatcher							
Fork-tailed Flycatcher							
Eastern Kingbird							
Tropical Kingbird							
Gray Kingbird							
Western Kingbird							
Piratic Flycatcher							
White-ringed Flycatcher							
Boat-billed Flycatcher							
Bright-rumped Attila							
Sulphur-bellied Flycatcher							
Streaked Flycatcher							
Golden-bellied Flycatcher							
Gray-capped Flycatcher							
Social Flycatcher							
Great Kiskadee							
Rufous Mourner							
Panama Flycatcher							
Brown-crested Flycatcher							
Nutting's Flycatcher							
Great-crested Flycatcher							
Ash-throated Flycatcher							

	1	2	3	4	5	6	7
Dusky-capped Flycatcher							
Olive-sided Flycatcher							
Western Wood-pewee							
Eastern Wood-pewee							
Tropical Pewee							
Dark Pewee							
Ochraceous Pewee							
Yellow-bellied Flycatcher							
Acadian Flycatcher							
Alder Flycatcher							
Willow Flycatcher							
White-throated Flycatcher							
Least Flycatcher							
Yellowish Flycatcher							
Black-capped Flycatcher							
Tufted Flycatcher							
Ruddy-tailed Flycatcher							
Tawny-chested Flycatcher							
Cocos Flycatcher							
Sulphur-rumped Flycatcher							
Black-tailed Flycatcher							
Bran-colored Flycatcher							
Royal Flycatcher							
White-throated Spadebill							
Stub-tailed Spadebill							
Golden-crowned Spadebill							
Yellow-olive Flycatcher							
Yellow-margined Flycatcher							
Eye-ringed Flatbill							
Black-headed Tody-flycatcher							
Common Tody-flycatcher							
Slate-headed Tody-flycatcher							
Northern Bentbill							
Scale-crested Pygmy-tyrant							
Black-capped Pygmy-tyrant							
Rufous-browed Tyrannulet							
Yellow Tyrannulet							
Torrent Tyrannulet							
Yellow-bellied Elaenia							
Lesser Elaenia							
Mountain Elaenia							
Greenish Elaenia							
Scrub Flycatcher							
Northern Beardless-tyrannulet							
Southern Beardless-tyrannulet							
Mistletoe Tyrannulet							
Yellow-crowned Tyrannulet							

	1	2	3	4	5	6	7
Zeledon's Tyrannulet							
Brown-capped Tyrannulet							
Yellow-bellied Tyrannulet							
Slaty-capped Flycatcher							
Sepia-capped Flycatcher							
Olive-striped Flycatcher							
Ochre-bellied Flycatcher							

Swallows

	1	2	3	4	5	6	7
Purple Martin							
Brown-chested Martin							
Gray-breasted Martin							
Cliff Swallow							
Cave Swallow							
Barn Swallow							
Southern Rough -winged Swallow							
Northern Rough -winged Swallow							
Blue-and-white Swallow							
Bank Swallow							
Tree Swallow							
Mangrove Swallow							
Violet-green Swallow							

Jays, Crows, etc.

	1	2	3	4	5	6	7
White-throated Magpie-jay							
Brown Jay							
Black-chested Jay							
Azure-hooded Jay							
Silvery-throated Jay							

Dippers

	1	2	3	4	5	6	7
American Dipper							

Wrens

	1	2	3	4	5	6	7
Sedge Wren							
Banded-backed Wren							
Rufous-naped Wren							
Plain Wren							
Rufous-and-white Wren							
Striped-breasted Wren							
Bay Wren							
Riverside Wren							
Banded Wren							

	1	2	3	4	5	6	7
Black-throated Wren							
Black-bellied Wren							
Spotted-breasted Wren							
Rufous-breasted Wren							
House Wren							
Ochraceous Wren							
Timberline Wren							
White-breasted Wood-wren							
Gray-breasted Wood-wren							
Rock Wren							
Nightingale Wren							
Whistling Wren							
Song Wren							

Catbird

	1	2	3	4	5	6	7
Gray Catbird							

Thrushes, Robins, etc.

	1	2	3	4	5	6	7
White-throated Robin							
Clay-colored Robin							
Pale-vented Robin							
Mountain Robin							
Sooty Robin							
Black-faced Robin							
Wood Thrush							
Swainson's Thrush							
Gray-cheeked Thrush							
Veery							
Black-headed Nightingale-thrush							
Slaty-backed Nightingale-thrush							
Ruddy-capped Nightingale-thrush							
Orange-billed Nightingale-thrush							
Black-billed Nightingale-thrush							

Gnatcatchers and Gnatwrens

	1	2	3	4	5	6	7
White-lored Gnatcatcher							
Tropical Gnatcatcher							
Long-billed Gnatwren							
Tawny-faced Gnatwren							

CHECKLIST

	1	2	3	4	5	6	7
Waxwing							
Cedar Waxwing							
Silky-flycatchers							
Long-tailed Silky-flycatcher							
Black-and-yellow Silky-flycatcher							
Vireos, Greenlets, Shrike-vireos and Peppershrikes							
Rufous-browed Peppershrike							
Green Shrike-vireo							
White-eyed Vireo							
Mangrove Vireo							
Yellow-winged Vireo							
Yellow-throated Vireo							
Solitary Vireo							
Red-eyed Vireo							
Yellow-green Vireo							
Black-whiskered Vireo							
Philadelphia Vireo							
Warbling Vireo							
Brown-capped Vireo							
Scrub Greenlet							
Tawny-crowned Greenlet							
Lesser Greenlet							
Bananaquit							
Bananaquit							
Warblers							
Black-and-white Warbler							
Prothonotary Warbler							
Worm-eating Warbler							
Golden-winged Warbler							
Blue-winged Warbler							
Tennessee Warbler							
Three-striped Warbler							
Orange-crowned Warbler							
Nashville Warbler							
Flame throated Warbler							
Northern Parula							
Tropical Parula							
Yellow Warbler							
Mangrove Warbler							

	1	2	3	4	5	6	7
Magnolia Warbler							
Cape May Warbler							
Black-throated Blue Warbler							
Yellow-rumped Warbler							
Townsend's Warbler							
Black-throated Green Warbler							
Hermit Warbler							
Cerulean Warbler							
Blackburnian Warbler							
Yellow-throated Warbler							
Chestnut-sided Warbler							
Bay-breasted Warbler							
Blackpoll Warbler							
Pine Warbler							
Prairie Warbler							
Palm Warbler							
Ovenbird							
Northern Waterthrush							
Louisiana Waterthrush							
Kentucky Warbler							
Mourning Warbler							
MacGillivray's Warbler							
Connecticut Warbler							
Common Yellowthroat							
Masked Yellowthroat							
Olive-crowned Yellowthroat							
Gray-crowned Yellowthroat							
Yellow-breasted Chat							
Hooded Warbler							
Wilson's Warbler							
Canada Warbler							
American Redstart							
Slate-throated Redstart							
Collared Redstart							
Golden-crowned Warbler							
Black-cheeked Warbler							
Rufous-capped Warbler							
Buff-rumped Warbler							
Zeledonia							
American Orioles & Blackbirds							
Chestnut headed Oropendola							
Montezuma Oropendola							
Scarlet-rumped Cacique							
Yellow-billed Cacique							
Giant Cowbird							

	1	2	3	4	5	6	7
Bronzed Cowbird							
Melodious Blackbird							
Great-tailed Grackle							
Nicaraguan Grackle							
Orchard Oriole							
Black-cowled Oriole							
Yellow-tailed Oriole							
Spotted-breasted Oriole							
Northern (Baltimore) Oriole							
Streaked-backed Oriole							
Red-winged Blackbird							
Yellow-headed Blackbird							
Red-breasted Blackbird							
Eastern Meadowlark							
Bobolink							
Dickcissel							

Tanagers & Honeycreepers

	1	2	3	4	5	6	7
Golden-browed Chlorophonia							
Blue-hooded Euphonia							
Tawny-capped Euphonia							
White-vented Euphonia							
Scrub Euphonia							
Yellow-crowned Euphonia							
Thick-billed Euphonia							
Yellow-throated Euphonia							
Olive-backed Euphonia							
Spotted-crowned Euphonia							
Emerald Tanager							
Speckled Tanager							
Silver-throated Tanager							
Golden-hooded Tanager							
Plain-colored Tanager							
Rufous-winged Tanager							
Bay-headed Tanager							
Spangled-cheeked Tanager							
Green Honeycreeper							
Red-legged Honeycreeper							
Shining Honeycreeper							
Blue Dacnis							
Scarlet-thighed Dacnis							
Blue-and-gold Tanager							
Blue-gray Tanager							
Palm Tanager							
Scarlet-rumped Tanager							
Crimson-collared Tanager							
Summer Tanager							

	1	2	3	4	5	6	7
Hepatic Tanager							
Scarlet Tanager							
White-winged Tanager							
Western Tanager							
Flame-colored Tanager							
Olive Tanager							
Red-crowned Ant-tanager							
Red-throated Ant-tanager							
Black-cheeked Ant-tanager							
White-throated Shrike-tanager							
White-lined Tanager							
White-shouldered Tanager							
Tawny-crested Tanager							
Sulphur-rumped Tanager							
Gray-headed Tanager							
Dusky-faced Tanager							
Rosy Thrush-tanager							
Black-and-yellow Tanager							
Common Bush-tanager							
Sooty-capped Bush-tanager							
Ashy-throated Bush-tanager							

New World Sparrows, Finches

	1	2	3	4	5	6	7
Black-headed Saltator							
Buff-throated Saltator							
Grayish Saltator							
Streaked Saltator							
Black-faced Grosbeak							
Slate-colored Grosbeak							
Black-thighed Grosbeak							
Rose-breasted Grosbeak							
Black-headed Grosbeak							
Blue Grosbeak							
Blue-black Grosbeak							
Indigo Bunting							
Painted Bunting							
Yellow-faced Grassquit							
Slate-colored Seedeater							
White-collared Seedeater							
Variable Seedeater							
Yellow-bellied Seedeater							
Ruddy-breasted Seedeater							
Blue Seedeater							
Pink-billed Seed-finch							
Thick-billed Seed-finch							
Blue-black Grassquit							
Cocos Finch							

CHECKLIST

	1	2	3	4	5	6	7
Grassland Yellow-finch							
Slaty Finch							
Peg-billed Finch							
Slaty Flowerpiercer							
Large-footed Finch							
Yellow-thighed Finch							
Yellow-throated Brush-finch							
Chestnut-capped Brush-finch							
Black-headed Brush-finch							
Sooty-faced Finch							
Orange-billed Sparrow							
Olive Sparrow							
Black-striped Sparrow							
Prevost's Ground-sparrow							
White-eared Ground-sparrow							
Savannah Sparrow							
Grasshopper Sparrow							
Striped-headed Sparrow							
Rusty Sparrow							
Botteri's Sparrow							
Volcano Junco							
Chipping Sparrow							
Rufous-collared Sparrow							
Lincoln's Sparrow							
Wedge-tailed Grass-finch							

Siskins, Canaries, Finches, etc.

	1	2	3	4	5	6	7
Lesser Goldfinch							
Yellow-bellied Siskin							

Old World Sparrow

	1	2	3	4	5	6	7
House Sparrow							

NOTES

NOTES

NOTES

NOTES

NOTES

ABOUT THE AUTHOR

Aaron Sekerak first developed his outdoor interests while spending boyhood summers with his family on ranches in Wyoming. Larger spaces and wilder lands called, along with academic interests, which resulted in a B.Sc. from the University of Alaska in Fairbanks, and an M.Sc. and Ph.D. in Biological Sciences from the University of Calgary in Alberta, Canada.

As a professional environmental consultant for over 20 years, he performed biological field investigations, primarily in Arctic North America, and gained first-hand knowledge of ecosystems from the Aleutian Islands, Northern Alaska and Yukon, to the High Arctic Islands of Canada, and the Labrador Sea. Dr. Sekerak was a principal owner of a leading consulting company in Canada for many years. He formed a consulting base in Yellowknife, Northwest Territories, Canada, to perform specialized studies involving biological resources and aboriginal people. These activities resulted in scientific reports and formal publications. His interest in tropical biology resulted in the present publication. Dr. Sekerak resides near Victoria, British Columbia, but spends considerable time in Costa Rica, where he is in the process of organizing a tour company that specializes in birding walks, day trips and longer expeditions.

ABOUT THE ARTIST

Elissa Conger has a B.A. in Art History from Boston University and a B.F.A. in Sculpture from Maine College of Art. She has travelled extensively in Central America and makes her home in Portland, Maine, or wherever there are flowers.